Progress and Confusion

Progress and Confusion

The State of Macroeconomic Policy

edited by Olivier Blanchard, Raghuram Rajan,
Kenneth Rogoff, and Lawrence H. Summers

The MIT Press
Cambridge, Massachusetts
London, England

This book was set in Sabon by Toppan Best-set Premedia Limited. Printed and bound in the United States of America.

Library of Congress Cataloging-in-Publication Data

Names: Blanchard, Olivier (Olivier J.) editor.
Title: Progress and confusion : the state of macroeconomic policy / Blanchard, Olivier, Raghuram Rajan, Kenneth Rogoff, and Lawrence H. Summers, eds.
Description: Cambridge, MA : The MIT Press, 2016. | Includes bibliographical references and index.
Identifiers: LCCN 2015039939 | ISBN 9780262034623 (hardcover : alk. paper)
Subjects: LCSH: Monetary policy. | Fiscal policy. | Economic policy. | Macroeconomics.
Classification: LCC HG230.3 .P76 2016 | DDC 339.5—dc23 LC record available at
    http://lccn.loc.gov/2015039939

10 9 8 7 6 5 4 3 2 1

Contents

Capital Flows, Exchange Rate Management, and Capital Controls

The International Monetary and Financial System

Conclusion

1

A Road Map to "Progress and Confusion"

Olivier Blanchard and Rafael Portillo

On April 15–16, 2015, the IMF organized the third "Rethinking Macro Policy" conference. Held every two years since 2011, these conferences have brought together academics and policymakers to assess how the global financial crisis and its aftermath should change our views of macroeconomic policy. This time around, the focus was on the contours of policy in the future, once the global financial crisis is finally over. Will the macro framework look like the precrisis consensus, or will it be different? Have we made progress on this question, or does confusion remain?

The twenty-seven chapters in this book reflect the discussions that took place at the conference, covering many dimensions of macro policy. The chapters are organized into seven topics: the "new normal," financial regulation, macroprudential policies, monetary policy, fiscal policy, capital flows and exchange rate management, and the international monetary system. Given the breadth of issues, we thought we needed to provide a road map to guide the reader. For each topic we present a list of questions, then provide a summary of each chapter and where it fits within the broader policy debate. Not all of the questions are addressed in this volume, though some of them are discussed in the two previous conference volumes.[1]

The "New Normal"

At the core of the conference is the question of the new normal. Will the macro landscape of the future be similar to the precrisis landscape, one of decent growth and "normal" interest rates? Or are we in for a prolonged period of stagnation, negative real rates, and deflationary pressures, similar to the experience of the last few years?

Two of the book's editors provide opposing views on this issue. On the one hand, *Kenneth Rogoff* argues that we are in the adjustment phase of a "debt supercycle." Following the excessive expansion in credit that led to the global financial crisis, subsequent deleveraging has been a persistent drag on growth. This is typical of a financial crisis. But, he argues, these are not secular trends: as these headwinds subside, we should expect higher growth rates. The United States and the UK have already reached the end of the deleveraging cycle, while the euro zone is in the thick of it and China is starting to face challenges from the debt buildup of recent years. As for real interest rates, Rogoff makes the case that low *safe* rates mask much tighter financial conditions for many households and firms. As deleveraging comes to an end and financial conditions soften, safe real rates should again increase.

On the other hand, *Lawrence H. Summers* elaborates on his secular stagnation hypothesis, which he first put forward at an IMF conference in 2013.[2] He argues that events since then—lower yields, sluggish growth, and below-target inflation—provide further confirmation of the chronic excess of savings over investment, which he acknowledges is more global in nature than he originally thought. In this context, keeping the economy at potential may well require low or even negative real interest rates for the foreseeable future, with worrisome implications. Aggregate demand management may become harder as central banks become increasingly constrained by the zero lower bound. In addition, the risks to financial instability are likely to increase, as low or negative equilibrium real interest rates encourage bubbles and a greater search for yield. These concerns permeate many of the discussions throughout this book.

The two views have very different policy implications. For example, the secular stagnation view calls for boosting investment—including investment in public infrastructure—to raise aggregate demand and equilibrium real interest rates. Rogoff's view, on the other hand, that low safe rates mask tight financial conditions, suggests that greater public borrowing may end up crowding out the private sector even further.

What to make of these competing arguments? Much of it hinges on how to interpret movements in interest rates. Recent IMF work provides a somewhat nuanced view.[3] Debt overhang and deleveraging, and other cyclical factors, have played a role, which implies rates should increase as these factors subside. But the decrease in real rates does appear to be secular (and global): it started well before the global financial crisis and is therefore unlikely to disappear once the crisis is over. So we may continue to see low real rates, though not necessarily negative, for the foreseeable future.

Systemic Risk and Financial Regulation

The global financial crisis resulted from the interaction of excessive leverage in the financial system and the related interconnectedness and complexity of the balance sheets of banks and nonbanks. In other words, the crisis revealed the existence of large and previously undetected systemic risk. Since then, there have been efforts to better understand and measure the many dimensions of systemic risk. But where do we stand on these? Are some aspects easier to measure than others, such as leverage in the financial system versus risks from shadow banking, or solvency risks versus liquidity risks?

In addition, regulatory reforms have been pervasive, as the Dodd-Frank Act, the UK Vickers Commission, the work of the Financial Stability Board, and similar efforts attest. Are reforms succeeding in reducing systemic risk? Do they have unintended effects? More generally, do the ever-changing financial landscape and the incentives for the system to remain excessively leveraged imply regulatory reform is hopeless?

In his introduction to this part of the volume, *Paul A. Volcker* summarizes its two main themes: the importance of avoiding excessive leverage in the financial system, and the need to expand the regulatory framework beyond banks.

Viral V. Acharya's chapter shows there has been progress in measuring systemic risk, at least in banking. He presents a measure developed at NYU's Volatility Institute, called SRISK, and uses it to assess progress with regulatory reform. This measure provides a market-based estimate of banks' capital shortfalls during episodes of aggregate stress. By comparing a firm's leftover equity in the event of a hypothetical market collapse with the level implied by a capital ratio considered "prudent," and aggregating across all listed financial firms, SRISK provides a quantitative, time-varying indicator of financial fragility.

With the help of such a measure, Acharya paints a mixed picture of regulatory reform across the world. He sees considerable improvements in US banks since the crisis, thanks to capital injections and measures put in place following passage of the Dodd-Frank Act, including stress testing of systemically important financial institutions. But systemic risk in Europe remains more than twice as large as it was before the crisis, which Acharya argues is the result of insufficient recapitalization and ineffective stress tests (with an excessive focus on risk-weighted capital ratios instead of direct leverage). He also detects a large increase in systemic risk in Asia, especially China, following the massive increase in debt and leverage of recent years.

Anat R. Admati is pessimistic. She argues that the failure of financial regulation made evident during the global financial crisis has not been addressed. Conflicts of interest between creditors and shareholders can lead to excessive leverage, what Admati calls the "leverage ratchet effect." This effect is particularly acute in banking because of the implicit guarantees regarding debt and the expectation of support from central banks and governments, which weakens creditor discipline. Capital regulations should correct these distortions. But they still allow extremely high levels of indebtedness, in part because of the complex system of risk weighting, which distorts investment decisions and increases systemic risk.

For Admati, the solution is clear: *much* higher capital ratios, at least 15 percent of banks' total (non-risk-weighted) assets, are needed. This is much higher than the Basel III minimum (3 percent proposed for testing—final calibration to be determined) or the new ratios set by US agencies (5–6 percent).[4] She also calls for more discussion of measurement issues, such as how to account for derivatives exposures, and argues that debt-like securities (e.g., contingent convertible capital bonds, or CoCos, or nonequity total loss-absorbing capacity instruments), which can in principle be converted into equity, are dominated by equity for the purpose of regulation, because triggering conversions in times of stress will prove exceedingly difficult.

Banks are only part of the picture; nonbanks and markets have been taking an increasing role in financial intermediation.[5] In this context, *Philipp Hildebrand* looks at liquidity risks in financial markets and the role of asset managers. Recent episodes of asset-price swings and widened bid-ask spreads have raised the issue of whether stricter regulation, by reducing banks' market-making role, has created systemic liquidity risk. Hildebrand is skeptical of the argument, arguing instead that there has long been a "liquidity illusion" and that all financial market participants need to adapt to deal with liquidity risks. He also argues that asset management companies are not themselves a source of systemic risk, as they have small balance sheets and are not leveraged, though some of their products may expose investors to illiquidity risks. He supports stress testing of investment funds.

Robert E. Rubin argues that market-based financial systems will inevitably experience episodes of booms and busts, even if regulation can reduce their likelihood and severity. In the current environment, he sees significant potential for systemic risk in the shadow banking world, which has grown rapidly in recent years yet is still not well understood. He calls for greater efforts toward cataloguing the asset classes, organizations, and activities involved and toward developing the right set of regulatory tools.

Macroprudential Policies

Macroprudential tools are the new policy kids on the block. A standard example is maximum loan-to-value ratios, which can be adjusted depending on the state of the housing market. In principle, these tools can target the many dimensions of financial risk, allowing fiscal and monetary policy to deal with their traditional mandates. But do macroprudential policies work? Why not just set tighter, non-time-varying, regulatory requirements? And how should macroprudential policies and monetary policy be combined? Also, these policies can have important distributional effects. How do we deal with their political economy implications?

Paul Tucker takes a view focused directly on the stability of the financial system. He defines a macroprudential regime as one in which regulatory parameters are adjusted dynamically to maintain a desired degree of resilience in the financial system. He emphasizes resilience (inversely related to the frequency with which crises occur) rather than fine-tuning the credit cycle, arguing that the latter is too ambitious and risks missing what is essential. Implicit in the framework is the idea that the base regulatory regime—around which the parameters are adjusted—is not designed for the "exuberant" states of the world and therefore, on its own, cannot guarantee financial stability. For Tucker, this is the choice that policymakers have already made, in part because of concerns about the effect of permanently very tight regulations on the provision of financial services to the economy (as well as regulatory arbitrage).

Tucker lists some desirable features of a macroprudential regime, building in part on similar efforts in the monetary policy debate from previous decades. First, in light of the changing financial landscape, macroprudential policies need to encompass both banks and nonbanks. Second, discretion is inevitable, which implies policymaking must be constrained by a well-defined objective set by democratically elected officials. Third, to the extent possible, policymakers need to avoid making first-order distributional *choices*. Fourth, the process for making macroprudential policies should be as transparent and systematic as possible, with regular stress testing playing an important role. Finally, to the extent that macroprudential policies are housed at the central bank, a separate structure for making decisions can help separate macroprudential from monetary policy and underpin incentives to take both missions seriously.

Whereas Tucker views macroprudential policies as clearly different from monetary policy, *Hyun Song Shin* makes the case that the distinction is not always clear. Both policies affect the demand and the supply of credit, and as a result, there can be some tension in moving macroprudential and monetary policy in opposite directions. In such a scenario, households and firms are being told to "simultaneously borrow more and borrow less." Shin argues that monetary policy is increasingly constrained by global financial conditions, especially in emerging market economies (EMEs). Macroprudential policies are not so constrained, and may therefore play an important role in the macro framework. He cautions, however, that their effectiveness may be limited by the changing financial landscape.

Lars E. O. Svensson tackles the question of the relative roles of monetary and macroprudential policies from a different angle. He applies a quantitative cost-benefit analysis to Sweden to assess whether monetary policy should target financial stability. Svensson finds that the benefits of moderate increases in interest rates for financial stability (in terms of reducing the likelihood and severity of a crisis) are very small and are overwhelmed by the much larger costs in terms of increased unemployment. He concludes that monetary policy is not the right tool to deal with financial stability and that macroprudential policies are much better suited to this task.

Monetary Policy in the Future

The global financial crisis and the zero lower bound on interest rates forced central banks to experiment with many new policy tools and approaches, with the central bank balance sheet growing exponentially. The questions going forward are many. How much should we move away from the old inflation-targeting framework? Should we put these new tools back on the shelf? What is the optimal size of the central bank balance sheet, and are there negative externalities from central banks' holding long-term government bonds? And, given the origins of the crisis, how can we better incorporate financial sector issues into the policy framework?

José Viñals provides a comprehensive overview of the key challenges posed to monetary policy by the global financial crisis, focusing on whether monetary policy can sustain financial stability *in addition to* price and output stability or whether this task should rest exclusively or primarily with macroprudential policy. He highlights that effective use of macroprudential policy can make monetary policy work better over the cycle by reducing the likelihood of a zero lower bound constraint on it, owing to the lower likelihood and severity of financial crises. He also elaborates on a number of associated policy challenges: the very fine balancing act that communication on monetary policy has needed to strike between informing the public's expectations of future action and conveying a sense of existing uncertainty about economic prospects, and the difficult trade-offs that monetary policy faces in EMEs and small open economies receiving large capital inflows with a correspondingly elevated risk of a sudden stop.

Two chapters present opposing views of monetary policy in the United States. *Ben Bernanke* offers a strong defense of the current framework. He argues that the Fed's adoption of an explicit inflation target has strengthened the anchoring of inflation expectations and gave the Fed more scope to ease monetary policy during the global recession. For him, a framework focused on targets rather than on instruments is robust to changes in the structure of the economy, and therefore is preferable to following a simple rule for the fed funds rate. The latter would unduly constrain monetary policy. Bernanke is also of the view that unconventional monetary policy tools (large-scale asset purchases and forward guidance) should eventually go back on the shelf, with the fed funds rate taking center stage again. He does acknowledge, however, a potential role for a larger central bank balance sheet going forward, mainly to provide an elastically supplied safe short-term asset (Fed liabilities).

For *John B. Taylor*, the monetary policy framework has instead been excessively discretionary, going back to the early 2000s. In his view, the resulting deviations from instrument rules–based policies were a key factor in the crisis and then again in the sluggish performance of the economy during the global recession period. He also argues that these deviations have extended beyond the United States, through the adoption of quantitative easing by other major central banks (for example), while also creating unpleasant monetary policy spillovers for EMEs. Taylor therefore advocates "renormalizing" monetary policy, by which he means return to a rules-based approach, suggesting that legislation might help. Such legislation would require the Fed to describe its rule or strategy for adjusting its policy instruments.

John Geanakoplos adds to the debate by arguing that central banks need to pay much more attention to financial conditions, and puts forward the concept of the credit surface. The credit surface traces the rates at which firms and households can borrow on the basis of their credit score and the value of their collateral, and it reflects the fact that default risk is an inherent element of the financial landscape. He argues that such a measure provides a much better view of financial conditions than the riskless interest rates central banks typically focus on. Geanakoplos goes on to argue that central banks need to intervene more directly on the credit surface in order to limit the booms and busts associated with credit and leverage. To do so, he advocates greater use of macroprudential tools, such as variations in loan-to-value ratios, and a more active lending role by central banks. But he also goes one step further, calling for policymakers to seriously consider debt forgiveness as a policy tool.

But are central banks taking on too much? For *Gill Marcus* the crisis forced central banks to take extraordinary actions, extending beyond their traditional focus. Additional responsibilities have been or are being added, including a greater focus on financial stability, the deployment of macroprudential tools, and so forth These actions have generated unrealistic expectations about what central banks can achieve, while also creating the perception that they have become too powerful. The distinction between fiscal and monetary policy has blurred as a result, and central bank independence is increasingly coming under pressure. Marcus acknowledges there are no easy solutions to this problem, as a return to the narrower inflation mandate may also undermine central banks' credibility.

Fiscal Policy in the Future

When the financial system froze, and monetary policy no longer worked, most advanced economies relied on fiscal policy to limit the decrease in demand, and in turn in output. However, these measures coincided with collapsing fiscal revenues and the materialization of contingent liabilities (including from the financial sector), resulting in a dramatic increase in ratios of public debt to GDP. This led to a policy shift from stimulus to debt stabilization. As we look now to the future, the experience raises a number of issues. Should we use fiscal policy more actively for macroeconomic purposes, and if so, under what conditions? What are safe public debt levels? Can automatic stabilizers be improved? In addition, the struggles of the EU since the crisis have placed fiscal rules at the forefront of the debate. Can one design better rules? And how can fiscal policy better incorporate risks?

Vitor Gaspar focuses on two aspects of policy. First, he calls for improved analysis of fiscal risks. One lesson from the crisis is that risks are highly correlated, asymmetric, and nonlinear. Efforts to better measure, prevent, and minimize these risks are imperative for fiscal policy not to become a source of future (debt) crises. Second, he emphasizes the importance of fiscal stabilization to reduce macroeconomic volatility and support growth. Gaspar introduces the fiscal stabilization coefficient (FISCO), a measure of fiscal countercyclicality, in which a higher coefficient implies a greater stabilization role. He outlines various measures that can increase countercyclicality, such as automatic tax deductions during recessions. He warns, however, against asymmetric stabilization because of its implications for ratcheting debt levels.

Martin Feldstein discusses when to use fiscal policy to stimulate investment and aggregate demand. The traditional objection to using fiscal policy as a macroeconomic tool is that recessions do not last long, and by the time discretionary fiscal measures are implemented, it is typically too late. Feldstein makes the point that some recessions, in particular those associated with financial crises, are long enough that discretionary policy can and should be used. He notes, however, that fiscal activism need not mean changes in the overall budget deficit or surplus but may come from changes in the composition of the budget, such as an increase in the investment tax credit financed by an increase in corporate taxation.

Marco Buti looks at the future of rules-based fiscal policy in the EU and the importance of flexibility. He argues that fiscal rules need to achieve a "double act": they need to ensure debt sustainability but also help stabilize the economy. The stabilizing role is especially important in currency unions, and yet has not been sufficiently emphasized in both the design and the implementation of the EU fiscal framework. More broadly, he argues, the current framework suffers from excessive complexity and lack of enforcement ability, both reflecting deeper political economy issues, namely, the lack of trust between the main actors in the coordination game. Despite these challenges, Buti points to recent efforts to make better use of the flexibility allowed within the current system to achieve a more growth-friendly fiscal stance and foster structural reforms, which he equates to designing "smarter" rules. The hope is that such efforts will allow a more effective implementation of the existing framework and an overall improvement in European fiscal policy.

Finally, *J. Bradford DeLong* makes a provocative case for both higher government spending and higher public debt levels in the twenty-first century. He argues that the economy will increasingly shift toward sectors (education, health care, information goods) in which market failures are pervasive. As a result, the relative size of the public sphere should expand. In addition, the rate at which the government borrows (r) is lower than the rate at which the economy grows (g), and has been so for close to two hundred years. If this is the case ($r < g$), the economy may be dynamically inefficient, in which case the textbook answer is for governments to increase, not decrease, current debt levels. If the low interest rates in fact reflect a demand by people for safety, then it still makes sense for the state to issue safe debt and use it for productive investment. (This is where the discussion about the "new normal," and what is in store for future interest rates, becomes highly relevant.)

If the interest rate is less than the growth rate, then public debt can be thought as fundamentally safe: the public debt-to-GDP ratio will decrease, even if the government never repays the debt. There are clearly limits to this argument. If the demand for safe assets driving low interest rates reflects some distortion that may be corrected in the future, then higher debt levels may not be sustainable. Or higher debt levels may increase the risk of self-fulfilling runs. DeLong acknowledges these risks but argues that historically, fiscal crises in industrial powers have been caused by fundamental news rather than by sudden changes in the demand for government debt. He also argues that governments will always be able to impose financial repression, if necessary, which reduces the risk of debt blowups.

Capital Inflows, Exchange Rate Management, and Capital Controls

The crisis has reinforced the notion that international capital flows can be very volatile, with EMEs being particularly vulnerable. Policymakers have responded with a panoply of tools: macroprudential measures aimed at shaping flows, foreign exchange intervention, and capital controls have all become part of the policy landscape. But do these tools work? When should they be used, and how should they be articulated with the rest of the toolbox? And what does the experience since the crisis say about the optimal opening of the capital account, even in the long run?

All three chapters in this part of the volume provide, to varying degrees, justifications for some of the nonconventional tools adopted by EMEs to deal with a volatile external environment.

Maurice Obstfeld places this discussion within the broader context of the system of flexible exchange rates that emerged following Bretton Woods. He argues that the very success of floating rates in promoting real and especially financial integration is now spurring efforts to reintroduce elements of market segmentation. There is an increasing acknowledgment that flexible exchange rates cannot fully insulate economies from the global financial cycle and the policy spillovers in the form of capital flows. In this context, capital controls can be considered a second-best option. Macroprudential policies would be preferable, but he argues that their effects on capital flows are not well understood.

Luiz Awazu Pereira da Silva makes the case for the "pragmatic" approach to policymaking implemented in Brazil, and EMEs more generally, following the crises of the 1990s and further enhanced after the global financial crisis. Initially, the approach consisted of a "textbook" component (a floating exchange rate, fiscal discipline, and inflation targeting), combined with nonstandard policies (self-insurance via reserves buildup and foreign exchange interventions to smooth exchange rate volatility). More recently, with the surge in capital inflows and the risks to financial stability, he argues that the approach has been successfully enhanced to include macroprudential policies, to avoid excessive credit growth, and refinements in the foreign exchange interventions policy to facilitate hedging by private firms.

For *Agustín Carstens*, the use of nonconventional tools in EMEs reflects a response to the financial risks created by the use of unconventional policies in advanced economies (which he nonetheless justifies in light of the domestic conditions in those countries). He sees "competitive reserve accumulation" in EMEs as an effort to mitigate the real and financial effects of capital surges and prepare for the associated flow reversals. In this regard, he argues, reserve accumulation can be considered a macroprudential tool. Carstens is, however, skeptical of bank-based macroprudential policies, given the market-based nature of the flows, as well as of the imposition of capital controls.

The International Monetary and Financial System

The financial crisis played out on a global scale, and the international monetary system was tested as never before. Central banks had to extend swap lines. The IMF created new programs to provide liquidity. Large capital flows, and large changes in exchange rates, triggered talk of currency wars. More broadly, spillovers from unconventional policies from advanced economies to the rest of the world have increasingly come into focus, as attested by the previous discussion. But are these spillovers well understood? Can we live with the existing system? If international coordination is necessary, what form should it take? Can we design cross-border financial regulation and limit the risks of international arbitrage? Should we reexamine the rules of the game for exchange rates?

Jaime Caruana makes the case that there is a blind spot in the international monetary system: the combination of domestically focused policies ("local" rules) and global markets does not constrain the buildup and international transmission of financial imbalances. Though Caruana acknowledges that better integration of financial stability considerations into a domestic macro framework can help, his view is that countries, especially large advanced economies, need to internalize the so called "spillbacks"—the feedback from the effects of their policies on other countries back onto their own countries—in their policy decisions. More research is needed to determine the nature and magnitude of these spillbacks. Caruana also makes the case for greater international cooperation, including through global rules of the game (an argument further developed by Raghuram Rajan later in this part of the book).

Zeti Akhtar Aziz reviews international policy coordination since the crisis. She sees progress in the coordination of financial stability policies through the creation of new international agencies such as the Financial Stability Board and the strengthening of cross-border supervisory arrangements, such as the implementation of global recovery and resolution plans. She cautions against unilateral measures, such as ring-fencing of national financial systems, arguing that such measures would constitute a retreat from desirable financial globalization.[6] Aziz sees little progress in the coordination of macro policies, with the exception of regional arrangements, such as the Chiang Mai initiative of multilateral currency swaps among Asian central banks.

Ricardo J. Caballero identifies a weakness in the international financial system. There is, he argues, a global shortage of safe assets, which he sees as a main factor behind low real interest rates and secular stagnation (the "safety trap"). For Caballero, quantitative easing in advanced economies, of the type focused on long-term government bonds, and reserve accumulation in EMEs are aggravating the problem by further reducing the supply of long-term safe assets. He argues that quantitative easing by advanced countries' central banks is particularly counterproductive, given its limited direct real effects (which implies that much larger purchases are needed) and the triggering of further reserve accumulation by EMEs. Two recommendations follow: (1) to go further in the global pooling of risks by strengthening IMF facilities and extending swap arrangements so that there is less need for self-insurance by central banks in EMEs, and (2) to pay increasing attention to the global spillovers from policies in advanced economies.

Finally, *Raghuram Rajan* goes further in his critique of the international monetary system. He argues there is excessive focus in reigniting weak growth in advanced economies, which he labels "the growth imperative." This imperative is pushing central banks to engage in policies (e.g., quantitative easing) whose effects, he argues, are to shift demand away from other countries and to increase leverage and financial vulnerabilities. Rajan makes an explicit call for multilateral organizations such as the IMF to develop new rules of the game with regard to exchange rates, and to explicitly assess whether countries' policies are consistent with these rules.

Conclusion

In light of these discussions, does progress or confusion prevail with regard to the future of macro policy? In the final chapter, *Olivier Blanchard* concludes the answer is both. For example, he argues that there is agreement that macroprudential policies have to be become part of the toolkit. But there is a great deal of uncertainty about the type of tools, given the changing shape of the financial system. In the monetary policy area, Blanchard agrees that many lessons have been learned. But there is no clear agreement on some of the key issues, such as the right size of central bank balance sheets or the type of instruments. And on fiscal policy, confusion remains about what constitute safe levels of debt.

Notes

1. See Blanchard et al. (2012) and Akerlof et al. (2014).

2. See Summers (2015).

3. See IMF, *World Economic Outlook* (2014b), chap. 3.

4. Looking at banking crises since 1970, recent research at the IMF (Dagher et al. 2015) finds that a risk-weighted capital ratio of 15–22 percent would have been sufficient to fully absorb bank losses in approximately 90 percent of them, or about 9–13 percent in non-risk-weighted terms.

5. See IMF, *Global Financial Stability Report* (2014b), among others.

6. Obstfeld's chapter in the previous section raises an interesting counterpoint. He sees regulatory efforts to ring-fence domestic financial systems as attempts to regain national sovereignty over financial policy. These efforts may be segmenting global banks' internal capital markets and reducing efficiency, but Obstfeld argues that this may be worthwhile if it helps reduce risks to financial stability worldwide.

References

Akerlof, George, Olivier Blanchard, David Romer, and Joseph Stiglitz. 2014. *What Have We Learned?* Cambridge, MA: MIT Press.

Blanchard, Olivier, David Romer, Michael Spence, and Joseph Stiglitz. 2012. *In the Wake of the Crisis.* Cambridge, MA: MIT Press.

Dagher, Jihad, Giovanni Dell'Ariccia, Luc Laeven, Lev Ratnovski, and Hui Tong. 2015. "Bank Capital: How Much Is Enough?" Submitted manuscript. Washington, DC: International Monetary Fund.

International Monetary Fund. 2014 a. "Perspectives on Global Interest Rates." In *World Economic Outlook*, chap. 3. Washington, DC: International Monetary Fund, April.

International Monetary Fund. 2014 b. "Improving the Balance between Financial and Economic Risk Taking." In *Risk Taking, Liquidity, and Shadow Banking: Curbing Excess while Promoting Growth*, chap. 1. Global Financial Stability Report. Washington, DC: International Monetary Fund, October.

Summers, Lawrence. 2015. "Have We Entered an Age of Secular Stagnation? IMF Fourteenth Annual Research Conference in Honor of Stanley Fischer, Washington, DC." *IMF Economic Review* 63 (1): 277–280.

The "New Normal"

2

Debt Supercycle, Not Secular Stagnation

Kenneth Rogoff

I want to address a narrow yet fundamental question for understanding the current challenges facing the global economy: Has the world sunk into "secular stagnation," with a long future of much lower per capita income growth driven significantly by a chronic deficiency in global demand? Or does weak postcrisis growth reflect the post-financial-crisis phase of a debt supercycle where, after deleveraging and borrowing headwinds subside, expected growth trends might prove higher than simple extrapolations of recent performance might suggest?[1]

In this chapter I argue that the financial crisis/debt supercycle view provides a much more accurate and useful framework for understanding what has transpired and what is likely to come next. Recovery from financial crises need not be symmetric; the United States and perhaps the United Kingdom have reached the end of the deleveraging cycle, while Europe, owing to weaknesses in the construction of the eurozone, is still very much in the thick of it. China, having markedly raised economy-wide debt levels in response to the crisis originating in the West, now faces its own challenges from high debt, particularly local government debt.

The Case for a Debt Supercycle

The evidence in favor of the debt supercycle view is not merely qualitative but also quantitative. The run-up to and aftermath of the 2008 global financial crisis has unfolded like a garden variety post–World War II financial crisis, with very strong parallels to the baseline averages and medians that Carmen Reinhart and I documented in our 2009 book, *This Time Is Different*.[2] The evidence is not simply the deep fall in output and subsequent very sluggish U-shaped recovery in per capita income that commonly characterize recovery from deep systemic financial crises. It also includes the magnitude of the housing boom and bust, the huge leverage that accompanied the bubble, the behavior of equity prices before and after the crisis, and certainly the fact that increases in unemployment were far more persistent than after an ordinary recession that is not accompanied by a systemic financial crisis. Even the dramatic increases in public debt that occurred after the crisis are quite characteristic.

Of course, the crisis had unique features, the most important of which was the eurozone debt drama, which exacerbated and deepened the problem. Emerging market economies (EMEs) initially recovered relatively quickly, in part because many entered the crisis with relatively strong balance sheets. Unfortunately, a long period of higher borrowing by both the public sector and corporations has left EMEs vulnerable to an echo of the advanced economies' financial crisis, particularly as growth in China slows and the US Federal Reserve System contemplates raising interest rates.

Modern macroeconomics has been slow to come to grips with the analytics of how to incorporate debt supercycles into canonical models, but there has been much progress in recent years,[3] and the broad contours help explain the now well-documented empirical regularities. As credit booms, asset prices rise, which raises their value as collateral, thereby helping to expand credit and raise asset prices even more. When the bubble ultimately bursts, often catalyzed by an underlying adverse shock to the real economy, the whole process spins into a harsh and precipitous reverse.

Of course, policy played an important role. However, there has been far too much focus on orthodox policy responses and not enough on heterodox responses that might have been better suited to a crisis greatly amplified by a financial market breakdown. In particular, policymakers should have more vigorously pursued debt write-downs (e.g., subprime debt in the United States and periphery country debt in Europe), accompanied by bank restructuring and recapitalization. In addition, central banks were too rigid in their inflation target regimes; had they been more aggressive in getting out in front of the crisis by pushing for temporarily elevated inflation rates, the problem of the zero lower bound might have been avoided. In general, the failure to more seriously consider the kinds of heterodox responses that EMEs have long employed in part reflected an inadequate understanding of how advanced economies have dealt with banking and debt crises in the past.[4]

Fiscal policy (one of the instruments of the orthodox response) was initially very helpful in avoiding the worst possible outcomes, but then many countries tightened prematurely, as IMF managing director Christine Lagarde rightly noted in her opening speech at the "Rethinking Macro Policy III" conference. Slowing the rate of debt accumulation was one motivation, as she noted, but let us not have collective amnesia. Overly optimistic forecasts played a central role in every aspect of most countries' response to the crisis. No one organization was to blame, as virtually every major central bank, finance ministry, and international financial organization was repeatedly overoptimistic. Most private and public forecasters anticipated that once a recovery began, it would be V-shaped, even if somewhat delayed. In fact, the recovery took the form of the very slow U-shaped recovery predicted by scholars who had studied past financial crises and debt supercycles. The notion that the forecasting mistakes were mostly due to misunderstanding fiscal multipliers is thin indeed. The timing and strength of both the US and UK recoveries defied the predictions of polemicists, who insisted that very slow and gradual normalization of fiscal policy was inconsistent with recovery.

Secular Stagnation

Of course, secular factors have played a role, as they always do in both good times and bad. Indeed, banking crises almost invariably have their roots in deeper real factors driving the economy, with banking crises typically being an amplification mechanism rather than a root cause.

What are some particularly obvious secular factors? Well, of course, demographic decline has set in across most of the advanced world and is on the doorstep of many EMEs, notably China. In the long run, global population stabilization will be of huge help in achieving sustainable global economic growth, but the transition is surely having profound effects, even if we do not begin to understand all of them.

Another less trumpeted secular factor is the inevitable tapering off of rising female participation in the labor force. For the past few decades, the ever-greater share of women in the labor force has added to measured per capita output, but the main shift is likely nearing an end in many countries, and so will no longer contribute to growth.

Then there is also the supercycle of Asia's rise in the global economy, particularly China. Asian growth has been pushing up IMF estimates of global potential growth for three decades now. As China shifts to a more consumption-based domestic-demand-driven growth model, its growth will surely taper off, with significant effects around the globe on consumers' real incomes and on commodity prices, among other factors. As Asian growth slows, global growth will likely tend back toward its fifty-year average.

Going forward, perhaps the most difficult secular factor to predict is technology. Technology is the ultimate driver of per capita income growth in the classic Solow growth model. Some would argue that technology is stagnating, with computers and the Internet being a relatively modest and circumscribed advance compared to past industrial revolutions. Perhaps, but there are reasons to be much more optimistic. Economic globalization, communication, and computing trends all suggest an environment highly conducive to continuing rapid innovation and implementation, not a slowdown. Indeed, I personally am far more worried that technological progress will outstrip our ability to socially and politically adapt to it than that innovation is stagnating. Of course, because of tight credit in the aftermath of the financial crisis, some technological developments may have been "trapped" by lack of funding. But the ideas are not lost, and the cost to growth is not necessarily permanent.

What of Solow's famous 1987 remark, "You can see the computer age everywhere but in the statistics"? Perhaps, but one has to wonder to what extent the statistics accurately capture the welfare gains embodied in new goods during a period of such rapid technological advancement. Examples abound. In advanced economies, the possibilities for entertainment have expanded exponentially, with consumers having at their fingertips a treasure trove of music, films, and TV programs that would have been unimaginable twenty-five years ago. Health improvements through the use of low-cost statins, ibuprofen, and other miracle drugs are widespread. It is easy to be cynical about social media, but the fact is that humans enormously value connectivity, even if GDP statistics really cannot measure the consumer surplus from these inventions. Skype and other telephony advances allow a grandmother to speak face-to-face with a grandchild in a distant city or country. Disruptive technologies such as the transportation network Uber point the way toward vastly more efficient uses of the existing capital stock. Yes, there are negative trends, such as environmental degradation, that detract from welfare, but overall it is quite likely that measured GDP growth understates actual growth, especially when measured over long periods. It is quite possible that future economic historians, using perhaps more sophisticated measurement techniques, will evaluate ours as an era of strong growth in middle-class consumption, in contradiction to the often polemic discussion one sees in public debate on the issue.

All in all, the debt supercycle model and the secular stagnation view of today's global economy may present two different views of interpreting the same phenomenon, but one is far more speculative than the other. The debt supercycle model matches up with a couple of hundred years of experience with similar financial crises. The secular stagnation view does not capture the heart attack the global economy experienced; slow-moving demographics do not explain sharp housing price bubbles and collapses.

Low Real Interest Rates Mask an Elevated Credit Surface

What about the very low value of real interest rates? Low rates are often taken as prima facie evidence by secular stagnation proponents, who argue that only a chronic demand deficiency could be responsible for steadily driving down the global real interest rate. The steady decline in real interest rates is certainly a puzzle, but a host of factors could account for it. First, we do not actually observe the true economic real interest rate; that would require a utility-based price index that is extremely difficult to construct in a world of rapid change in both the kinds of goods we consume and the way we consume them. My guess is that the true real interest rate is higher, and perhaps this bias is larger than usual. Correspondingly, true economic inflation is probably considerably lower than even the low measured values that central banks are struggling to raise.

Perhaps more important, in a world where regulation has sharply curtailed access for many smaller and riskier borrowers, low sovereign bond yields do not necessarily capture the broader credit surface the global economy faces.[5] Whether by accident or by design, banking and financial market regulation has hugely favored low-risk borrowers (governments and cash-heavy corporations), knocking out other potential borrowers who might have competed up rates. Many of those who can borrow face higher collateral requirements. The elevated credit surface owes partly to inherent riskiness and slow growth in a postcrisis economy, but policy has also played a large role. Many governments, particularly in Europe, have rammed sovereign bonds down the throats of pension funds, banks, and insurance companies. Financial repression of this type effectively taxes not only middle-income savers and pensioners (who receive low rates of return on their savings) but also potential borrowers (especially middle-class consumers and small businesses), which these institutions might have financed to a greater extent had they not been required to be so overweight in government debt.

Surely global interest rates are also affected by the massive balance sheet expansions that most advanced country central banks have engaged in. I don't believe this is as important as the other effects I have discussed (even if most market participants would say the reverse). Global quantitative easing by advanced economies and sterilized intervention operations by EMEs have also surely had a very large impact on bringing down market volatility measures.

The fact that global stock market indices have hit new peaks is certainly a problem for the secular stagnation theory, unless one believes that profit shares are going to rise massively further. I won't pretend there is one simple explanation for the stock-bond disconnect (after all, I have already listed several). But one important observation follows the work of my colleague Robert Barro. Barro has shown that in canonical equilibrium macroeconomic models (which could be Keynesian, but his is not), small changes in the market perception of tail risks can lead both to significantly lower real risk-free interest rates and to a higher equity premium. Another one of my colleagues, Martin Weitzman, has espoused a different variant of the same idea based on how people form Bayesian assessments of the risk of extreme events.

Indeed, it is not hard to believe that the average global investor changed his or her general assessment of all types of tail risks after the global financial crisis. The fact that EM investors are playing a steadily increasing role in global portfolios also plausibly raises generalized risk perceptions, since many of these investors inhabit regions that are still inherently riskier than advanced economy countries. I don't have time to go into great detail here, though I have discussed the idea for many years in policy writings[6] and have explored the idea analytically in recent work with Carmen and Vincent Reinhart.[7] Of course, a rise in tail risks will also initially cause asset prices to drop (as they did in the financial crisis), but then subsequently they will offer a higher rate of return to compensate for risk. All in all, a rise in tail risks seems quite plausible, even if massive central bank intervention sometimes masks the effect on market volatility measures.

What are the policy differences between the debt supercycle model and the secular stagnation view? When it comes to government spending that productively and efficiently enhances future growth, the differences are not first order. With low real interest rates and large numbers of unemployed (or underemployed) construction workers, good infrastructure projects should offer a much higher rate of return than usual.

However, those who would argue that even a very mediocre project is worth doing when interest rates are low have a much tougher case to make. It is highly superficial and dangerous to argue that debt is basically free. To the extent that low interest rates result from fear of tail risks à la Barro and Weitzman, one has to worry that the government itself might be exposed to the same kinds of risks the market is worried about, especially if overall economy-wide debt and pension obligations are near or at historical highs already. Obstfeld has argued cogently that governments in countries with large financial sectors need to have ample cushion, as otherwise government borrowing might become very expensive in precisely the states of nature where the private sector has problems.[8] Alternatively, if one views low interest rates as giving a false view of the broader credit surface (as Geanakoplos argues), one has to worry whether higher government debt will perpetuate the political economy policies that are helping the government finance debt but making it more difficult for small businesses and the middle class to obtain credit.

Unlike secular stagnation, the debt supercycle is not forever. As the economy recovers, collateral values will recover and, eventually, the economy will be positioned for a new rising phase of the leverage cycle. Over time, financial innovation will bypass some of the more onerous regulations. If so, real interest rates will rise, though the overall credit surface facing the economy will flatten and ease.

Sundry Unrelated Issues

Let me conclude by briefly touching on a few further issues. First, it is unfortunate that in the debate over the size of government, there is far too little discussion of how to make government a more effective provider of services. The case for having a bigger government can be strengthened when combined with ways for finding out how to make government better. Education would seem to be a leading example. Second, inequality in advanced economy countries is certainly a problem and plausibly plays a role in the global shift to a higher savings rate. Tax policy should be used to address these secular trends, perhaps starting with higher taxes on urban land, which seems to lie at the root of inequality in wealth trends. I am puzzled again, however, that those who claim to be interested in inequality from a fairness perspective pay so much attention to the world's upper middle class (the middle class of advanced economy countries) and so little attention to the true global middle class. Shouldn't a factory worker in China get the same weight in global welfare as one in France? If so, the past thirty years have largely been characterized by historic decreases in inequality,[9] not rises, as many seem to believe. In any event, these are all important issues, but they should not be confused with longer-term output-per-capita trends.

Concluding Remarks

The case for describing the world as being in a debt supercycle is both theoretically and empirically compelling. The case for secular stagnation is far thinner. It is always very difficult to predict long-run future growth trends, and although there are some headwinds, it seems at least as likely that technological progress will outperform over the next two decades as that it will exhibit a sharp slowdown.

Again, the United States appears to be near the tail end of its leverage cycle and Europe is still deleveraging, while China may be nearing the downside of a leverage cycle. Though many factors are at work, the view that we have lived through a debt supercycle, marked by a severe financial crisis, is far more constructive for policy analysis than the view that the world is suffering from long-term secular stagnation as a result of a chronic shortfall of demand.[10]

Notes

1. Stephanie Lo and Kenneth Rogoff, "Secular Stagnation, Debt Overhang and Other Rationales for Sluggish Growth, Six Years On," BIS Working Paper 482, Bank for International Settlements, January 2015, http://www.bis.org/publ/work482.htm.

2. Carmen M. Reinhart and Kenneth S. Rogoff, *This Time Is Different: Eight Centuries of Financial Folly* (Princeton, NJ: Princeton University Press, 2009).

3. For a survey, see John Geanakoplos, "Leverage, Default, and Forgiveness: Lessons of the American and European Crises," *Journal of Macroeconomics* 39, pt. B (March 2014): 313–333.

4. Carmen M. Reinhart, Vincent Reinhart, and Kenneth Rogoff, "Dealing with Debt," *Journal of International Economics* 96, Suppl. 1 (2015): S43–S55, http://www.sciencedirect.com/science/article/pii/S0022199614001214.

5. Geanakoplos, "Leverage, Default, and Forgiveness."

6. Kenneth Rogoff, "The Stock-Bond Disconnect," Project Syndicate, March 9, 2015, http://www.project-syndicate.org/commentary/equity-low-interest-rates-by-kenneth-rogoff-2015-03.

7. Reinhart, Reinhart, and Rogoff, "Dealing with Debt."

8. Maurice Obstfeld, "On Keeping Your Powder Dry: Fiscal Foundations of Financial and Price Stability," faculty paper, Department of Economics, University of California, Berkeley, June 14, 2013, http://eml.berkeley.edu/~obstfeld/fiscalfoundations.pdf.

9. Kenneth Rogoff, "Where Is the Inequality Problem?," Project Syndicate, May 8, 2014, http://www.project-syndicate.org/commentary/kenneth-rogoff-says-that-thomas-piketty-is-right-about-rich-countries--but-wrong-about-the-world.

10. Lo and Rogoff, "Secular Stagnation."

3

Rethinking Secular Stagnation after Seventeen Months

Lawrence H. Summers

I salute Olivier Blanchard and the IMF for so open a dialogue at the conference on so wide a range of macroeconomic hypotheses. What I want to do in this chapter is talk about three things: I want to express why I think that the risk of secular stagnation is an important problem throughout the developed world. I want to contrast the secular stagnation viewpoint with two views that I regard as heavily overlapping—the debt supercycle view that Ken Rogoff has put forward and the savings glut view that Ben Bernanke has put forward—and explain why I think they're very similar but, as far their nuances of difference are concerned, I prefer the secular stagnation view. And then I want to reflect on the policy implications of this general view of the global economy over the next decade.

What has happened in the seventeen months since I first broached the possibility of secular stagnation at another conference that Olivier organized?[1] Interest rates have sharply declined in the United States, where quantitative easing was ended; in Japan, where it was continued; and in Europe, where it was initiated. And index bond yields remain remarkably low over quite long periods of time. Growth has remained sluggish, and growth forecasts have been revised downward to a substantial extent (table 3.1, figure 3.1).

Real forward rates over the 2020–2025 period, which should clearly be after the hangover of the financial crisis, are negative in Japan and the euro area and barely positive for the United States (table 3.2). The so-called five-year indexed bond yields are negative or barely positive. And nowhere in the G-7 is market-expected inflation over a ten-year period likely to reach the 2 percent target.

So even as we have moved a year and a half further away from the crisis, market pricing has actually moved in all the directions you would

Table 3.1
Ten-Year Interest Rates, April 2015 and November 2013 (Initial IMF Speech on Secular Stagnation)

Rates	USA 11-8-2013	Now	Japan 11-8-2013	Now	Germany 11-8-2013	Now	UK 11-8-2013	Now
Nominal	2.80	2.01	0.59	0.34	1.76	0.16	2.77	1.59
Real	0.63	0.20	−0.37	−0.74	0.22	−1.23	−0.47	−1.12
Inflation	2.17	1.82	0.96	1.08	1.53	1.39	3.24	2.71

Sources: Bloomberg; Gürykaynak, Sack, and Wright (2006, 2008).

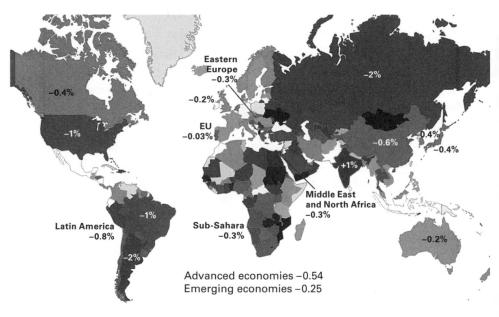

Figure 3.1
Changes to Medium-Term GDP Forecast since October 2013, Five-Year Effects.
Source: IMF, *World Economic Outlook,* October 2013 and April 2015.

Table 3.2
Real Rates, 2020–2025 (%)

USA	0.28
Japan	−0.14
Euro	−0.88

Table 3.3
Breakeven Ten-Year Inflation (%)

Canada	1.79
France	1.42
Germany	1.39
Italy	1.26
Japan	1.08
Sweden	1.45
UK*	1.81
USA	1.82

Note: *CPI inflation.
Source: Bloomberg.

expect if you thought that there was a chronic excess of savings over investment (table 3.3).

Now, Ken Rogoff argues the debt supercycle view, that the current weakness is the temporary result of overindebtedness.[2] It seems to me that there is a pretty good way of distinguishing between one aspect of the debt supercycle theory and that of secular stagnation in what the markets are telling us. The debt supercycle view does not have a ready explanation for the low level of real interest rates, nor does it have a ready explanation for the fact that real interest rates have fallen steadily. In fact, real interest rates have trended downward over fifteen years regardless of whether measured for the United States through TIPs (figure 3.2), or measured globally by the IMF, or measured in almost any way you can measure (e.g., figure 3.3), and had already reached quite low levels in the aftermath of the last recession in 2003.

For instance, figures 3.2 and 3.3 show US TIPS rates and the average level of world real interest rates. If you looked at the trend from before the crisis in 2007 and extrapolated the trend to now, you would not be wildly off. And yet the whole debt overhang idea is that what is really defining life right now is that we were dealing with some overhang of the crisis, so if that were true, there should be no way to dictate the current level of real interest rates from stuff that happened prior to the crisis. And I would argue that it is closer to right to say that real rates are spot on the trend.

Ken Rogoff suggests an alternative hypothesis for explaining the low level of real interest rates, which is a generalized increase in the level of risk in the world. I agree with him that if there was a substantial and generalized increase in perceived risk, you might expect that to lead to a decline in real interest rates. You would also, however, expect it to lead to a decline, rather than an increase, in asset values, given that it was those assets that had become more risky. You would expect it to manifest itself in a measurable and clear increase in implied volatilities, as reflected in options markets. You would expect it to reflect itself in a dramatic

Figure 3.2
TIP Real Wages Have Fallen Steadily. US TIPS Ten-Year Real Yield.
Source: Bloomberg.

increase in the pricing of out-of-the-money puts. But the opposite has occurred. It is far cheaper today to buy insurance against the Dow falling below 12,000 than it was a year ago, or two years ago, or four years ago. If one thinks about the market pricing of risk, it seems that risk has declined rather than increased. And it seems to me that the length of time that markets are forecasting low real interest rates makes the stagnation fairly secular or the debt supercycle very long, at which point the distinction blurs.

And what is the temporary debt overhang–induced headwind that is thought to be present in a major way today but that will be gone in three years? Corporate balance sheets are flush. The spread between LIBOR and other yields are low. Debt service ratios are at abnormally low levels. Whatever your indicator of repair from the financial crisis, it has mostly happened. And yet with interest rates of zero, the US economy is still likely to grow by only 2 percent this year. I do not see a good reason to be confident that the situation will be significantly better three years from now.

So, first, it is not like real interest rates are in some kind of extraordinary place relative to what you would have thought based on pre-2007 trends. Second, there is no obvious theory as to what the removable headwinds

Figure 3.3
Along with Rates in the Rest of World. Rest of World Real Rate.
Note: 10 Year Yield – 5 Year Prior Inflation, weighted by PPP GDP.
Source: Bloomberg, IMF.

will be from this point on. And third, any debt overhang would itself be endogenous. Why did we have a vast erosion of credit standards by 2005? Why were interest rates in a place that enabled such bubbles? Because that was what was necessary to keep the economy going with adequate aggregate demand through that period. So even if a debt overhang were occurring, it would in a sense be a mechanism through which secular stagnation or oversaving produced damage. It is not an alternative to the idea of secular stagnation.

What about Ben Bernanke's idea that there this a savings glut?[3] The idea that there is a chronic excess of saving over investment (i.e., secular stagnation) and the idea that there is a savings glut kind of sound the same. That is because in many respects they are the same. As best I can tell, there are two questions on which Ben Bernanke and I have somewhat different judgments. One difference—where I would amend my views in his direction—has to do with the importance of taking into account the open economy aspects in thinking about this question of secular stagnation. I very much agree that a structural increase in savings that took place internationally would lead to the low real rates that I described. If I had my remarks at the IMF last year and in 2013 to do again, I would put more emphasis than I did at the time on the importance of the international aspects of increased saving relative to investment. But in either event, the fundamental reality is the same: an increase in saving leads to lower interest rates, which leads to a shortfall of demand.

In a forthcoming paper with Gauti Eggertsson, Neil Mehrotra, and Sanjay Singh, I further explore the open economy aspects of secular stagnation. We show that secular stagnation can persist on a global basis so long as the world real interest rate is below zero.[4] When that is the case, countries with relatively attractive investment opportunities (but barriers to external investment) will be wary of increased foreign investment because capital inflows could cause their domestic interest rates to fall below zero, thereby risking domestic secular stagnation. Alternatively, a country mired in secular stagnation will be relatively better off if it spreads that stagnation to its trading partners. Put simply, secular stagnation is a contagious malady.

I think it is important for understanding the global economy and a crucial issue for US economic policy that Europe and to some extent Japan are indeed exporting their secular stagnations. They are exporting their secular stagnation by having a very low equilibrium interest rate, leading to capital outflows, leading to currency depreciation, leading to the shift in demand toward Europe and Japan and leading toward a shift in the shipping demand away from the United States.

Ten years ago, when Ben first started talking about a savings glut,[5] there was a substantial and legitimate concern that countries were pursuing mercantile policies either because of the economic development advantages of running substantial trade surpluses or because of a desire to build up reserves so as never to have to deal with the IMF. This led to substantial capital exports. Today there is much less of that going on, with the notable exception of Germany. Rather, today many emerging market economies are each in their own way having substantial troubles, and the environment is much less attractive for capital than would have been expected five years ago in Brazil, in Russia, in China, and in South Africa. It is not so much more attractive in India as to offset all of that, and so for a different reason you are seeing a shift toward capital exports from emerging markets.

So, yes, the rest of the world is providing savings to the industrial world, and the rest of the industrial world is providing savings to the United States. That is an important part of the savings glut, and an important driver of secular stagnation.

The other difference is Ben's suggestion that the savings glut is a relatively transitory phenomenon that will be repaired. Perhaps in the fullness of time it will. I think it is very difficult to read market judgments about real interest rates as suggesting that that scenario is likely. It is very difficult to read the IMF forecasts—with continuing downward revisions in medium-term growth—as suggesting that we are in a process of repair and healing, rather than suffering from a more serious problem. So, it's my judgment that for the relevant medium-term policy horizon (as I have no useful views about 2040 or 2050) the challenge of absorbing savings in productive investment will be the overriding challenge for macroeconomic policy.

What are the implications of that view? First, there is a compelling case for pro-productive investment policy. Pro-productive investment policy raises supply and raises demand. When countries initiate it domestically it leads their exchange rates to appreciate and, therefore, has favorable international spillovers. It is a question of values and a question of specifics to what extent the right pro-investment policies involve public investment or involve incentives or the removal of barriers to private investment. But if one accepts this diagnosis, the most straightforward response is a focus on pro-investment policies. For the United States there is a compelling case, at a time when net federal infrastructure investment is zero, for an increase in infrastructure investment. And there is also a compelling case for a set of measures that would free up and stimulate energy investment in the private sector, and also a compelling case for corporate tax reform. The details will vary from country to country, but the clearest response and the one that avoids the most difficulties is a pro-investment response.

Second, monetary policies. I think it is a mistake to overdo the exogeneity of monetary policy. Here Ben Bernanke was very clear, and I thought exactly right, in his blog, in explaining that if monetary policy is seeking to regulate economies for full employment, the real interest rates that are set will respond to the broader structural factors that determine equilibrium real interest rates.[6] I am worried about the view that if equilibrium real rates have to be very low, then monetary policy just needs to figure out how to make them very low with some combination of pre-commitments, revised inflation targets, and quantitative easing. I worry about that view not because I think doing nothing is better in the face of fiscal inaction but because I think the catalogue of risks associated with pursuing negative real interest rates is significant. The risks are to financial instability and for the creation of bubbles in an environment where interest rates are significantly less than growth rates, and for the international spillovers that may result from such policies. I relate to the concerns that the public sector will build infrastructure badly, and that that will be inefficient, and we should not be advocating that. But I do not understand why there is not a concern that the incremental investment projects that the private sector does not undertake now with a zero percent interest rate, but would choose to undertake with a negative 1 percent interest rate, will be projects that are of particular value. And I worry about the substantial impetus to financial engineering that hyper-low interest rates generate.

So my judgment is that whether we call it a savings glut, a debt supercycle, secular stagnation, or a quacking duck, we need to recognize the reality that the defining challenge is going to be absorbing all the savings in a satisfactory way in the global economy for the next decade.

The first priority for policy should not be financial engineering in either the private sector or the public sector but a concerted effort to identify and find the means of financing the most productive investment opportunities globally.

Notes

1. Lawrence H. Summers, "IMF Fourteenth Annual Conference in Honor of Stan Fischer," May 2015, http://larrysummers.com/imf-fourteenth-annual-research-conference-in-honor-of-stanley-fischer.

2. Kenneth Rogoff, "Debt Supercycle, Not Secular Stagnation," *VoxEU*, Centre for Economic Policy Research, April 22, 2015, http://www.voxeu.org/article/debt-supercycle-not-secular-stagnation.

3. See Ben S. Bernanke, "Why Are Interest Rates So Low, Part 2: Secular Stagnation" (blog post, *Ben Bernanke's Blog,* March 31, 2015, http://www.brookings.edu/blogs/ben-bernanke/posts/2015/03/31-why-interest-rates-low-secular-stagnation), for Bernanke's recent post on secular stagnation, and "On Secular Stagnation: A Response to Bernanke" (http://larrysummers.com/2015/04/01/on-secular-stagnation-a-response-to-bernanke) for my response.

4. Gauti B. Eggertsson, Neil Mehrotra, Sanjay Singh, and Lawrence H. Summers, "A Contagious Malady? Open Economy Dimensions of Secular Stagnation," forthcoming, 2015. For a prepublication pdf, see https://www.imf.org/external/np/seminars/eng/2015/secularstag/pdf/Eggertsson_pres.pdf.

5. Ben S. Bernanke, "The Global Savings Glut and the U.S. Current Account Deficit," remarks by Governor Ben S. Bernanke before the Virginia Association of Economists, the Sandridge Lecture, March 10, 2005, http://www.federalreserve.gov/boarddocs/speeches/2005/200503102.

6. Ben S. Bernanke, "Why Are Interest Rates So Low?," blog post, *Ben Bernanke's Blog,* March 30, 2015, http://www.brookings.edu/blogs/ben-bernanke/posts/2015/03/30-why-interest-rates-so-low.

References

Gürkaynak, Refet S., Brian Sack, and Jonathan H. Wright. 2006. "The U.S. Treasury Yield Curve: 1961 to the Present," Federal Reserve Finance and Economics Discussion Series 2006-28, 2006. http://www.federalreserve.gov/pubs/feds/2006/200628/200628abs.html.

Gürkaynak, Refet S., Brian Sack, and Jonathan H. Wright. 2008. "The TIPS Yield Curve and Inflation Compensation," Federal Reserve Finance and Economics Discussion Series 2008-05, 2008. http://www.federalreserve.gov/pubs/feds/2008/200805/200805abs.html.

Systemic Risk and Financial Regulation

4

A Note from the Session on Systemic Risk and Financial Regulation

Paul A. Volcker

Three participants—two distinguished academics and a prominent ex-central banker and financial executive—presented overlapping analyses of the challenge for "macroprudential" supervision.

Several themes stood out. One was common and not unexpected: the fundamental importance of strong capital requirements for commercial banks, and more generally, concerns about excessive leverage throughout the financial system.

Within that context, however, substantial differences in analysis were evident. One was concern about the potential weakness of relying on "risk-based" measures of capital, given the difficulty of identifying the sources of risk, current and potential. The usefulness of contingent capital instruments (i.e., those characterized by mandatory convertibility at times of stress) was debated, as was the role of stress tests in varying circumstances.

More fundamental differences were apparent in concerns about the stiff regulation of commercial banks inducing other financial institutions to undertake more maturity and credit transformation outside the regulatory framework. That concern may be more evident in the United States, with its more developed shadow banking system.

Though session chair, I could not refrain from expressing my own concerns. Years ago, I was a strong proponent of the view that, if a strong banking system could be assured by official oversight or otherwise, then other financial institutions and markets could be lightly supervised, and left free to fail. That view, in my mind, is no longer tenable when non-banks in the United States have come to account for more total financing, often with high leverage, than commercial banks themselves.

Finally, there was discussion of the importance of shifting cultures in financial institutions toward an emphasis on short-term performance and impersonal "counterparty" trading as opposed to building customer relationships. It is a difficult area. Some hope was expressed that in practice, a better "culture" could be encouraged by sensible regulation and supervision. A small ray of hope thus emerged to conclude the session.

5

A Comparative Analysis of Financial Sector Health in the United States, Europe, and Asia

Viral V. Acharya

This chapter uses recent methodology for estimating capital shortfalls of financial institutions during aggregated stress to assess the evolution of financial sector health since 2007 in the United States, Europe, and Asia. Financial sector capital shortfalls reached a peak at the end of 2008 and in early 2009 for the United States and Europe; however, they declined thereafter steadily only for the United States, with Europe reaching a similar peak in the fall of 2011 during the southern periphery sovereign crises. In contrast, the financial sector in Asia had little capital shortfall in 2008–2009, but the shortfall has increased steadily since 2010, notably for China. These relative patterns can be explained based on the regulatory responses in the United States to improve the capitalization of the financial sector, the lack of such an adequate response to recapitalize the financial sector in Europe, and the undertaking of bank-leverage-based fiscal stimulus in China.

In particular, the chapter exploits a theoretically well-founded notion of the systemic risk contribution of financial firms—their *expected capital shortfall in a crisis*—and measures it using publicly available market and balance sheet data. This approach allows a comparative analysis of the global financial sector health since early 2007, focusing on similarities and differences among the United States, Europe, and Asia.

The reason for selecting capital adequacy as a measure of systemic risk is simply that undercapitalized financial sectors lead to significant loss of economic output through the withdrawal of efficient intermediation services and possibly the misallocation of resources. In particular, when a large part of the financial sector is funded with fragile, short-term debt (or conversely, is not funded with adequate equity capital) and is hit by a common shock to its long-term assets, there may be en masse failures of financial firms. In such a scenario, it is not possible for any individual firm to reduce its leverage or risk without significant costs since other financial firms are attempting to achieve the same outcome. Since deleveraging and risk reduction are privately costly to owners of the financial firms, firms delay such actions, operating as undercapitalized firms that are averse to efficiently expanding the provision of intermediation to households and corporations and keen to pursue risky strategies (gambling for resurrection) that offer them some chance of recovering but at the cost of a greater chance of further stress. If further stress develops, there may be a complete disruption of payments and settlement services, which can cause trade and growth to collapse, as occurred for several years during the Great Depression as well as in the fall of 2008 during the global recession.

The adverse impact of undercapitalized financial sectors on the allocation of economic resources has been the focus of an important body of empirical research. This theme has been confirmed again in the European countries following the financial crisis of 2007–2009. The lack of adequate recapitalization and cleaning up of European banks' balance sheets prevented an efficient allocation of credit for an extended period of time. Popov and van Horen (2013) report that it has taken European banks much longer to recover in terms of their global syndicated lending than other banks. Acharya and Steffen (2015) demonstrated that undercapitalized European banks put on "carry trades" by using short-term funding to purchase risky government bonds of the southern periphery, a bet that did not pay off and resulted in a combined sovereign and banking crisis for Europe in the fall of 2011.

In light of these adverse consequences of undercapitalized financial sectors, it is natural to single out expected capital shortfall of the financial sector as a way of measuring its systemic risk or vulnerability to a future crisis. Section 1 introduces the measure we employ, *SRISK*, based on the work of Acharya, Pedersen, Philippon, and Richardson (2010a, 2010b, 2010c) and Acharya, Engle, and Richardson (2012). Section 2 assesses global financial sector health since 2007 using *SRISK* as the measure of systemic risk. Section 3 discusses the divergence observed in the United States, Europe, and Asia in terms of the evolution of financial sector health since 2007.

1. *SRISK,* a Measure of Financial Sector Health

Acharya (2009) and Acharya, Pedersen, Philippon, and Richardson (2010a, 2010b, 2010c) argue that systemic risk should be described in in the context of a firm's overall contribution to systemwide failure. The intuition is that when capital is low in the aggregate, it is not possible for other financial firms to step into the breach. This breakdown in aggregate financial intermediation is the reason why there are severe consequences for the broader economy, such as a credit crunch and fire sales of assets.

Acharya, Engle, and Richardson (2012) implement this intuition by proposing a measure of systemic risk contribution of a financial firm, called *SRISK* and measured as the expected capital shortfall of a firm in a crisis. In particular, the *SRISK* of firm i at time t is defined as the capital that the firm is expected to need (conditional on available information up to time $t - 1$) to operate "normally," that is, not face a run of its creditors, should another financial crisis occur. Symbolically it can be defined as

$$SRISK_{i,t} = E_{t-1}\left(Capital\ Shortfall_i \,|\, Crisis\right). \tag{1}$$

To calculate *SRISK*, we first need to evaluate the losses that an equity holder would face if there is a future crisis. To do this, the volatilities and correlations of an individual financial firm's equity return and the global marketwide return are allowed to change over time, assuming the two return series are conditionally (i.e., each day) multivariate normal, and simulated for six months into the future many times. Whenever the broad index falls by 40 percent over the next six months, a rather pessimistic scenario that captures the kind of market collapse witnessed during the Great Depression in 1930s and the global recession in 2007–2009, this is viewed as a crisis, and the firm's equity return is drawn from the joint distribution assumptions described above. For the crisis scenarios, the expected loss of equity value of firm i is called the long-run marginal expected shortfall, or *LRMES*. This is just the average of the fractional returns of the firm's equity in the crisis scenarios.

The capital shortfall can be directly calculated by recognizing that the book value of debt will be relatively unchanged during this six-month period while equity values fall by *LRMES*. Assume k is a prudential capital ratio, which we take as 8 percent (and 5.5 percent for Europe, to adjust for the differences between the European IFRS and US GAAP accounting standards in the treatment of netting of derivatives). Then we can define the *SRISK* of firm *i* at time *t* as

$$
\begin{aligned}
SRISK_{i,t} &= E_{t-1}\left(\left(k\left(Debt + Equity\right) - Equity\right)|Crisis\right) \\
&= k\left(Debt_{i,t}\right) - \left(1 - k\right)\left(1 - LRMES_{i,t}\right)Equity_{i,t},
\end{aligned}
\tag{2}
$$

where $Equity_{i,t}$ is the market value of equity today, $Debt_{i,t}$ is the notional value of nonequity liabilities today, and $LRMES_{i,t}$ is the long-run marginal expected shortfall of equity return estimated using available information today. This measure of the expected capital shortfall captures many of the characteristics considered important for systemic risk, such as size and leverage. These characteristics tend to increase a firm's capital shortfall when there are widespread losses in the financial sector. But a firm's expected capital shortfall also provides an important addition, most notably the *comovement* of the financial firm's assets with the aggregate market in a crisis.

Given the simple formulaic structure for *SRISK*, we can also understand changes in *SRISK* over time as coming from changes in its components, the book value of nonequity liabilities, the market value of equity, and the market value of equity times the *LRMES*, as follows:

$$
\begin{aligned}
\Delta SRISK_i &= SRISK_{i,t} - SRISK_{i,t-1} \\
&= \Delta Debt_i + \Delta Equity_i + \Delta Risk_i, where \\
\Delta Debt_i &= k\left(Debt_{i,t} - Debt_{i,t-1}\right), \\
\Delta Equity_i &= -\left(1 - k\right)\left(Equity_{i,t} - Equity_{i,t-1}\right), and \\
\Delta Risk_i &= \left(1 - k\right)\left(LRMES_{i,t}Equity_{i,t} - LRMES_{i,t-1}Equity_{i,t-1}\right),
\end{aligned}
\tag{3}
$$

where the changes in *Debt, Equity,* and *Risk* are measured over the period from $t - 1$ to t, and, together with the appropriate weights from the *SRISK* formula in (2), combine to explain the change in *SRISK* over the period from $t - 1$ to t.

2.   Assessing Global Financial Sector Health using *SRISK*

To operationalize *SRISK* and compare it across countries and regions, the NYU Stern School of BusinessVolatility LAB (VLAB) includes all publicly listed financial firms in a country with active trading in common equity that are in the top 10 percent of firms in a year by size (see the appendix to this chapter for sample size distribution by year). To identify firms with capital shortfall, firms with positive *SRISK* are identified. All positive values of *SRISK* for a country or region in a given year are aggregated to obtain the overall *SRISK* for that country or region. In what follows, all references to the current or the present moment refer to October 10, 2014.

Figures 5.1–5.6 and table 5.1 summarize our overall findings for aggregate *SRISK* across the three regions (the United States, Europe, and Asia, with an emphasis on China):

1. Figure 5.1 plots the aggregate *SRISK scaled by the GDP* for the three regions and China and is the central figure of this chapter.

In the case of the United States, systemic risk appears to have peaked in the fall of 2008 and early 2009, with an estimated capital shortfall of the

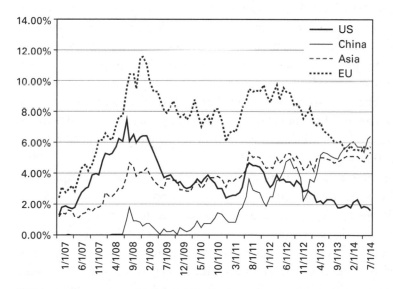

Figure 5.1
SRISK Normalized by GDP Comparison.
Notes: This figure plots the sum of *SRISK* for publicly traded financial firms (see inclusion criteria in the appendix to this chapter) in a given week, scaled by the country's (or sum of the countries') latest GDP figure available that week, for the United States, China, Asia (including China), and Europe. The *SRISK* data are from the NYU Stern Volatility Lab (http://vlab.stern.nyu.edu/welcome/risk) from January 1, 2007, until end of September 2014. The country GDP data are from Bloomberg.

financial sector at close to 8 percent of GDP (over $1 trillion). This is of the order of magnitude of the capital injections and other forms of federal support for the financial sector following the collapse of Lehman Brothers in the form of TARP legislation, FDIC guarantees, and Federal Reserve liquidity provision. Since then, the systemic risk appears to have steadily come down since the spring of 2009, with current levels (2 percent of GDP) being as low as in January 2007. The one exception is August 2011, when the systemic risk in the United States rises again around the debt-ceiling political crisis in the United States and the eurozone sovereign debt and financial sector crisis.

Similar to what is seen for the United States, the systemic risk of the European financial sector also reaches its peak in the fall of 2008 and early 2009 (12 percent of GDP, or about $2.25 trillion), but reveals an important difference: it reaches another peak of 10 percent of GDP ($2 trillion) in August 2011, coincident with the eurozone sovereign debt crisis. In other words, Europe appears to have witnessed serial episodes of dramatic capital shortfalls in the financial sector. While systemic risk has come down since this second peak, its current levels (6 percent) remain at more than twice those in January 2007 (2 percent of GDP), another striking difference with the United States. This illustrates well that the European financial sector is far less healthy at present than the US financial sector and also relative to itself prior to the global financial crisis of 2007–2008.

The picture of systemic risk estimate for Asia is, however, quite different from that for the United States and Europe. The estimated capital shortfalls for the Asian financial sector show a steady trend upward all the way from January 2007 to date, with some local peaks, but overall having risen by close to $1 trillion from a quarter trillion (2 percent of GDP) to currently around $1.25 trillion (6 percent of GDP). China, which, along with Japan, is the largest financial sector in Asia, mirrors this trend, as shown in figure 5.1. The Chinese financial sector shows little estimated capital shortfall until the middle of 2010, but since then it has had a meteoric rise, with present estimates putting it at over a half trillion dollars (6 percent of China's GDP).

2. Figure 5.2 helps us understand the diverging patterns of systemic risk for the United States, Europe, and Asia in terms of leveraging or

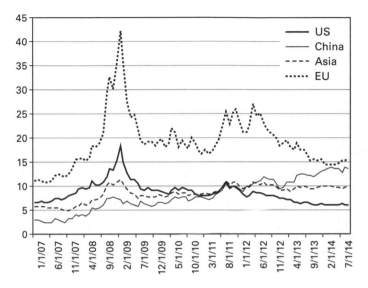

Figure 5.2

Aggregate Leverage Comparison.

Notes: This figure plots the aggregate (quasi-) leverage for publicly traded financial firms (see the inclusion criteria in the appendix to this chapter) for the United States, China, Asia (including China), and Europe. Quasi-leverage of a financial firm is its quasi-market assets (market value of equity + book value of nonequity liabilities) divided by the market value of equity. Quasi-leverage of financial firms in a region is weighted by the market value of equity of financial firms to obtain the aggregate quasi-leverage. The leverage data are from the NYU Stern Volatility Lab (http://vlab.stern.nyu.edu/welcome/risk) from January 1, 2007, until end of September 2014.

deleveraging of the financial sector by plotting the aggregate quasi-leverage of the respective financial sectors.[1] It illustrates succinctly that the leverage time series for these financial sectors tracks closely the evolution of the estimated systemic risk of these financial sectors. In other words, the financial sector in the United States experienced a significant leverage increase until the spring of 2009, and since then has been deleveraging at a rapid pace; the European financial sector experienced leverage rises until the summer of 2009, but also in the period close to and leading up to the fall of 2011, and has been deleveraging to some extent since then but not to January 2007 levels; in contrast, the Asian (and Chinese) financial sectors have been ramping up leverage at a steady pace all along from 2007 to date.

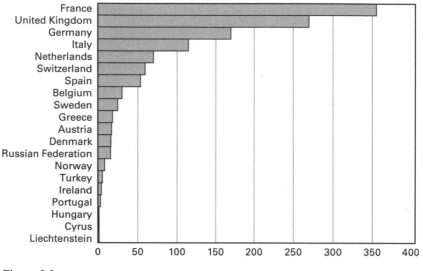

Figure 5.3
Global Systemic Risk by Country: Europe.
Notes: This figure plots the top twenty country-level values in Europe of the sum of *SRISK* in USD billion for publicly traded financial firms (see inclusion criteria in the appendix to this chapter) in a country as of October 10, 2014. The *SRISK* data are from the NYU Stern Volatility Lab (http://vlab.stern.nyu.edu/welcome/risk).

It is interesting that at present, the leverage in the US financial sector is down to 5 (i.e., five units of assets for one unit of market value of equity), lower than 10 for Asia, and around 15 for China and Europe. Equally interestingly, the leverage of the financial sector in Europe has been pervasively greater than that of the financial sectors in the United States and Asia.

Similarly, figures 5.3 and 5.4 help us understand the contributors (at country level) to current systemic risk assessment in Europe. In terms of absolute contributions to the estimated capital shortfalls (figure 5.3), France leads the way, at $350 billion, over a fourth of the current shortfall estimate for Europe. Even on a per GDP basis (figure 5.4), France leads the way, with its estimated capital shortfall being around 13 percent of its GDP, a rather sizable fraction of GDP to put aside to recapitalize the banking sector should future stress require public injections of capital.

While Switzerland and the UK are expected to rank high on a per GDP basis given the relatively large balance sheets of their financial

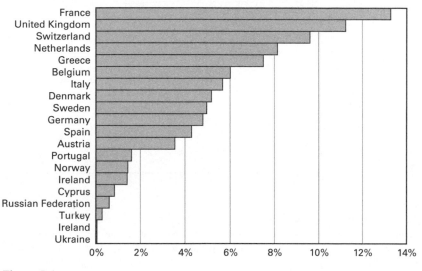

Figure 5.4
European *SRISK* Normalized by GDP.
Notes: This figure plots the top twenty country-level values in Europe of the sum of *SRISK* for publicly traded financial firms (see inclusion criteria in the appendix to this chapter) in a country, scaled by the country's latest GDP figure available as of October 10, 2014. The *SRISK* data are from the NYU Stern Volatility Lab (http://vlab.stern.nyu.edu/welcome/risk). The country GDP data are from Bloomberg.

sectors compared to the national balance sheets, France topping this list is somewhat surprising and highlights the relative undercapitalization of its banking sector (in terms of its quasi-market leverage). Notably, while Germany ranks high in figure 5.3 in terms of absolute size of estimated capital shortfalls, on a per GDP basis it looks much healthier than France.

And figures 5.5 and 5.6 help us understand countries that contribute to the systemic risk in Asia at the present date. China and Japan together account for most of the estimated capital shortfall in Asia (figure 5.5). On a per GDP basis, however, Japan is substantially higher, at over 11 percent shortfall relative to GDP, whereas China is somewhat smaller, at over 6 percent.

3. Finally, while China's systemic risk relative to its GDP appears manageable, particularly given its vast reserves, it is intriguing what explains its dramatic rise seen in figure 5.1, from practically zero to now half a trillion dollars, or 6 percent of GDP. Table 5.1 provides

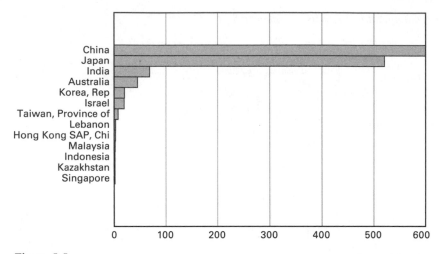

Figure 5.5
Global Systemic Risk by Country: Asia.
Notes: This figure plots the top thirteen country-level values in Asia (including Australia and New Zealand) of the sum of *SRISK* in USD billion for publicly traded financial firms (see inclusion criteria in the appendix to this chapter) in a country as of October 10, 2014. The *SRISK* data are from the NYU Stern Volatility Lab (http://vlab.stern.nyu.edu/welcome/risk).

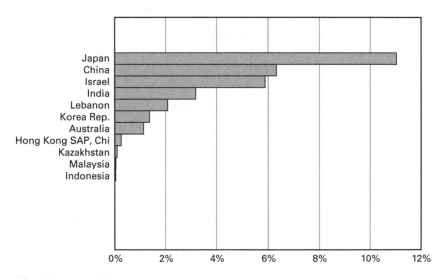

Figure 5.6
Asia *SRISK* Normalized by GDP.
Notes: This figure plots the top eleven country-level values in Asia (including Australia and New Zealand) of the sum of *SRISK* for publicly traded financial firms (see inclusion criteria in the appendix to this chapter) in a country, scaled by the country's latest GDP figure available as of October 10, 2014. The *SRISK* data are from the NYU Stern Volatility Lab (http://vlab.stern.nyu.edu/welcome/risk). The country GDP data are from Bloomberg.

Table 5.1
Decomposition of Change in SRISK

Institution	SRISK(t)	SRISK(t − 1)	ΔSRISK	ΔDebt	ΔEquity	ΔRisk
Bank of China Ltd.	105,580.9	−4,396.9	109,977.8	90,325.2	20,038.1	−385.5
China Construction Bank Corp.	84,956.1	−12,500.5	97,456.6	90,456.5	15,262.1	−8,261.9
Industrial and Commercial Bank of China Ltd.	77,991.2	−71,501.9	149,493.1	114,137.7	48,781.9	−13,426.4
Bank of Communications Co. Ltd.	44,484.7	−678.7	45,163.4	38,475.8	6,314.8	372.7
China CITIC Bank Corp. Ltd.	33,828.5	−3,342.2	37,170.7	32,863.6	5,290.3	−983.2
China Merchants Bank Co. Ltd.	29,608.3	−14,607.5	44,215.8	38,062.1	5,430.3	723.4
Shanghai Pudong Development Bank	25,899.8	−4,037.5	29,937.3	29,607.2	−1,414.7	1,744.8
Industrial Bank Co. Ltd.	24,856.8	−8,643.1	33,499.9	33,119.3	−1,822.7	2,203.2
China Minsheng Banking Corp. Ltd.	17,584.8	−4,891.7	22,476.5	27,422.5	−6,765.6	1,819.6
Huaxia Bank Co. Ltd.	11,742.1	2,068.4	9,673.7	12,193.5	−2,690.4	170.6

Notes: This table shows the change in *SRISK* between the beginning of 2010 ($t − 1$) and October 10, 2014 (t), in USD billion for publicly traded financial firms (see inclusion criteria in the appendix to this chapter) in China, with the top ten values of *SRISK* as of October 10, 2014. The change in *SRISK* is decomposed further into change due to changes in book value of nonequity liabilities (*Debt*), in market value of equity (*Equity*), and in market value of equity times *LRMES*, the measure of downside beta of the firm's equity to a global market correction of −40 percent (*Risk*). The *SRISK* data and its component changes are from the NYU Stern Volatility Lab (http://vlab.stern.nyu.edu/welcome/risk).

an intuitive understanding of this rise using the decomposition of change in *SRISK* between the end of 2009 and October 10, 2014, for the highest *SRISK* contributors in the Chinese financial sector into its three components ($\Delta Debt, \Delta Equity, \Delta Risk$), as explained in the concluding remarks of section 3.

The top four banks in the list are the largest state-owned commercial banks in China. Together they contribute to over half of the estimated capital shortfall for China. However, all these banks had negative *SRISK* at the end of 2009; that is, they were in fact in capital surplus. What is remarkable in table 5.1 is that almost all of the change in *SRISK* can be attributed to the increase in debt liabilities ($\Delta Debt$) for these banks. Indeed, while their debt liabilities have increased, equity valuations have suffered, so that the increase in *SRISK* is also to the result of declines in equity (positive $\Delta Equity$). Interestingly, their downside risk on a per dollar of equity basis has improved, so that the risk contribution ($\Delta Risk$) is negative. Together, these observations suggest massive *financial* leveraging of the largest banks in China from 2010 to date, which has increased the systemic risk of the financial sector to nontrivial levels, and way beyond that for the United States on a per GDP basis.

3.   What Explains the Divergence in the Evolution of the Global Financial Sector Health since 2007?

In summary, the financial sector capital shortfalls reached a peak around the end of 2008 and early 2009 for the United States and Europe; however, they declined thereafter steadily only for the United States, with Europe reaching a similar peak in the fall of 2011 during the sovereign debt crises in the southern periphery states of Europe. In contrast, the financial sector in Asia had little capital shortfall in 2008–2009 but the shortfall has increased steadily since 2010, notably for China and Japan. What explains these relative patterns? I argue below that these patterns can be explained based on the regulatory responses in the United States, the lack thereof in Europe, economic stagnation in Japan, and the bank leverage–based fiscal stimulus in China.

Following the collapse of Lehman Brothers, the United States put in place first a substantial rescue package in the form of TARP recapitalization of the financial sector up to $750 billion, FDIC deposit and loan guarantee programs, and the Federal Reserve's liquidity support of the financial sector as well as of the markets at large, in addition to the government conservatorship of the mortgage agencies, Fannie Mae and Freddie Mac. While these measures were not adequate to calm the volatility in markets, which remained substantially high even in early 2009, the stress test–based recapitalization in spring 2009 (the Supervisory Capital Assessment Program, SCAP) ensured that banks injected a further $200 billion in capital into the balance sheets (required capital-raising by regulators was $75 billion). These measures significantly calmed worries over the health of the financial sector in the United States. Following this, the Dodd-Frank Act was enacted in 2010 and various measures were put in place to rein in systemic risk, again notably an annual stress test of the systemically important financial institutions identified by the newly created Financial Stability Oversight Council. All of these measures have ensured substantial deleveraging of the US financial sector balance sheets, as seen in figures 5.1 to 5.3, to the point that they appear to be among the healthiest in the global economy at present.

In contrast to the United States, the regulatory response in Europe to the financial sector meltdown of 2007–2008 was half-baked. While the governments and central banks were quick to assist the ailing financial sector with asset and liability guarantees as well as liquidity injection, there was no substantial recapitalization of the financial sector on a scale similar to the TARP recapitalization for the US financial sector. This lack of recapitalization, in the presence of massive guarantees, meant that the financial sector had poor incentives during the recovery phase. Many undercapitalized banks invested in risky assets to rebuild equity capital, transferring risks in the process to the government, by undertaking "carry trades" on the southern periphery states' sovereign debt funded with retail and wholesale deposits (Acharya and Steffen 2015). This created a rather unfortunate nexus between financial and sovereign credit risks in the eurozone, bringing about twin crises in the fall of 2011, with the deteriorating macroeconomic and financial health in Spain and Italy (Acharya 2014). This nexus of sovereign and financial sector credit risks—first, the undercapitalized financial sector taking leveraged exposures to risky sovereigns, and second, further distress of risky sovereigns' inflicting collateral damage on the financial sector—appears to have had significant real consequences. Acharya, Eisert, Eufinger, and Hirsch (2014) show that even relatively large borrowers in Europe whose lead banks have been from the southern periphery countries have been hoarding cash and cutting back investment and employment, behaving as though they were financially constrained, an effect that is not seen for borrowers whose lead banks are from the core European countries, which are, in turn, relatively better capitalized.

The carry-trade strategies and the undercapitalization of banks that induced them were left unchecked, and in fact were encouraged, by regulators, who conducted stress tests with little bite compared to the SCAP exercise of the United States. As Acharya, Engle, and Pierret (2014) document, the European stress tests granted zero risk weights to risky southern periphery states' sovereign debt so that effectively not much capital was raised by banks in response, and in fact the worst banks, such as Dexia, in terms of risks were found to require the least capital on the stress tests. Acharya and Steffen (2014) document that the pattern was hardly different with the Asset Quality Review and Comprehensive Assessment of the European Central Bank in 2014. Nevertheless, there is some overall improvement in the health of the financial sector relative to the fall of 2011 owing to the extraordinary liquidity injection and the ECB's promises to purchase securities from the market starting in December 2011.

Finally, the case of Asia can be explained by the continuing economic malaise in Japan since the regulatory failure in 1990s to recapitalize the banking sector, and the debt-based stimulus in China to ensure high growth rates in the short run even as the global economy suffered in the wake of the crisis of 2007–2008. In the case of Japan, the financial sector leverage remains high or increasing despite the continued macroeconomic weakness, which has only had temporary relief from "Abenomics," explaining the continuing rise of systemic risk in Japan since 2007.

The case of China, in contrast, is relatively straightforward. After the global financial and economic crisis of 2007–2008, Chinese state-owned banks have leveraged massively, including through the use of off-balance-sheet liabilities (not captured in *SRISK* analysis), to fund real estate and infrastructure projects, many of which are at unsustainable price levels and subject to high nonperforming rates. From 2008 to 2013, total credit outstanding in the Chinese economy grew from 125 percent to 240 percent. Much of this increase came about from stimulus expenditures undertaken since 2008 by local municipal governments. These local governments, being prohibited from raising debt directly, set up special-purpose financing vehicles, which raised debt from shadow banks ("trusts") in China to invest in infrastructure and real estate development. The local government debt is backed mainly by revenues from land sales, but with house prices inevitably slowing down in the past few years from their astronomical growth rate before, the shadow banks—many of which are implicitly supported by parent state-owned banks—are exposed to significant losses, which has created the possibility of runs as well as of undercapitalized banks.

While China appears to have the time and resources (a large quantity of reserves and a high domestic savings rate), in addition to tight control of its banks and housing markets, the question is whether, like the United States in the post-Lehman era, it will make the tough recapitalization decisions for its banks before its own crisis comes to fruition, or whether, like Japan in the 1990s and Europe since the global recession, it will let undercapitalized banks continue to operate as zombie banks engaged in the misallocation of economic resources.

Appendix

Table 5A.1
Number of Total Firms per Region

Year	USA	China	Asia	EU
2007	155	30	336	353
2008	159	39	373	389
2009	148	52	409	395
2010	148	58	429	397
2011	156	66	453	405
2012	157	70	458	404
2013	156	70	457	394
2014	153	70	451	385

Note: Using publicly listed financial firms in each country with active trading in common equity that are also in top 10 percent of financial firms by size (market equity), the number of total firms included in SRISK calculations in each year and geography are as above.

Note

1. Quasi-market leverage is the notion of leverage in *SRISK,* which is the quasi-market value of assets divided by the market value of equity. This is in contrast to the regulatory notion of leverage, which corresponds to risk-weighted assets divided by a measure of the book value of the equity of a financial firm.

References

Acharya, V. V. 2009. "A Theory of Systemic Risk and Design of Prudential Bank Regulation." *Journal of Financial Stability* 5 (3): 224–255.

Acharya, V. V. Forthcoming. "The Nexus between Financial Sector and Sovereign Credit Risks." In *Toulouse Lectures in Economics.* Princeton, NJ: Princeton University Press.

Acharya, V., T. Eisert, C. Eufinger, and C. Hirsch. 2014. "Real Effects of the Sovereign Debt Crisis in Europe: Evidence from Syndicated Loans." Faculty paper, New York University Stern School of Business. http://pages.stern.nyu.edu/~sternfin/vacharya/public_html/pdfs/realeffects2014.pdf.

Acharya, V. V., R. Engle, and D. Pierret. 2014. "Testing Macro-prudential Stress Tests: The Risk of Regulatory Risk Weights." *Journal of Monetary Economics* 65:36–53.

Acharya, V. V., R. Engle, and M. P. Richardson. 2012. "Capital Shortfall: A New Approach to Ranking and Regulating Systemic Risks." *American Economic Review* 102 (3): 59–64.

Acharya, V. V., L. H. Pedersen, T. Philippon, and M. P. Richardson. 2010 a. "Measuring Systemic Risk." In *Regulating Wall Street: The Dodd-Frank Act and the New Architecture of Global Finance,* ed. V. V. Acharya, T. Cooley, T., M. Richardson, and I. Walter. New York: John Wiley & Sons.

Acharya, V. V., L. H. Pedersen, T. Philippon, and M. P. Richardson. 2010 b. "Taxing Systemic Risk." In *Regulating Wall Street: The Dodd-Frank Act and the New Architecture of Global Finance,* ed. V. V. Acharya, T. Cooley, M. Richardson, and I. Walter. New York: John Wiley & Sons.

Acharya, V. V., L. Pedersen, T. Philippon, and M. Richardson. 2010 c. "Measuring Systemic Risk." Technical report. Department of Finance, New York University Stern School of Business. http://papers.ssrn.com/sol3/papers.cfm?abstract_id=1573171.

Acharya, V. V., and S. Steffen. 2014. *Benchmarking the European Central Bank's Asset Quality Review and Stress Test: A Tale of Two Leverage Ratios.* Brussels: Center for European Policy Studies.

Acharya, V. V., and S. Steffen. 2015. "The Greatest Carry Trade Ever? Understanding Eurozone Bank Risks." *Journal of Financial Economics* 115:215–236.

Becker, B., and V. Ivashina. 2015. "Reaching for Yield in the Bond Market." *Journal of Finance* 70 (5): 1863–1902.

Becker, B., and M. Opp. 2014. "Regulatory Reform and Risk-Taking: Replacing Ratings." Working paper, University of Berkeley Haas School of Business.

Calomiris, C., and R. Herring. 2013. "How to Design a Contingent Convertible Debt Requirement That Helps Solve Our Too-Big-To-Fail Problem." *Journal of Applied Corporate Finance* 25 (2): 66–89.

Koijen, R. S. J., and M. Yogo. 2013, "Shadow Insurance." Working paper, London Business School and Federal Reserve Bank of Minneapolis.

Popov, A., and N. van Horen. 2014. "Exporting Sovereign Stress: Evidence from Syndicated Bank Lending during the Euro Area Sovereign Debt Crisis." Working paper, *Review of Finance*. doi: 10.1093/rof/rfu046.

6

Rethinking Financial Regulation: How Confusion Has Prevented Progress

Anat R. Admati

The failure of financial regulation can, and did, cause significant harm to the economy. I argue that confusion about the nature of the problems in the financial system and about the trade-offs associated with key regulations has prevented progress in making the financial system safer and healthier. This system, little changed since the financial crisis, still endangers and distorts the economy unnecessarily.

In 2007–2009, a crisis that started in the US housing market had powerful ripple effects around the globe. These effects were largely the result of an increase in opacity and interconnectedness, which created powerful contagion mechanisms, transmitting default risks from financial institutions to their direct and indirect counterparties and to the rest of the economy. Concerns with systemic risk led central banks and governments to provide extraordinary and unprecedented support to many financial institutions. Despite this support and continued actions by central banks, the economy has suffered substantial and long-lasting harm. Excessive mortgage lending created a heavy debt burden for households, exacerbating the effects.

If financial crises were like unpreventable natural disasters, we might have to accept them as inevitable. But the extreme fragility of the financial system that gives rise to systemic risk and crises is rooted in the incentives of people within the system and in the failure of regulations to counter these incentives. Beyond the risk of acute crises, the same forces that cause excessive fragility also make the financial system inefficient, distort credit markets, and harm the economy. Much can be done to improve this system. Unfortunately, regulatory reform efforts have been unfocused. Regulations remain inadequate, and their flaws further exacerbate the problems.

Why the System Is So Fragile and Distorted

In taking deposits and issuing short-term debt, banking institutions naturally engage in borrowing. Borrowing creates leverage, which magnifies risk and increases the likelihood of distress, insolvency, and default. Borrowing also gives rise to conflicts of interest. Decisions made by borrowers acting in their own interest may harm creditors and others who have less control. The presence of overhanging debt creates inefficiencies, possibly leading borrowers to make risky value-reducing investments while at the same time passing up worthy investments that do not have enough upside. In banking, such distortions may result in biases in favor of speculative trading or credit card and subprime lending and against creditworthy business loans.

Borrower-creditor conflicts also distort funding decisions. Once debt is in place, borrowers may choose to take on additional debt, even though increasing indebtedness makes distress, default, and bankruptcy more likely and harms creditors. These same conflicts of interest lead managers and shareholders in indebted corporations to resist any actions that would reduce indebtedness and make existing debt safer, such as retaining profits and avoiding payouts to shareholders, selling assets to buy back debt, or issuing new equity to fund new investments. The conflicts of interest again lead to inefficiency, for example by increasing the likelihood that the firm's assets would be depleted by the deadweight costs of bankruptcy. The harm can spill to others.

The tendency for leverage to become addictive is underappreciated and often ignored in the academic literature. In 2015, my colleagues and I (see Admati et al. 2015) examined the bias against reducing leverage and in favor of increasing it attributable to borrower-creditor conflicts of interest, which we termed *the leverage ratchet effect*. We study this effect in the presence of other frictions, including bankruptcy costs, taxes, and asymmetric information, to study corporate leverage adjustments. The analysis is highly relevant for banking.

Although corporate tax codes generally favor debt over equity funding, outside of banking it is rare for healthy corporations to operate with less than 30 percent equity relative to total assets, and some thriving companies borrow very little. Retained profits are a preferred source of funding that does not involve borrowing. The reason is that, outside of banking, the interest rates creditors charge and the conditions or covenants attached to debt contracts reflect the likelihood of default, bankruptcy costs, and the potential for managerial actions to harm creditors, including by ratcheting up leverage and risk and passing up worthy investments.

Banker-depositor conflicts have always caused excessive fragility in banking. Since banks' assets are often opaque, concerns about the quality of the assets can lead to panics and runs. Such concerns are less likely, however, if banks have significant equity funding from owners or shareholders, which allows them to continue to pay their debts and invest even after losses. In the nineteenth century, when banks in the UK were unlimited-liability partnerships, they routinely funded 50 percent of their investments by equity, and their owners' personal assets could be tapped to pay depositors. Deposit insurance and central bank supports have made depositor runs less likely. At the same time, the use of equity in banking has persistently declined over the last century.

The safety net provided to the financial system has expanded significantly in recent decades. Concerns with systemic risk have created the expectation of supports from central banks and governments. Implicit guarantees have translated to outsized and distortive subsidies to banking institutions and to the entire financial sector. Because of the interconnectedness of the system, bailouts and supports flow from borrowers (institutions and even sovereigns) to their creditors and counterparties. The bailouts of AIG and of the Greek governments provide examples of this effect. Distressed households, however, have not received much direct relief.

The safety net weakens or eliminates creditor discipline, protecting financial institutions from the burden that heavy borrowers and their creditors experience elsewhere. Guarantees perversely feed, enable, and reward the addiction to leverage and risk that accompanies heavy borrowing because of conflicts of interest, as discussed earlier.

Worse, guarantees also enable and encourage inefficient growth, complexity, opacity, and herding behavior, all of which increase systemic risk. The largest and most systemic institutions, which benefit most from implicit guarantees, gain competitive advantage over less privileged companies, and have incentives and ability to grow and expand their scope and scale beyond banking and finance. The expansion of opaque derivatives markets that enable taking and hiding more risks, often with counterparties within the system, has also contributed to the interconnectedness and fragility of the financial system.

In this situation, regulations must protect the public and correct the distortions, restoring the vanishing market discipline and countering the flawed incentives. Yet financial regulations have not kept up with market developments. Regulations aimed to control the funding mix in banking, so-called capital regulations, still tolerate extremely high levels of indebtedness.

Capital regulations also rely in recent years on a complex system of risk weighting that further distorts investment decisions and increases systemic risk. For example, as the interest rate the Greek government promised prior to its debt restructuring in 2012, sometimes higher than 15 percent, contained significant compensation for default risk, the debt had zero risk weight. Banks could buy Greek debt entirely with borrowed money, benefiting from large spreads until losses arrived, causing some, such as Dexia and the Cypriot banks, to fail. During the financial crisis, many institutions suffered devastating losses from investments that regulators had assumed to be safe but that were actually risky, such as AAA-rated mortgage securities.

Because equity levels in banking remain extremely low overall, banks can use the highly imperfect risk weights to ratchet up their actual leverage and risk while satisfying the regulations. Regulations also allow banks to use their own models to determine the risk weights, which make the weights manipulable.

Compensation practices that encourage risk taking, and significant governance problems, also contribute to the fragility and inefficiency of the financial system. The largest financial institutions are the largest of all corporations by asset size and arguably the most complex. Investors and regulators are unable to understand and evaluate the risks these institutions and the system are exposed to. Repeated scandals involving fraud, manipulation, and other wrongdoing show that boards and executives are unable or unwilling to control the actions of individuals within the institutions.

When risk is taken on, someone must bear the downside. The business of banking has become focused on finding ways to pass downside risk to others and to obscure this fact. A few, mostly within the system, benefit disproportionately from the upside, while the economy suffers from significant collateral harm. Laws and regulations have failed to address these problems.

The Muddled Debate

All the contagion mechanisms that create systemic risk, including direct contractual dominos, inferences from weakness of one institution about the strength of others, a credit crunch owing to lenders' distress, and the intensity of asset sales in deleveraging, would be alleviated if institutions were more resilient to shocks and able to absorb more losses without becoming distressed. Society stands to benefit greatly from requiring that the funding mix of banking institutions, particularly those considered systemic, includes much more equity. Progress in designing and implementing such regulations, however, has been prevented by confusion and politics.

Prior to the financial crisis, the relevant international agreement for minimal capital regulations, Basel II, allowed banks to reduce their equity levels below 3 percent of their total assets. Many regulated institutions that had satisfied Basel II or even tougher requirements failed, or survived only thanks to massive support from central banks and governments. Basel III, the reformed 2010 international agreement, sets a minimum "leverage ratio" of 3 percent equity relative to total assets. (US regulations require 5 percent for large bank holding companies and 6 percent for deposit-taking institutions.) The remaining regulatory ratios are stated relative to risk-weighted assets. The actual meaning of all these ratios depends on how different assets are accounted for and how risk weights are calculated. Details, including how to treat derivatives and off-balance-sheet commitments, matter greatly.

Bankers and regulators routinely claim that capital levels in banking have increased dramatically, quoting a percentage change relative to previous ratios and ignoring the fact that accounting-based and risk-weight-based capital ratios can be misleadingly reassuring, and that actual indebtedness levels in banking remain inappropriate and dangerous. In a September 14, 2010, column in the *Financial Times* titled "Basel: The Mouse That Didn't Roar," Martin Wolf said cynically, "Tripling the previous requirements sounds tough, but only if one fails to realize that tripling almost nothing does not give one very much." With equity levels sometime below 1 percent of total assets under previous requirements, the same is true for a six- or tenfold increase. The question is not the percentage increase relative to previous failed regulations but what is reasonable and desirable, and the costs and benefits of significantly tighter requirements. On these issues, confusion prevails and progress has stalled.

Ahead of Basel III's approval by G-20 leaders in 2010, I helped organize a letter, signed by twenty academics from finance and banking, which stated: "Basel III proposals fail to eliminate key structural flaws in the current system. Banks' high leverage, and the resulting fragility and systemic risk, contributed to the near collapse of the financial system. Basel III is far from sufficient to protect the system from recurring crises. If a much larger fraction, at least 15 percent, of banks' total, non-risk-weighted, assets were funded by equity, the social benefits would be substantial. And the social costs would be minimal, if any." The figure of 15 percent was meant to indicate that Basel requirements are entirely in the wrong range.[1]

The letter, which also pointed out some of the problems with the risk weights system, concluded by stating: "Ensuring that banks are funded with significantly more equity should be a key element of effective bank regulatory reform. Much more equity funding would permit banks to perform all their useful functions and support growth without endangering the financial system by systemic fragility. It would give banks incentives to take better account of risks they take and reduce their incentives to game the system. And it would sharply reduce the likelihood of crises." Our recommendations, and the more detailed proposals in Admati and Hellwig (2013a, chap. 11), have not been followed.

A large collection of flawed claims by bankers and others, including academics, are brought up to support the mantra in banking that "equity is expensive." My colleagues and I have classified claims to fallacies (false statements), irrelevant facts (e.g., claims that confuse private and social costs), and myths (implausible theoretical constructions that selectively ignore important parts of reality) (see Admati et al. 2013). The fallacies show confusions about balance sheet mechanics and about basic notions in finance, such as that leverage magnifies risk, that riskier investments generally require higher expected returns, that targeting specific return levels is not the same as creating value for investors, and that rearranging how risk is borne by different investors does not by itself change funding costs.

Misleading jargon also serves to confuse. One fallacy involves insidious confusion about the meaning of the word "capital" in banking, stemming from terms like "capital reserve" and expressions like "hold" or "set aside" capital. Such terminology suggests falsely that bank capital is idle cash reserve. Confusion between private and social costs is reflected in terms like "capital (sur)charge" that falsely suggest a relevant social cost for higher equity requirements.

Banking institutions are better able to serve the economy, providing appropriate and consistent liquidity and credit and other financial services, if they have more equity and less debt funding. The institutions have significant discretion over how they use their funds, and providing blanket subsidies to their *debt* funding is perverse because it increases systemic risk and creates more inefficiencies. Subsidies, if deemed desirable, must not be delivered in ways that harm.

Theoretical models of banking and empirical studies that purport to inform policy often make inappropriate, even fallacious, assumptions, while ignoring key forces such as the inefficiencies and harm from high leverage, poor governance, and flawed regulations. Models that significantly distort reality provide poor policy guidance.

Instead of increasing equity requirements, regulators have recently focused on trying to force large systemic institutions to issue hybrid, debtlike securities that could in principle convert to equity in certain scenarios. These securities are dubbed TLAC (Total Loss Absorbing Capacity), GLAC (Gone-concern Loss Absorbing Capacity), CoCos (contingent convertible capital instruments) or bail-inable debt.

There are numerous problems associated with using hybrid debtlike securities instead of equity. For example, triggering the conversion of these securities to equity or forcing them to absorb losses often requires that someone with authority determine that a large and complex institution is near or at insolvency, which is very difficult. Market instabilities are likely to start in anticipation of any trigger, which may scare policymakers away from forcing the conversion. Indeed, in 2008–2009, none of the hybrid securities that had counted as regulatory capital and that were supposed to absorb losses actually did absorb losses (except at Lehman Brothers), even in institutions that received massive support. It is baffling that regulators believe next time could be different.

Using common equity instead of debtlike hybrid securities is a simpler and more reliable approach to making sure systemic institutions are better able to absorb their losses without harming the economy.[2] There is no relevant sense in which hybrid securities, assuming they actually work, are cheaper or better than equity. The fact that the securities become useful in resolution is irrelevant, because if equity were used instead, resolution would be less likely to be needed at all, which is better.

Basic finance suggests that if downside risk is borne by investors and not by taxpayers, rearranging risk among investors does not by itself change funding costs. Shareholders, who are entitled to the upside, are the most natural targets for bearing downside risk, and loss absorption by shareholders does not require unreliable and potentially destabilizing triggers. The rationale for using debtlike securities in capital regulations is based on flawed claims.

Excuses and Politics

Some arguments against financial regulation do not concern the merit of specific tools, but rather raise concerns about the scope and enforcement of regulations. A common claim is that tighter regulations would lead activities to move to the unregulated "shadow banking system," consisting of money market funds, hedge funds, asset management firms, and other institutions that are regulated differently, or more lightly, than banking institutions.

For laws and regulations to be effective, their design and enforcement must work. The shadow banking system grew and became harmful largely because regulated institutions used it to hide risks. For example, special-purpose vehicles funded almost entirely with debt were sponsored and implicitly guaranteed by regulated institutions. Regulated institutions purchased credit protection from AIG to an extent that the institutions became exposed to AIG's credit risk, a fact that regulators failed to notice. Accounting rules allow risk exposures to be disguised using off-balance sheet entries and derivatives. The crisis made clear that risk claimed or believed to be eliminated may in fact appear elsewhere. The lesson is that regulators must monitor the system more effectively and do better in enforcing regulations, using their authority to insist that the system become less opaque and to intervene when risks build up.

Shadow banking does not actually operate in the dark. Some institutions or activities may not require much regulation, while others require better regulation. Money market funds, for example, add fragility to the system and must be regulated more effectively than they are. Turning the shadow banking excuse on its head, the largest banking institutions can be viewed as the most dangerous "shadow hedge funds," with privileges that enable extreme opacity and leverage. Shining a brighter light on these reckless and dangerous institutions and reducing the excessive risk and costs they impose on the economy would be highly beneficial.

A related and frequently cited argument against regulation is that international coordination, or a "level playing field," is necessary. In many ways the search for harmonization has led to a race to the bottom in regulation. The flawed notion that countries should support "their" banks in global competition, even at the cost of endangering and harming their citizens, has brought disaster to Ireland, Iceland, and Cyprus.

The Opportunity and the Challenge

The economy suffers when banking institutions are allowed to be persistently distressed and possibly insolvent. Delaying recognition of losses, tolerating and even supporting weak institutions over an extended period, is misguided. Unless their indebtedness is reduced, and with supports always given in the form of debt, banks are less likely to make new loans that help the economy. Their weakness can even interfere with the transmission of central banks' policies. If an institution is unable to sell shares to investors, it may be too opaque or weak. Instead of the prompt corrective action needed, excessive forbearance has become the norm. The result has been harmful cycles of boom, bust, and crises.

We may be unable to write tractable dynamic stochastic general equilibrium models that properly capture the complex dynamics of systemic risk, and we may not have the data to measure it. Hansen (2013) warned recently: "We should not underestimate the difficulty of measuring systemic risk in a meaningful way…. Caution should prevail about the impact of model misspecification on the measurements and the consequences of those measurements." It is also difficult to predict whether the next financial crisis will be triggered by interest rates changes, sovereign debt defaults, or a cybersecurity attack. The policy focus must be on making the system more resilient so that shocks are less harmful and less distorted, so it can serve the economy better. Current regulations do much too little toward these goals, allowing the financial system to remain dangerous and unhealthy.

Perhaps the biggest challenge in financial regulation is the lack of political will. Politicians have other priorities; they seem to view banks more as a source of funding than as a source of risk. The harm from failing to design and enforce effective financial regulation is large but abstract, and there is little personal accountability throughout the system, including for regulators or politicians.

Confusion, however, has also played an important role in preventing progress. When the debate is muddled and the trade-offs are misunderstood by so many, narrow interests are more likely to succeed in affecting policy. Rethinking the issues is therefore important and useful.

Notes

I thank Olivier Blanchard, Martin Hellwig, Paul Pfleiderer, and John Talbott for helpful comments. The material in this chapter is based on Admati and colleagues (2013, 2015), Admati and Hellwig (2013a, 2013b, 2015), and Admati (2014a, 2014b). Hellwig (2014) provides a related and more detailed discussion of systemic risk and macroprudential regulation. Pfleiderer (2014) discusses how models can be misused. Links to most of these references (and more) are available at http://bankersnewclothes.com and https://www.gsb.stanford.edu/faculty-research/excessive-leverage.

1. "Healthy Banking System in the Goal, Not Profitable Banks," *Financial Times*, November 9, 2010 (the full text is available at https://www.gsb.stanford .edu/faculty-research/excessive-leverage/healthy-banking-system-goal). Among the signatories are Franklin Allen, Markus Brunnermeier, John Cochrane, Eugene Fama, Charles Goodhart, Stewart Myers, Jean Charles Rochet, Stephen Ross, William Sharpe, and Chester Spatt. In an interview, Eugene Fama suggested 50 percent would be appropriate, and John Cochrane in a review of Admati and Hellwig (2013a) in the *Wall Street Journal* on March 1, 2013, captured the key idea, to shift the main loss absorption to investors, by saying that equity should be raised "until it does not matter." Additional multisignatory letters in February and July 2011 protested allowing banks to resume dividend payments and responded to a flawed commentary by Alan Greenspan, respectively.

2. This point was made in the 2010 letter by twenty academics cited earlier, and discussed in more detail in Admati, DeMarzo, and colleagues (2013, sect. 8) and Admati and Hellwig (2013a, chap. 11).

References

Admati, Anat R. 2014 a. "The Compelling Case for Stronger and More Effective Leverage Regulation in Banking." *Journal of Legal Studies* 43:s35–s61.

Admati, Anat R. 2014 b. *Examining the GAO Report on Expectations of Government Support for Bank Holding Companies.* Testimony for hearing of Senate Committee on Banking, Housing and Urban Affairs Subcommittee on Financial Institutions and Consumer Protection, July 31. http://www.banking.senate.gov/public/index.cfm?FuseAction=Files. View&FileStore_id=3e6b2c82-dce3-4fa1-a764-04fe9e447792.

Admati, Anat R., Peter M. DeMarzo, Martin F. Hellwig and Paul Pfleiderer. 2013. "Fallacies, Irrelevant Facts, and Myths in the Discussion of Capital Regulation: Why Bank Equity is Not Socially Expensive." Working Paper 13-7. Stanford University Graduate School of Business, October (first draft August 2010). http://papers.ssrn.com/sol3/papers.cfm?abstract_id=2349739##.

Admati, Anat R., Peter M. DeMarzo, Martin F. Hellwig and Paul Pfleiderer. 2015. "The Leverage Ratchet Effect." Working Paper 3029. Stanford University Graduate School of Business, December (first draft March 2011). http://papers.ssrn.com/sol3/papers.cfm?abstract_id=2304969.

Admati, Anat R., and Martin F. Hellwig. 2013a. *The Bankers' New Clothes: What's Wrong with Banking and What to Do about It.* Princeton, NJ: Princeton University Press.

Admati, Anat R., and Martin F. Hellwig. 2013b. "Does Debt Discipline Bankers? An Academic Myth about Bank Indebtedness." Working Paper 132. Stanford University, Rock Center of Governance, February. http://papers.ssrn.com/sol3/papers.cfm?abstract_id=2216811.

Admati, Anat R., and Martin F. Hellwig. 2015. "The Parade of Bankers' New Clothes Continues: 31 Flawed Claims Debunked." Working Paper 143. Stanford University, Rock Center of Governance, December. http://papers.ssrn.com/sol3/papers.cfm?abstract_id=2292229.

Hansen, Lars Peter. 2013. "Challenges in Identifying and Measuring Systemic Risk." In *Putting Macroprudential Policy to Work.* Occasional Studies 12–7, ed. Aerdt Houben, Rob Kijskens and Mark Teunissen. Amsterdam: De Nederlandsche Bank.

Hellwig, Martin F. 2014. "Systemic Risk and Macro-Prudential Policy." In *Putting Macroprudential Policy to Work.* Occasional Studies 12–7, ed. Aerdt Houben, Rob Kijskens and Mark Teunissen, 42–77. Amsterdam: De Nederlandsche Bank.

Pfleiderer, Paul. 2014. "Chameleons: The Misuse of Theoretical Models in Finance and Economics." Working Paper 3020. Stanford University Graduate School of Business, March. https://www.gsb.stanford.edu/faculty-research/working-papers/chameleons-misuse-theoretical-models-finance-economics.

7

Systemic Risk and Financial Regulation: Where Do We Stand?

Philipp Hildebrand

Financial Regulation Has Gone a Long Way toward Taming Systemic Risk in Banks

The Basel III/Financial Stability Board agenda has clearly helped bring about a global banking system that is much more resilient to insolvency and liquidity risks. If we consider both quantity and quality, capital buffers in the world's most significant banks today are at least six times higher than before the crisis; living wills and "bail-inable" capital should help further to contain the too-big-to-fail problem; and key supervisors everywhere are showing proactiveness with stress tests, which is key to having a dynamic view of risks. Equally important, investors are continuing to push for further changes and risk reduction in the business models of global banks.

So, while banks have by no means become risk free, I struggle to see further major banking regulation initiatives that would be critical at this stage. Personally, I still feel that more ambitious capital standards and less of everything else would likely have been a more effective and certainly much simpler way to respond to the crisis, but from a practical perspective, this is now a moot point. What I would say is that the priority now should be to hold the line and not roll back these improvements, and to have the courage to implement the crisis provisions now available if and when the time comes.

It is therefore sensible for the regulatory focus to have shifted to systemic liquidity risk and systemic risks from nonbanks, including asset managers. I will focus on these two types of risk.

Has Financial Regulation Created a New Systemic Risk in the Form of Liquidity Scarcity?

My short answer is no.

A number of recent market episodes have shown that even in some of the world's most liquid markets, prices can swing widely, and bid-ask spreads widen enormously, possibly suggesting a lack of liquidity. Some examples are the October 2015 flash rally in US Treasury prices after a weak data release (an eight-standard-deviation shock!); the 15 percent intraday swing in the value of the Swiss franc against the euro when the central bank dropped the exchange rate floor on January 15; or the 2.5 percent intraday move in the value of the USD against the euro on March 20, 2015 (after a Fed chair statement perceived, perhaps too hastily, as dovish), only to correct with an equally sharp swing the next day.

Conventional wisdom would have it that (1) such developments are very worrying and (2) they are the unforeseen and unfortunate result of the regulatory tightening imposed on banks, which can no longer afford the now much higher costs of market-making.

Both these contentions strike me as highly suspect, for a couple of reasons. First, in all these episodes, the bulk of the sharp price deviation was corrected within days, without any trace of a lasting misalignment or market malfunction. Second, we have (I hope) learned from the precrisis years that ultra-low volatility breeds excessive risk taking. Higher volatility is therefore welcome if it serves as a reminder that market prices can and do fluctuate.

That said, it is true that banks have cut their dealer inventory significantly in response to new capital requirements and changes in their business models, by about 20 percent overall, and this cut has been heavily skewed toward corporate bonds. (As a result, there is a sort of bifurcation in liquidity, with sovereign bond markets more highly liquid than before the crisis and corporate bond markets less so.)

What is much less clear is that reduced dealer inventory is the driver of large price swings (i.e., low liquidity) *in response to unexpected news*. Rather, one would expect it to lead to reduced liquidity all the time, as pointed out by Markus Brunnermeier recently.[1] But if we look at indicators such as transaction volumes or bid-ask spreads, we find very little evidence of that.

Most likely what is to blame for these wild price swings is the combination of an extensive search for yield from asset owners who find themselves forced by their liabilities to respond to the persistent highly unconventional monetary policy stance and the impact it has on the entire yield curve. This in turn leads to crowded trades in higher-risk positions. When you combine this with procyclical bank risk management models in which volatility can lead to capital shocks and fire sales, you certainly have a credible explanation for what we have witnessed on several occasions during the past year. (The data in the IMF's April 2015 Global Financial Stability Report [GFSR] chapter showing increasing herding in most markets over the past five years lends credence to this hypothesis.)[2]

In summary, the new regulations, aimed at making banks safer, have effectively curtailed what one might think of a liquidity illusion caused by intensive market-making by banks. This means that the liquidity risk previously borne by banks must now in part be borne by other market participants. With liquidity premia currently highly compressed because of unconventional monetary policies, there is likely underestimation by market participants of the liquidity risks they face. If they have not made necessary adjustments in their liquidity management practices by the time monetary policy normalizes, we could be in for repeated situations of extreme volatility.

Incidentally, this is an underappreciated channel through which highly accommodating monetary policy may fuel financial instability: not by fueling bubbles, as the typical narrative would have it, but by creating a liquidity illusion that could catch many unprepared when it dissipates.

Against this backdrop, some are asking, will other market players with deep pockets, such as asset managers, step in and make markets? I expect not, and I think it would be wrong if they did. Our objective cannot be to recreate the liquidity illusion that existed pre-Basel III. Rather, the entire market and its plumbing need to evolve, and all market participants need to adjust to a world in which liquidity cannot be taken for granted, and price it accordingly.

Are Large Asset Managers a Source of Systemic Risk?

Again the answer is no, though some of their activities and products may be.

It is very important to make a clear distinction between asset management entities and activities or products. As I will explain, the risks reside predominantly with the latter.

The bulk of global financial assets are managed by asset owners, not by asset management companies. And asset management companies themselves to a very significant extent do what asset owners tell them to do.

Asset management entities themselves pose minimal credit and counterparty risk, again for a couple of reasons:

Asset managers' balance sheets are many orders of magnitude smaller than those of banks, and these balance sheets do not embed any significant leverage.

Even if a major asset manager were to go under, whether struck by bankruptcy or by lightning, counterparty risk would be limited because the asset manager doesn't hold the assets it manages (they are held by custodians). Moreover, an asset management company does not trade securities on its own account but only as a fiduciary on behalf of clients.

An important question is whether large asset managers can be a source of herding, or can otherwise cause wide swings in valuations.

Size needs to be put into perspective:

The assets under management (AUM) of even the largest asset management companies represent only a fraction (about 2–3 percent) of the universe of global financial assets, most of which—between two-thirds and three-quarters, depending on estimates—are managed in-house.

The AUMs of large asset managers tend to be split among a multitude of *independent* investment strategies, which have no reason to be correlated more closely among themselves than strategies of different asset managers.

Certainly, some of the individual funds' positions may be large in certain markets, but there are exposure limit rules—both internal ones and, what is quite important, those stemming from investment mandates given by asset owners. Concentrated exposure is also curtailed by way of counterparty rules imposed by trading platforms. So I don't think there really is much risk of a "large fish in a small pond" effect.

Moreover—and this is often not sufficiently appreciated—asset allocations within each fund of a large asset manager are typically quite sticky, at least when measured at the asset-class level, for multiple reasons.

First, a large proportion of assets are passively managed. In other words, they are not subject to discretionary allocation decisions but instead track an index, which actually results in countercyclical invest-ment decisions as long as the index doesn't change (as securities whose prices fall must be purchased in larger amount to retain the same weight in the portfolio as in the index).

Second, of the remaining actively managed funds, the overwhelming majority are subject to investment mandates imposed by asset owners and requiring relatively fixed allocations to given asset classes. So portfolio managers' decisions could certainly move the prices of certain securities, but they couldn't really destabilize entire asset classes, which is what we are presumably talking about with the concept of systemic risk.

One can certainly think of extreme cases in which a fund or several funds of a large asset management company might be forced to sell sig-nificant fund holdings. Typically this could happen in the event of large redemptions, which are, of course, possible in open-end funds.

Here it is perhaps helpful to look at history. The data suggest that at least so far, redemption concerns are overblown:

A recent Oliver Wyman/Morgan Stanley study, corroborated also by the IMF's April 2015 GFSR, found that over the past twenty years, redemptions on average have not exceeded around 5–6 percent of the AUM of a fund over the worst three months, even in times of great mar-ket stress, including the global financial crisis.[3]

Moreover, redemptions, even if they snowball, as happened over the past year to one large asset manager, do not necessarily lead to fire sales or herding, for the following reasons:

First, virtually all funds have some form of liquidity buffer (including cash, repo lines, credit facilities, and so forth).

Second, internal liquidity management practices, which seek to match buyers and sellers internally before going to the market, can certainly be helpful in such circumstances, particularly in the presence of large positions.

Third, asset owners can and do switch asset managers without any sale needing to occur at all. Indeed, this is a common practice among institutional investors. Or they can choose to redeem their shares in kind rather than in cash.

Last—and here I depart from the IMF analysis—with the exception of cases of reputational concerns with a given asset manager, I am not at all convinced that the market impact of mass redemptions is worse when asset holdings are pooled in mutual funds than in a completely atomistic market. If all the individuals who take fright on seeing bad economic news managed their assets directly through smart apps on their phones, would they be less prone to sell? It seems to me the answer is no. At least in theory, one would expect the greater professionalism of mutual fund managers, as well as the presence of internal market and liquidity buffers, to mitigate a rush to the exit from a particular asset class.

In sum, I don't see how nonleveraged asset managers, even very large ones, constitute a source of systemic liquidity risk.

But we need to be aware that there are certainly possible risks from open-end funds that promise generous liquidity to their clients while being invested in less liquid assets. The fact that they have not materialized despite many episodes of market stress is comforting, but it shouldn't breed complacency, as the scale of these funds relative to the market increases continuously and, as noted earlier, underlying liquidity conditions are changing by becoming more demanding.

What Can Usefully Be Done to Contain What Does Exist in Terms of Systemic Liquidity Risks?

I find myself in general agreement with the recommendations of the IMF's April 2015 GFSR study, but let me emphasize a few points:

- There are market structure issues: encouraging greater standardization of bond issues, electronic trading on exchanges, and so on certainly makes sense.

  Regulation of mutual funds may need to focus more on circuit breakers against potential mass redemptions, such as fees, gates, share pricing that internalizes the cost of redemptions, and greater incentives to invest in vehicles that investors can get out without reducing the size of the fund, such as ETFs, where investors get out by selling their shares on the secondary markets, or closed-end funds, where investors can sell their shares only if a willing buyer is available.

- What is most important, in my view, is that both supervisors and risk managers need to step up their surveillance of exposures to high price volatility, that is, crowded trades, particularly for assets that are less likely to be dubbed safe assets in a stress episode. This may mean accepting lower returns in the short run but will surely lead to higher risk-adjusted ones. In that spirit, I fully support the idea of stress testing of funds, as already practiced in Europe by the European Securities and Markets Authority and as announced by the SEC in the United States.

- Last but not least, there is a need for the asset managers' supervisory community to continue to develop a strong financial stability focus alongside its well-established consumer protection one. This is easier said than done because while the two go together—consumers who feel well protected are less likely to run—the issues have nothing in common: to caricature, securities regulators struggle to grasp financial stability issues, and bank regulators, who are now on top of the latter, struggle to understand the asset management business. Things have improved already, but having worked on both sides of this divide, I know this will be a big challenge, but one that is critical to tackle.

Notes

1. See Markus Brunnermeier, "Liquidity Illusion and Segmentation," presentation at the Stanford Conference, "Financial Market Adaptation to Regulation and Monetary Policy," Palo Alto, March 20, 2015, https://www.gsb.stanford.edu/sites/default/files/Brunnermeier%2C%20Markus%20-%202015a%20Liquidity%20Stanford.pdf.

2. See International Monetary Fund, "The Asset Management Industry and Financial Stability," in *Navigating Monetary Policy Challenges and Managing Risks,* Global Financial Stability Report, IMF, April 2015, http://www.imf.org/external/pubs/ft/gfsr/2015/01/.

3. See Oliver Wyman/Morgan Stanley, "Liquidity Conundrum: Shifting Risks, What It Means," Blue Paper, March 19, 2015, http://www.oliverwyman.com/content/dam/oliver-wyman/global/en/2015/mar/2015_Wholesale_Investment_Banking_Outlook.pdf.

8

Shadow Banking as a Source of Systemic Risk

Robert E. Rubin

My colleagues on the panel are highly respected and deeply experienced experts on central bank issues. In this chapter I express my views as a practitioner, and those views are based on my experience at Goldman Sachs, where I had responsibility for some, and then all, of the firm's trading and arbitrage activities; my years in the Clinton administration; and my present activity advising several investment organizations and as a continuing participant in the national policy dialogue. I will focus on three issues: the possibility of market excesses, the likelihood of future market and financial destabilization, and systemic risk in shadow banking. A few other issues I cannot take up because of time limitations I will list anyway, because they are on my mind and because I think they are important to anyone involved with investment or policy.

These issues include the monetary policy risks in having expanded the Fed balance sheet so greatly; the fallacy, in my view, of the argument that these risks can be largely avoided by tightening through increasing interest rates on excess reserves or using reverse repos—what I call the magic wand argument; the substantial limitations on the ability of econometric models to predict future economic conditions or responses to policy; and finally, the daunting and hugely consequential question of where the combination of dysfunctional government in the United States, the euro zone, Japan, and elsewhere on fiscal and structural issues joined with expansive monetary policy will lead for the currencies and for financial and economic conditions in the United States and around the world.

Now I will turn to my three focal topics, starting with excesses. I would guess that we would all agree that there has been a substantial reaching for yield along the risk curve for some years now, owing to the low interest rates on US Treasuries, which I think were predominantly a result of multiple factors other than QE2 and QE3, which I think had limited effect on rates. Having said that, I do think QE2, and even more QE3, heightened the reaching for yield by creating a sense of comfort in the financial arena that the Fed could and would keep rates down.

I don't have a judgment as to whether this extensive reaching for yield has, in fact, led to excesses. But that is a realistic possibility, with the US stock market at roughly all-time highs, the revival of covenant light and even noncovenanted lending, the vast increase in fixed income ETFs, euro-zone sovereign debt in the troubled countries selling at what to me, at least, is inexplicable yields on a risk-adjusted basis, and much else. And if there are excesses, they will inevitably fall of their own weight at some unpredictable time.

However, even if markets are not broadly in excess now relative to long-term fundamentals, they will be periodically and unpredictably in the future. In my view, markets are a psychological phenomenon in the short term, oscillating between the fear and greed rooted in human nature, while on average reflecting fundamentals over the longer term. Market-based financial systems over the centuries have always experienced periodic excesses on the upside and then, in reaction, overshooting on the downside, when excesses inevitably fall of their own weight. And I don't see any reason to think that all of human history with respect to market-based financial systems should change now. Thus, I think there is a high likelihood of periodic market and financial system destabilization at unpredictable times in the future.

Moreover, future destabilization may begin—and, almost by definition, will begin—in unexpected places. Goldman Sachs was almost destroyed by the unexpected bankruptcy of Penn Central in 1970. We then put in place measures to prevent any similar situation posing such a dire threat again. But I have never forgotten the comment of John Whitehead, one of our senior partners. He said that our actions would prevent a future Penn Central–type crisis for our firm, but that the next crisis would come from some totally unexpected place, and beyond that, there would surely be future crises. If you look at the history of market-based financial systems, that is what has happened repeatedly.

I don't believe that regulation will ever succeed in preventing excesses, and therefore significant market and financial cyclicality, as long as we have a market-based financial system. But regulation can and should try to reduce the probability of excesses, the likely severity of excesses, and the market and economic effects of downturns when they occur, such as by reducing the vulnerability of organizations involved with the financial system through constraining leverage.

The reforms put in place in response to the financial crisis—for example, the Consumer Financial Protection Bureau, the measures on derivatives, and increased capital requirements—have presumably in large measure accomplished those purposes with respect to banks, other than for the too-big-to-fail issue. In my view, nothing yet done or proposed would solve this important issue under conditions of serious systemwide duress.

More recently, attention has increasingly turned to shadow banking, and so will my remarks. The shadow banking system has long existed, but now many functions of traditional banks are rapidly and substantially gravitating toward the shadow banking world, in part because of the increased constraints on banks and dramatic changes in technology.

For example, market-making, and therefore market liquidity, has always been greatly facilitated by market-makers creating profit-seeking constructions around positions acquired through market-making activities. With proprietary trading now barred for banks, and with the great difficulties in distinguishing between market-making and proprietary trading, bank market-making and market liquidity have declined substantially. And both market-making and now, at an incipient level, the provision of capital to meet primary issuance demand are moving to multiple other platforms, including hedge funds, broadly defined.

Similarly, the increase in capital requirements has deterred various kinds of smaller and medium-sized lending by banks, and this regulatory constraint, plus the capacity for credit evaluation and for interaction with borrowers created by big data and other technological developments, is leading to rapid growth of this type of credit extension by nonbanks, including private equity funds and organizations established for these purposes.

More broadly, the shadow banking world involves a vast array of institutions, asset classes, and activities, and it is growing rapidly. There seems an enormous potential for systemic risk in this world. Let me briefly mention three examples. If excesses develop in financial assets, sooner or later those asset prices will destabilize, and hedge funds and other asset managers, who are highly sensitive to short-term results, could engage in a rush to the exit with those assets, and even with good assets, in order to increase liquidity. That could trigger broad financial market duress. Moreover, while leverage obviously exacerbates the pressure to liquidate, that can occur even when leverage is limited.

Another example is the vast increase in the size of fixed income ETFs. They promise constant liquidity, but the assets of those funds might not be salable in an orderly fashion in times of significant market stress. Heavy redemptions could thus lead to highly destabilizing market dumping. As just one more example, there are new regulations with respect to derivatives, and while they are useful, I don't think they get to the heart of the matter. The outstandings in derivatives are vast. Under normal conditions, that all works. But in times of market stress, correlations move in all kinds of unpredictable ways, and many participants find they have risks different from, and multiples greater than, they had expected. And this could lead to serious market and economic duress, and to unexpected counterparty credit failures. I published a book in 2003 in which I suggested that margin and capital requirements be greatly increased for all users of derivatives—a view I had held going back to my days at Goldman Sachs—and I still think that is critically important, to reduce derivative use, to provide a larger cushion, and to better protect against systemic risk.

I could go on endlessly listing asset classes, types of organizations, and types of activities in shadow banking that could generate systemic risk. Moreover, that situation is not limited to the United States. In today's instantaneously interconnected world, systemic risks in shadow banking abroad can rapidly and powerfully affect us.

One regulatory answer put forth in response to this systemic risk in shadow banking is macroprudential regulation. I interpret that term, in this context, as financial regulations for shadow banking analogous conceptually—though not necessarily with respect to specifics—to financial regulations for the banking system. However, despite work going on with respect to some aspects of shadow banking, in very large measure, as far as I can see, this challenge still needs to be met. In my view, meaningful macroprudential regulation requires meeting three hugely complex and highly time-consuming challenges:

1. Creating a comprehensive catalogue of the shadow banking world, including asset classes, types of organizations, and types of activities. Today, to the best of my knowledge, no one comes close to having identified the full reach of shadow banking or the systemic risks it poses, and doing so will involve a lot of ambiguities and uncertainties. Moreover, while this project would be a monumental undertaking for the United States alone, it should also, perhaps as a separate undertaking, at some point, include the significant shadow banking systems elsewhere.

2. Developing a menu of tools to address the possible systemic risks posed by the shadow banking world. This menu might include, as examples to consider but not recommendations, capital changes, margin requirements, leverage constraints, and possibly position or concentration limits of some sort, or measures tailored to particular shadow banking issues. At best, these tools will be quite imperfect, given the complexities of the various aspects of shadow banking and the complexities around the effects of regulatory measures under conditions of systemic stress. In this context of regulation, while asset classes and organizations are important, I would probably focus especially on activities because systemically risky activities can occur within institutions that are sound and cause serious trouble in the financial system. For example, a large asset manager could be strong enough to withstand very large shocks but have derivative activities, hedge funds, ETFs, or money market funds that could, under stressful conditions, trigger or contribute to serious risks for the financial system.

3. Devising a plan for effective implementation and coordination of macroprudential regulation, once the first two challenges are met. This third challenge is daunting, given our large number of regulatory institutions and the Federal Stability Oversight Council's limited powers. It becomes even more daunting once shadow banking outside of our borders is considered.

In theory, the Office of Financial Research, housed in the Treasury Department, is empowered to undertake these studies. But as a practical matter, far greater resources will be needed, and other regulatory institutions, especially the Fed, could contribute capacity. Perhaps the best way forward is first to recognize the imperative for these studies, and then have the FSOC develop a collaborative plan to get it done. But that, I suspect, is a lot easier said than done.

I think the timeframe for accomplishing this whole project will be lengthy. However, each of the three components could be divided into subsets, in order to move forward in some areas while continuing to work on others. Also, even a strong program would provide far from perfect protections, given the uncertainties and unpredictability in markets, the wide swath of shadow banking, the enormous complexities with respect to each of the three steps, and the inevitability of unforeseen developments.

Thus, I believe, contrary to the views of many, that the Fed should take systemic risk into consideration in monetary policy decisions, even though excesses and bubbles are impossible to identify with high convictions except ex post. That doesn't mean that the formal criteria should be expanded from the current two, combating inflation and promoting full employment, but simply that systemic risk should be considered.

I'll make one final observation: all judgments relating to markets and financial systems are obviously about probabilities, though, as Stan Fischer once said to me, while every thoughtful decision maker recognizes that, relatively few have deeply internalized that probabilistic mind-set and actually operate that way. Moreover, the judgments about probabilities with respect to markets, policy responses, and the like should be treated as having a great deal of uncertainty about them, and that uncertainty itself should be appropriately weighed in decision making. Thus, creating strong regulatory protection, and measuring costs versus benefits, should allow for the possibility that developments, especially under stress conditions, will be at substantial variance with the most likely projected case and may even be outside the range of projected possibilities. Effectively regulating shadow banking is imperative, and it is a complex challenge.

Macroprudential Policies: Gathering Evidence

9

Macroprudential Policy Regimes: Definition and Institutional Implications

Paul Tucker

Policymakers and economists spent decades debating the design of monetary institutions before the wave of central bank independence measures in the 1990s. We now need to turn our eyes to a fresh institution-building challenge: macroprudential regimes. Even for skeptics, this is an important endeavor as, wisely or unwisely, these regimes are increasingly springing up around the world.

There is not yet agreement, however, on the meaning of "macroprudential." Too often the term is used as a synonym for financial stability policy more generally; we don't need two words for one thing. It is important that the IMF, the Bank for International Settlements and the Financial Stability Board coalesce around a common definition that can become embedded in usage.

A Definition of Macroprudential Policy

I define macroprudential policy to be a regime under which policymakers can dynamically adjust regulatory parameters to maintain a desired degree of resilience in the financial system.

Policy instruments—requirements on firms, funds, or structures set out in rules, regulations and international accords—are not completely static under such regimes. Nor are they time-contingent. They are to be state-contingent, varying as needed with threats to stability. That does not mean that they vary a lot. The better the design and calibration of the base regulatory regime, the less cause there will be to vary them. But where necessary, they can be varied to sustain the financial system's resilience.

In terms of the objective—maintaining the resilience of the system—this is not, therefore, a regime for *fine-tuning* the credit cycle. That would be too ambitious. It is hard to know whether temporarily raising, say, capital requirements for banks would tighten or relax the supply of credit in the short run. Any macroprudential measure will reveal not only the action itself but also information about the authorities' views on the state of the financial system. In contrast to monetary policy, where the data on the economy are in the public domain, a prudential policymaker has lots of private information about vulnerabilities in individual financial institutions and the linkages among those institutions. If the market is surprised that the policymaker is concerned enough to act, credit conditions might tighten sharply if market participants conclude, on the basis of the information newly available to them, that the actions taken are insufficient. If, by contrast, the market has been ahead of the authorities in spotting a lurking threat to stability and so is relieved that the policymaker is finally waking up, credit conditions might even ease. There are many scenarios in-between.[1]

Hence my proposed focus is less on trying actively to manage credit conditions and rather more on aiming to sustain a desired degree of resilience in the system. That has the merit of concentrating on the big issue in this field. The greatest social cost of a vicious credit cycle occurs if the eventual bursting of the bubble causes the implosion of the financial system, cutting off the supply of essential services. It is an ambitious enough goal, but a vital one, to get policymakers to prevent the ceiling collapsing in future. Big picture, the ceiling can be reinforced even if the authorities' actions reveal disturbing information about the financial weather.

Filling Out the Concept

How should we think about dynamic adjustment—state-contingent adjustment—of regulatory parameters in order to sustain a desired degree of systemic resilience? Implicitly there are three things going on here, which need to become more explicit.

First of all, I am assuming that society has, or should have, a desired degree of systemic resilience. Does it want to avoid a big crisis once every million years, every thousand years, every one hundred fifty years? It seems clear that seventy years, roughly the gap from the crisis of the 1920s–1930s to the 2007–2009 crisis, is more than the public of either North America or Europe is prepared to bear. But I doubt whether society wants to rule out a crisis for the next five million years, since that would most likely entail banning huge swaths of financial activity.

Second, the macroprudential authority is assumed to have a picture (or model) of the exposures and interconnectedness of the financial system. It uses that to gauge the prospective effects of possible shocks—causing a sharp rise in defaults or trading losses—on the system's residual resilience, and thus whether actual resilience falls short of desired resilience. Of course, that picture of the *structure* of the system will be flawed to a greater or lesser extent, and so has to be kept under review.

The third thing implicit in this conception of prudential regimes is the riskiness of the world. If you like, abstractly, what is the underlying stochastic process generating unexpected losses to financial institutions—the first-round losses that the system's structure transmits across firms, funds and markets?

Big picture, we can think of the underlying risk process in the financial system as a whole as being at any time in one of three broad modes— normal, exuberant, or depressed. If that is right or helpful as a picture, then a very important policy question is whether or not to calibrate the base regulatory requirements designed to keep the system safe and sound—minimum capital requirements, minimum collateral requirements on derivatives transactions, and so forth—to exuberant states of the world. An argument against doing so is essentially ignorance and uncertainty. We do not know enough about the properties of the financial system to be confident about the effects on the supply of credit or of other financial services of calibrating the base regulatory requirements against the most vicious exuberant states of the world. This is a key moment in the argument. I am identifying a "prudent" approach to policy where self-conscious ignorance prompts policymakers to step back from calibrating the base regulatory regime to exuberant states of the world. That may be a mistake, but it *is* the choice made by international and national policy-makers in the years following the 2007–2009 crisis.

If the regime is calibrated to a "normal" underlying risk-generation process, then we know that those regulatory requirements will be insufficient when the world moves into highly exuberant mode. In those circumstances, capital requirements or margin requirements or haircut requirements or whatever need to be changed in order to sustain the desired degree of resilience. Similarly, if the structure of the system changed in ways that made the propagation of first-round losses more contagious, the core regulatory parameters might need to be recalibrated, if only temporarily while deeper solutions were designed.

To be clear, this is not changing the goalposts. The goalposts stay fixed: the tolerance for crisis embedded in the desired degree of systemic resilience.

A Metaphor

A metaphor might help. In the spirit of Knut Wicksell, most monetary authorities think of themselves as moving around their policy interest rate in order to keep the actual short-term real rate (r) in line with estimates of the short-run *equilibrium* real rate (r^*) as shocks occur to aggregate demand or supply. By analogy, macroprudential policy involves moving around, say, the actual capital requirement applied to intermediaries (K) in order to keep it in line with what is necessary to deliver the desired degree of resilience (K^*).

The metaphor is of course imperfect in some respects. The suggestion is not that macroprudential policy be actively used, with *frequent* regulatory recalibrations. Unlike r^*, K^* is not entirely market determined but reflects the regime's objective: how resilient the system should be. Nor is K the only instrument; leverage is not a uniquely useful measure of resilience. But I hope the metaphor helps to illuminate the thought of dynamic adjustment of regulatory instruments with a view to "neutralizing" the threats posed to stability by developments in the world.

Note that this conception of the purpose of macroprudential policy cuts through some of the current debates about its effectiveness. That work typically starts with questions about which among a range of instruments—whether tightening capital requirements or loan-to-value limits or other regulatory constraints—has the greatest and/or quickest effect on the rate of credit growth or asset-price appreciation. As already discussed, those questions are going to be incredibly hard to answer unless we can model the significance of the ex ante information asymmetries between the market and the authorities.

By contrast, the effectiveness of the conception of macroprudential policy outlined here is relatively straightforward. If, for a given balance sheet, core firms have to increase their tangible common equity by 10 percent, they will, broadly, be 10 percent more resilient against an unchanged risk environment. Even though the macroprudential intervention might reveal information about perceived threats to the system and so affect the price of risk in uncertain ways, the system itself is buttressed.

Instead, the hard part of the policymakers' task is to judge the extent to which a regulatory lever must be tweaked to maintain the desired degree of system resilience. That underlines how important the choice of the base requirements is. The more demanding they are, the less likely it is that the macroprudential policymaker will need temporarily to increase them. But wherever they are set, circumstances will eventually arise where maintaining a static regime will bring on disaster.

The Design of Macroprudential Regimes

From that general conception of the purpose and operation of macroprudential regimes flow some precepts or pointers for their design.

The Scope of Macroprudential Policy Regimes

In the first place, although I have used banking as the core example, this is not, in fact, only about banking supervision. It is not just about maintaining the stability of the banking system in the sense of de jure banks. Regulatory arbitrage is endemic in finance. The industry is a shape-shifter.

If the authorities were to focus exclusively on maintaining a resilient banking sector, then systemic risks will turn up with a terrifying inevitability in some manifestation of shadow banking or somewhere else in the financial system. So the scope of the regime needs to be broad.

If, then, macroprudential policy cannot just be about banking supervision, it must also be about the parts of the financial system that typically fall under the jurisdiction of securities regulators. That requires either reform of the mandates and mind-sets of securities regulators or, alternatively, a reshaping of the regulatory architecture to give one authority general macroprudential jurisdiction over the financial system as a whole.

Rules versus Constrained Discretion

Further, state-contingent adjustment of regulatory parameters is plainly not about writing detailed rules that are put out for extensive consultation in the usual way (in the US jargon, "notice-and-comment" rule-making). By the time any planned temporary adjustment had gone through such a process, it might be too late. Macroprudential policy, as conceived here, involves the exercise of discretion, and so needs to be carefully constrained to serve society's agreed-upon purposes.

Credible Commitment: An Independent Policymaker with Instrument but Not Goal Independence

Macroprudential regimes plainly face a problem of credible commitment. Dynamically adjusting the regulatory parameters to strengthen the system during a boom is likely to be unpopular. If the tools were in the hands of politicians, they might well decline to deploy them because, despite their better instincts, they would know that the credit or asset-price boom was making the electing public feel good, and so more likely to reelect them.

There might also be a strict time-inconsistency problem in the narrow sense of a social planner with unchanged preferences departing from a long-run optimal plan because it can improve on the plan in a single period. This question is underresearched.

The problem of credible commitment makes the case for a macroprudential regime of the kind I have described being in the hands of an independent institution, insulated from day-to-day politics. That institution need not necessarily be a jurisdiction's central bank, but it might be. I return to that below.

Whoever the policymakers are, they are going to be mighty powerful. That entails some constraints on institutional design if the regime is to enjoy democratic legitimacy.

First—and of course this echoes work on monetary policy a few decades ago—the goals should not be set by the independent unelected policymakers themselves. The objective should be decided by the people's elected representatives, after due public debate. That means more than elected politicians specifying a vague objective such as "preserve financial stability." It means that elected politicians also need to set or bless the standard of resilience for the system as a whole.

That is not going to be easy because, on the face of it, it amounts to asking politicians a question that many would not want to answer: "What is your tolerance for a crisis?" And yet a standard of resilience, and so a tolerance for crisis, *is* implicit in the minimum capital standards applied to banks and other financial institutions.

Taking into account the differences in other parts of system, that implicit standard should be applied elsewhere in the broadest sense, as follows: given the nature of the risks to stability from sector X, what requirement is needed to ensure that it is no more likely to bring down the ceiling than banking? That would entail making assumptions about the structure of each sector, its vulnerability to risk, and the wider systemic consequences of distress within the sector for the provision of core financial services. Technocrats and researchers need to find ways of having these debates with elected policymakers.

No First-Order Distributional Choices

Where a policy regime is delegated to an independent institution, insulated from day-to-day politics, that should not entail society delegating first-order distributional choices. The stress is on *choices*. The suggestion is not that these regimes cannot have distributional *effects*. Such effects might be foreseen by the politicians who are doing the delegating, whether or not they are expected to average out to zero over time.

If that design constraint is accepted, it poses some concrete questions for macroprudential regimes. For example, is it okay for independent agencies to *change* maximum loan-to-value (LTV) or loan-to-income ratios without the usual process of formal consultation? When I was in office, my view and Mervin King's view was that that would probably go a bit too far because there would inevitably be underserving losers whose voice had not been heard. I thought that the Bank of England found a neat solution to this a year or so ago (after my period of office): with mortgage credit rising quite rapidly, the BoE put a limit on the percentage of any bank's portfolio that could be accounted for by high-LTV mortgages. In other words, it did not ban the writing of or borrowing on high-LTV mortgages but instead focused on what it judged was required for the resilience of the system.

That's just one type of instrument. A lot of work would be needed if the constraint "no big distributional choices" were to be accepted. For each potential macroprudential instrument, it would be necessary to debate whether policy decisions would turn on the authority making a big distributional choice. If that is not debated in advance and decided by elected politicians, it will come back to bite these new policy regimes.

The Design of Multiple-Mission Central Banks

Finally, what does this mean for central banks?

Clearly, central banks are reasonable institutions to have these powers, but it then makes them *multi-mission* authorities. We have known for decades, both in theory and even more in practice, that there is a problem with institutions having multiple missions, because they have incentives to concentrate their efforts on the one that is most salient to the people and most observable to the outside world, which of course many people would think of as being monetary policy. So how on earth are these institutions, central banks, to handle multiple missions?

A few things can be said. First, I think that if a central bank has macroprudential responsibilities alongside monetary policy responsibilities, it should have separate committees. The committees would sensibly have overlapping membership in order to harness the benefits of housing them in the same agency, but ideally each would have a majority of members who were on that committee only.

Now that is what was done in the UK in the architectural reforms of 2012, and there is in fact a separate *micro*prudential policy committee as well. During the period when the new architecture was being designed and debated in the Westminster Parliament and beyond, a recurrent question was, why have three committees? My answer was, so that at each meeting, there is a majority of people in the room who are responsible for only that committee's mission and so will make sure it is always a serious meeting. However preoccupied those on two or three committees are with other matters, they will be incentivized to step up to the plate of the meeting they are in, because there's a bunch of people in the room who do only that.

A second imperative to help central banks in this new area is to make policy systematic, with the reasons for policy choices sufficiently transparent for the guiding principles to be observable and so capable of being subject to public scrutiny and debate. To be less transparent or systematic than in monetary policy could be damaging to a multi-mission central bank.

At first sight, this is a big deal. A problem that has plagued supervision and regulation is that not only are the outturns difficult to judge, but the outputs have sometimes been impossible to observe. I think the development since the crisis of systematic stress testing of firms' resilience potentially changes that in profound ways. The political economy significance of stress testing is that it is done once a year and is highly public: the scenario is public and the results are public. So politicians can have the Fed into Congress, the Bank of England into the Westminster Parliament, the ECB into the European Parliament, and say this scenario seemed a bit silly, too strong, too weak; the results seem implausible given the scenario, and so on. And, of course, that would be informed by masses of debate around the stress tests, in the way that monetary policy decisions are surrounded by debate.

Central banks should be in the business of encouraging debate about their stress tests. Debate, research and criticism will help them build and improve these regimes over the next decade or so.

Interactions with Monetary Policy and Central Bank Balance Sheet Operations

I have been describing a setup in which monetary policymakers and macroprudential policymakers can cooperate, even coordinate, but have separate objectives.

In some ways this bypasses suggestions that monetary policy should be the preferred instrument for addressing financial stability risks on the grounds that, as Jeremy Stein has pointed out, monetary policy gets into all the cracks, affecting all asset prices. But in fact, it gets into all of the cracks relevant to financial stability only under autarky, with capital controls and all the transactions within the economy denominated in the local currency. It does not get into all the cracks if households, businesses and intermediaries can borrow from abroad in foreign currency, as they can more or less everywhere. Time and again over the past half century we have seen stability problems rooted in, or at least brought to a head by, external or foreign currency indebtedness. That being so, even if societies were prepared to divert monetary policy from the goal of nominal stability, it could not substitute for a policy of maintaining the resilience of the financial system against the complete range of potential threats.

The approach outlined here allows the deployment of monetary policy instruments, and central bank balance sheet policy more generally, to return to being parsimonious once macroeconomic normality is regained. In the face of a stability-threatening boom, macroprudential policy action would be preferred over interventions based on selling parts of portfolios of private-sector securities to drive up credit spreads.

That leaves open the possibility of the authorities intervening in specific markets in a severe economic downturn when monetary policy has reached the zero lower bound. But that opens up a broader set of questions, not addressed here, about how to frame the proper role of central banks with respect to monetary/fiscal coordination.

Note

1. See Paul Tucker, "Banking Reform and Macro-prudential Regulation: Implications for Banks' Capital Structure and Credit Conditions," speech delivered at the SUERF/Bank of Finland Conference, "Banking after Regulatory Reform: Business As Usual," Helsinki, June 13, 2013, Bank of England, http://www.bankofengland.co.uk/publications/Documents/speeches/2013/speech666.pdf.

10

Macroprudential Tools, Their Limits, and Their Connection with Monetary Policy

Hyun Song Shin

In keeping with the title of the session, "Macroprudential Policies: Gathering Evidence," I will say something about the evidence, but I will also offer some broader reflections on the limits of macroprudential tools and their relationship with monetary policy.

A key aim of macroprudential policy is to moderate the procyclicality of the financial system. It does so by influencing the financial intermediation process; it operates on the assets, liabilities, and leverage of intermediaries (figure 10.1). In this respect, macroprudential policy and monetary policy share some similarities.

For instance, both policies affect the *demand for credit* by reallocating spending over time, either by postponing spending (i.e., by inducing consumers and firms to borrow less) or by bringing forward spending (i.e., by inducing them to borrow more). Both policies affect the *supply of credit* by influencing the funding cost of the intermediary. Macroprudential policies aim to reduce risk taking by constraining leverage, both that of borrowers and that of financial intermediaries. Even here, the parallels with monetary policy turn out to be closer than may be appreciated at first glance. Recent evidence on the "risk-taking channel" of monetary policy points to monetary policy working through intermediary leverage and risk taking more generally.[1]

However, there are two important differences between monetary policy and macroprudential policy.

The first difference is that macroprudential policy is aimed at specific sectors or practices. In some respects, macroprudential policy harks back to the directed credit policies used by many advanced economies up to the 1970s, although these were used to channel credit to favored sectors, as well as to constrain credit. The name is different, but the policies are

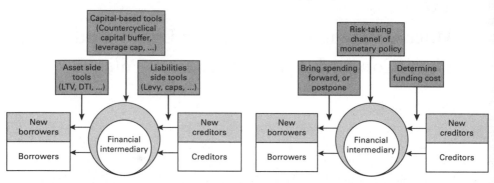

Figure 10.1
Comparison of Macroprudential Policy with Monetary Policy.

similar. In many cases, it is old wine in new bottles. In contrast, monetary policy influences risk taking more broadly, both within the domestic financial system and across borders, and is harder to circumvent.

On the other hand, the broader impact of monetary policy cuts both ways: domestic monetary policy is constrained by global conditions. This is the second difference between monetary policy and macroprudential policy. My BIS colleague Jaime Caruana will expand on this point. In a nutshell, the point is this. Currencies are global, but monetary policy is territorial, or rather the *mandated domain* of monetary policy is territorial.

A relevant and currently topical question is whether floating exchange rates are sufficient to insulate an open economy from global financial conditions. Hélène Rey's recent work has shed light on this question, and the initial evidence suggests that the answer is no.

In any event, actions speak louder than words, and judging from monetary policy actions actually pursued by central banks, the evidence is that central banks believe the answer to be no. Figure 10.2 updates the findings initially reported by Boris Hofmann and Bilyana Bogdanova cited above. The dashed line plots the average realized policy rate while the solid line plots the mean Taylor rule path, with the gray band showing the upper and lower bounds, depending on the particular version of the Taylor rule. While the actual policy rates chosen by central banks followed the Taylor rule rate fairly closely up to around 2003, they started to diverge thereafter, with the actual policy rate being lower than the Taylor rule rate for much of the period, especially for emerging

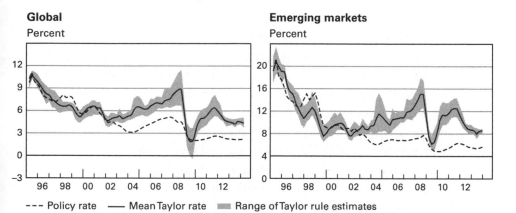

Figure 10.2
Policy Rates Compared to Taylor Rules.
Notes: See Boris Hofmann and Bilyana Bogdanova, "Taylor Rules and Monetary Policy: A Global 'Great Deviation'?," *BIS Quarterly Review,* September 2012, 37–49, http://www.bis.org/publ/qtrpdf/r_qt1209f.pdf. *Sources:* IMF, International Financial Statistics and World Economic Outlook; Bloomberg; CEIC; Consensus Economics; Datastream; national data; authors' calculations.

market economies (EMEs). One way to read these graphs is to suppose that the central banks would have chosen a path closer to the Taylor rule path in the absence of constraints from global financial conditions but that concerns about exchange rate appreciation stayed their hands and made them pursue monetary policies that were looser than the Taylor rule benchmark. However, more research would be necessary to ascertain whether such an interpretation is the correct one.

It is in this context—when external conditions constrain monetary policy—that macroprudential policy comes into its own, especially for EMEs. For the banking sector, policies aimed at constraining noncore liabilities may be one way to dampen procyclicality and lean against systemic risk.

Are monetary policy and macroprudential policy effective only when they tighten at the same time, or it is possible to tighten one but loosen the other? In other words, must the two policies pull in the same direction (be used as complements), or can they pull in opposite directions (be used as substitutes)?

Some recent discussions of macroprudential policies treat the two as being substitutes: monetary policy is loosened, and macroprudential policy is invoked to deal with the financial stability implications of a looser monetary policy. However, when they pull in opposite directions, households and firms are being told simultaneously to borrow more and borrow less. There is some tension between the two sets of policies, to say the least.

Initial research, including some conducted at the IMF, suggests that both monetary and macroprudential policies have some effect in constraining credit growth, and that the two tend to be complements, not substitutes, although results vary by type of shock.[2]

In my own study with Valentina Bruno and Ilhyock Shim on how macroprudential tools are actually deployed, we found that macroprudential policies and monetary policy often pull in the same direction. There is a modest positive correlation of around 0.2 between tightening macroprudential and monetary policy measures (table 10.1).[3] The small size of the positive correlation suggests that the complementarity of the two sets of policies is weak at best. In any case, it is one thing to show that the two sets of policies were used in the same direction. It is another to show that such a combination is optimal. To establish optimality, a theoretical investigation in a framework that is rich enough to accommodate all the competing forces would be necessary.

All of that said, we should be mindful of the limits to what can be achieved through macroprudential policy. Most macroprudential tools are aimed at the banking sector, especially the regulated banking sector. Their design is influenced by the experience of past crises. Watchwords are credit growth, leverage, maturity mismatch, complexity, and "too big to fail." While these factors are still relevant, it does not follow that all future bouts of financial disruption must follow the same mechanism as in the past.

The changing patterns of financial intermediation mean that we need to revise constantly our understanding of the relevant players in the financial system. Long-term investors have become increasingly important in recent years. Some of them are reaching for yield, but many long-term investors are chasing disappearing yield in their attempt to hedge duration, as government bond yields have plunged in recent weeks.

The German ten-year sovereign yield is 13 basis points this morning. The German thirty-year rate is down to 53 basis points. The Swiss ten-year rate is actually *negative*, at −14 basis points.

Figure 10.3 plots the duration gap for European insurers, and illustrates how insurance company liabilities tend to have longer duration than their assets. The gap is largest for German insurers.

Table 10.1
Correlation of Policy Changes in Asia-Pacific Economies

	Policy Rate	Non-Interest-Rate Monetary Policy Measures	Prudential Measures on Housing Credit	Prudential Measures on Banking Inflows and FX Exposures
Policy rate	1			
Non-interest-rate monetary policy measures	0.2214	1		
Prudential measures on housing credit	0.1599	0.1896	1	
Prudential measures on banking inflows and FX exposures	0.2018	0.2997	0.0925	1

Notes: Changes in the policy rate are actual policy rate changes. For changes in the other types of policy action, +1 is assigned for tightening actions, 0 for no change, and −1 for loosening actions. Quarterly data from 2004 to 2013 for Australia, China, Hong Kong SAR, India, Indonesia, Japan, Korea, Malaysia, New Zealand, the Philippines, Singapore, and Thailand.
Source: Adapted from table 15 in Valentina Bruno, Ilhyock Shim, and Hyun Song Shin, "Comparative Assessment of Macroprudential Policies," BIS Working Paper 502, Bank for International Settlements, June 2015, http://www.bis.org/publ/work502.htm.

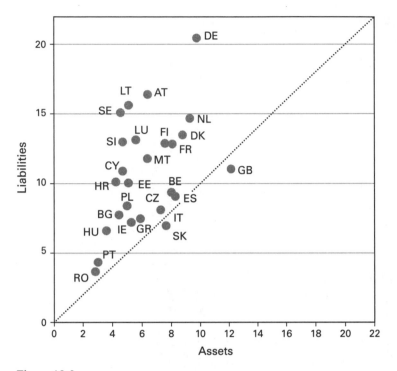

Figure 10.3
Duration of Assets and Liabilities of European Insurance Companies. *Source:* European Insurance and Occupational Pensions Authority (EIOPA).

Because of the duration mismatch, the duration of liabilities runs away from investors faster than the duration of assets increases as long-term yields fall. Investors who wish to match duration may need to chase long-dated bonds, pushing down their yields further. Like a dog chasing its tail, bidding up the price of long-dated bonds may succeed only in extending the duration of liabilities further.

The recent plunge in long-dated yields should give us pause for thought. The greater risk taking involved in chasing disappearing yield has pushed term premiums deep into negative territory. But other measures of risk premium—such as high-yield bond spreads or equity volatility premium—are sending mixed messages.

What if the deeply negative term premium is not just a sign of exuberance? What if it is also a sign of distress, of buyers forced into adding positions? We are reminded of the Stevie Smith poem, "Not Waving but Drowning."

These questions are worth asking, as the amplification forces that are driving long rates lower could just as well work in reverse, leading to sharply higher rates when yields eventually start to rise again. The further term premiums fall into negative territory, the sharper will be the snap-back when they reverse their decline.

Few of these forces are amenable to the macroprudential policies that have been deployed so far. Macroprudential policies have been aimed at the banking sector, in particular the regulated banking sector. The "snapback" risk in long-dated yields that comes with amplified falls in long-dated rates could not adequately be addressed with the types of macroprudential policies that have been tried or even contemplated. All this goes to show that macroprudential policy is more than a specific toolkit. It is about a perspective, or a frame of mind.

Notes

1. The term "risk-taking channel" was coined by Claudio Borio and Haibin Zhu, "Capital Regulation, Risk-Taking and Monetary Policy: A Missing Link in the Transmission Mechanism?," BIS Working Paper 268, Bank for International Settlements, December 2008, http://www.bis.org/publ/work268.pdf. Empirical studies have pointed to monetary policy shocks being a key determinant of inter-mediary leverage. See Valentina Bruno and Hyun Song Shin, "Capital Flows and the Risk-Taking Channel of Monetary Policy," *Journal of Monetary Economics* 71 (2015): 119–132.

2. See International Monetary Fund, *The Interaction of Monetary and Macro-prudential Policies* (Washington, DC: International Monetary Fund, January 29, 2013), https://www.imf.org/external/np/pp/eng/2013/012913.pdf. See also Eugenio Cerutti, Stijn Claessens, and Luc Laeven, "Macroprudential Policies: Ana-lysing a New Database," paper presented at the DNB-EBC conference, "Macro-prudential Regulation: From Theory to Implementation," Amsterdam, January 29–30, 2015; Kenneth Neil Kuttner and Ilyhock Shim, "Can Non-Interest Rate Policies Stabilize Housing Markets? Evidence from a Panel of 57 Economies," BIS Working Paper 433, Bank for International Settlements, November 2013, http://www.bis.org/publ/work433.pdf; and Ozge Akinci and Jane Olmstead-Rumsey, "How Effective Are Macroprudential Policies? An Empirical Investiga-tion," International Finance Discussion Paper 1136, Board of Governors of the Federal Reserve System, Washington, DC, May 2015, http://dx.doi.org/10.17016/IFDP.2015.1136.

3. See Valentina Bruno, Ilhyock Shim, and Hyun Song Shin, "Comparative As-sessment of Macroprudential Policies," BIS Working Paper 502, Bank for Interna-tional Settlements, June 2015, http://www.bis.org/publ/work502.htm.

11

A Simple Cost-Benefit Analysis of Using Monetary Policy for Financial Stability Purposes

Lars E. O. Svensson

Should monetary policy be used for financial stability purposes? Should monetary policy, as suggested by the Bank for International Settlements (2014), "lean against the wind"—for instance, against increases in housing prices and household debt—in an attempt to promote financial stability?

Jeremy Stein (2013) has put forward what is arguably the strongest argument in favor of leaning against the wind for financial stability purposes: "While monetary policy may not be quite the right tool for the job, it has one important advantage relative to supervision and regulation—namely that it gets in all of the cracks [of the financial system]."

However, when one thinks about this argument, I believe one must admit that a modest policy rate increase would most likely barely fill the bottom of these cracks. To fill the cracks, the policy rate may have to be increased so much that it would kill the economy.

This observation points to the need for a cost-benefit analysis of using monetary policy for financial stability purposes. If monetary policy should deviate from its mandate—for instance, from the Federal Reserve's objectives of price stability and maximum sustainable employment—it should be the case that the expected benefits exceed the costs of deviating from the objectives.

For instance, tighter monetary policy might limit the growth of housing prices and household debt somewhat. This might in some situations reduce the probability or the severity of a possible future financial crisis, or both. Because a financial crisis would most likely imply too low an inflation rate and too high an unemployment rate, tighter policy might then have the benefit of a better expected future macro outcome. But tighter policy will lower inflation and increase unemployment over the next few years. It may thus have costs in terms of a worse macro outcome during the next few years, with too low an inflation rate or too high an unemployment rate, or both. For a tighter policy to be justified, the expected benefits should exceed the expected costs. For policy to be optimal, it should be adjusted such that the expected marginal benefits equal the expected marginal costs.

The Swedish Riksbank's policy during 2010–2011 provides a clear example of leaning against the wind because of concerns about household debt. As discussed in Svensson (2010, 2015c), in June 2010, the Riksbank's forecast for CPIF inflation was below the inflation target, and the unemployment rate and the forecast for unemployment were far above the Riksbank's estimate of a long-run sustainable rate of unemployment.[1] Nevertheless, the Riksbank increased the policy rate from 0.25 basis points in June 2010 to 2 percent in July 2011 because of concerns about possible risks associated with rising housing prices and household debt. After this rapid rate increase, inflation fell to around zero, far below the target, and unemployment stayed up around 8 percent, far above any reasonable estimate of its long-run sustainable rate. In response to this, the Riksbank only slowly brought the policy rate down during 2012 and 2013. From the summer of 2014, the policy rate was brought down more quickly. In March 2015 it was lowered to –0.25 percent.[2]

The dramatic policy tightening in 2010–2011 was done without any previous analysis of the impact of monetary policy on any risks associated with household debt. It was arguably a seat-of-the-pants policy, justified by a gut feeling that the benefits must exceed the costs and disregarding existing evidence of small effects of the policy rate on debt and financial stability (Svensson 2010). Later, in July 2013, the Riksbank would present a framework that might justify its policy (Sveriges Riksbank 2013). According to this framework, tighter policy, by limiting household indebtedness, would reduce the probability and severity of a future financial crisis and its associated bad macro outcome. This way, the worse macro outcome over the next few years from the tightening could be seen as an insurance premium paid to ensure a better expected macro outcome in future. But no numbers or estimates were published that would justify its policy.

However, in early 2014 the Riksbank presented its own estimates of the impact of the policy rate on household real debt and the debt-to-income ratio (DTI) (Sveriges Riksbank 2014a). The Riksbank also regularly published, in its *Monetary Policy Report*, its estimates of the impact of alternative policy rate paths on inflation and unemployment (e.g., Sveriges Riksbank 2014b).[3] This makes it possible to assess the relative costs and benefits of the Riksbank's leaning against the wind, using the Riksbank's own estimated numbers together with estimates of the effect of real debt growth on the probability of a financial crisis in Schularick and Taylor (2012) and the effect of the DTI ratio on the depth of the recent crisis in Flodén (2014).

The Unemployment Cost of a Higher Policy Rate

Let me for simplicity express the cost and benefits of a higher policy rate in terms of unemployment (see Svensson 2015c for details). A higher policy rate results in a higher unemployment rate. According to Sveriges Riksbank (2014b, figures 2:13 and 2:15), a one-percentage-point higher policy rate during four quarters leads to about a 0.5-percentage-point higher unemployment rate during the next few years (Svensson 2015c, figure 4).[4] This increase in the unemployment rate then represents the *cost* of a higher policy rate, to be compared with any benefits of a higher policy rate.

The Benefits of a Higher Policy Rate

According to the Riksbank's framework, a higher policy rate should reduce household indebtedness. The reduced indebtedness would lower the *probability* of a future crisis, with its associated bad macroeconomic outcome, including low inflation and high unemployment. The reduced indebtedness would also, conditional on a crisis occurring, reduce the *severity* of a crisis—for instance, it would reduce the increase in the unemployment rate. The reduced probability of a crisis and the reduced severity of a crisis would constitute the *benefits* of a higher policy rate. What, then, are the benefits of a higher policy rate, according to the Riksbank's own estimates?

The Effect of a Higher Policy Rate on the Probability of a Crisis

What is the expected effect of a higher policy rate on the *probability* of a crisis? First, regarding the probability of a crisis, Sveriges Riksbank (2013) refers to Schularick and Taylor (2012). According to that paper, lower growth of real debt reduces the probability of a crisis occurring. More precisely, according to the authors' summary of their results, a one-percentage-point lower annual growth of real debt for five years (that is, 5 percent lower real debt in five years) would, everything else equal, reduce the probability per year of a crisis by about 0.4 percentage points.[5]

Second, according to the Riksbank's own estimate, a one-percentage-point higher policy rate during four quarters would result in 0.25 percent lower real debt in five years (see Svensson 2015c, figure 5, and Sveriges Riksbank 2014a, figure A20, for quarter 20).[6]

Altogether, this implies a reduction in the probability per year of a crisis by $0.25 \times 0.4/5 = 0.02$ percentage points, a very small reduction of the probability.

If one makes an assumption of how much higher unemployment would be in a crisis, the benefit of a lower probability of a crisis can be expressed in terms of expected lower unemployment. Sveriges Riksbank (2013, figure A10) assumes a crisis scenario in which the unemployment rate becomes about 5 percent higher. I will use that assumption.

If the probability of a crisis falls by 0.02 percentage points, that is, by 0.0002, the expected future unemployment rate will then fall by $0.0002 \times 5 = 0.001$ percentage points, that is, by 0.1 *basis* points. This is thus the benefit expressed in terms of lower expected future unemployment because of a lower probability of a crisis. It is clearly very small compared to the cost of a 0.5-percentage-point higher unemployment rate during the next few years.

Furthermore, according to Sveriges Riksbank (2014a, figure A20) and Svensson (2015c, figure 5), the policy rate has *no long-run effect on real debt* and thus no long-run effect on risks associated with real debt.

The Effect of a Higher Policy Rate on the Severity of a Crisis

What is then the expected effect of a higher policy rate on the *severity* of a crisis? First, according to a note by Riksbank deputy governor Martin Flodén (2014, table 1, column 2), a one-percentage-point lower DTI ratio might, all else equal, result in the increase in the unemployment rate in a crisis being 0.02 percentage points lower. Second, according to

Sveriges Riksbank (2014a, figure A22) and Svensson (2015c, figure 6), a one-percentage-point higher policy rate during four quarters would lead to a 0.44-percentage-point lower DTI ratio in five years.[7]

Altogether, this means that the increase in the unemployment rate might be $0.44 \times 0.02 = 0.009$ percentage points lower, that is, 0.9 basis points lower, if the crisis occurs with certainty. If the crisis occurs with the probability per year of 4 percent (the average probability of a crisis, according to Schularick and Taylor [2012], corresponding to a crisis, on average, every twenty-five years), the expected lower increase in the unemployment rate is only $0.04 \times 0.9 = 0.036$ basis points. Let me here assume a higher probability of a crisis, 10 percent per year. Then the expected lower increase in unemployment is still only $0.1 \times 0.9 = 0.09$ basis points, very small compared to the cost of a 0.5-percentage-point higher unemployment rate during the next few years.

Furthermore, according to Sveriges Riksbank (2014a, figure A22) and Svensson (2015c, figure 6), the policy rate has *no long-run effect on the DTI ratio* and thus no long-run effect on risks associated with the DTI ratio.

Adding Up Costs and Benefits in Terms of Unemployment

Adding up the two benefits of a higher policy rate, a lower probability of a crisis and a less severe crisis, we get an expected lower future unemployment rate of $0.1 + 0.09 = 0.19$ basis points. This is, of course, completely insignificant in comparison with the cost of a higher policy rate: a 0.5-percentage-point (i.e., 50-basis-point) higher unemployment rate during the next few years. The benefit is only about 0.4 percent of the cost, instead of the more than 100 percent required to justify the policy of leaning against the wind. Put differently, the cost is about 250 times the benefit, two orders of magnitude larger than the benefits. The cost and benefits are summarized in table 11.1.

There is, of course, considerable uncertainty about the Riksbank, Schularick and Taylor, and Flodén estimates that I have used, and there is also considerable uncertainty about the point estimate of the cost-benefit ratio that I have calculated from them. Nevertheless, there has to be extremely one-sided errors to result in a total error corresponding to two orders of magnitude.

Table 11.1

Costs and Benefit in Unemployment of a One-Percentage-Point Higher Policy Rate during four quarters

Cost: Higher unemployment during the next few years (basis points)	50
Benefit: Lower expected future unemployment (basis points)	
1. From a lower probability of a crisis (basis points)	0.1
2. From a smaller increase in unemployment in a crisis (basis points)	0.09
Total benefit (basis points)	0.19
Total benefit as a share of the cost (%)	0.38
Cost-benefit ratio	**263**

A Quadratic Loss Function

The above specifies the trade-off between the increase in the unemployment rate over the next few years and the associated possible reduction in the expected future unemployment rate. It can be seen as a simple linear calculation of the costs and benefits measured in unemployment. It has the advantage that it is independent of the initial conditions of the economy, in the sense that it does not depend on whether initially unemployment is above or below its long-run sustainable rate.

However, for monetary policy purposes, costs and benefits are usually expressed in terms of a quadratic loss function, for instance, a weighted sum of squared inflation deviations from an inflation target and squared unemployment gaps (deviations from its long-run sustainable rate). Let's consider losses in terms of a squared unemployment gap. Given the initial unemployment gap together with assumptions about the future unemployment gap before a crisis, we can calculate the cost and benefit in terms of the increased loss in the next few years and the expected reduction in the future loss from a reduction in the probability and severity of a crisis. The increased loss in the next few years is, of course, quite sensitive to whether the initial unemployment gap is positive, zero, or negative.

Assume that the initial unemployment gap is two percentage points and that the future unemployment gap in the absence of a crisis is zero.[8] For a one-percentage-point increase in the policy rate, the benefit (in the form of a reduction in the expected future loss from a lower probability and severity of a crisis) can be shown to be 0.38 percent of the cost (in the form of an increase in the loss because of a higher unemployment rate over the next few years). That is, the cost-benefit ratio is about 250.[9]

As mentioned, the quadratic loss depends on the assumed initial unemployment gap. If the initial unemployment gap is zero, the benefit is 3.4 percent of the cost, with a cost-benefit ratio of about 30, still much above 1.[10] Thus, even if the Swedish economy had had a zero unemployment gap in June 2010, a policy rate increase of one percentage point could, according to these calculations, not be justified (the actual policy rate increase from June 2010 to July 2011 was a full 1.75 percentage points).

This calculation of the quadratic cost and benefit can be extended to include the quadratic costs due to inflation deviations from target. It can be extended to include the sum of future costs and benefits, taking into account the expected length of a crisis and any discounting. It can be refined to take into account the precise time-series properties of the Schularick and Taylor (2012) estimates rather than using the effect of the five-year average growth rate of real debt. But because the expected future unemployment reduction is less than 1 percent of the unemployment rate increase during the next few years, it is clear that the result of a more complete cost-benefit analysis is unlikely to be much different from the simple calculations reported here. Svensson (2015a) pursues these issues further.[11]

The Effect of Inflation below Expectations

The calculation of costs and benefits above disregards the effect on real debt of actual inflation falling substantially below previous inflation expectations, which in Sweden have been at or a bit above the target expect very recently. Because the Riksbank's leaning against the wind has led to inflation much below not only the target but also below households' inflation expectations over the past few years, the real value of nominal debt has become higher than expected and planned for. As discussed in Svensson (2015c), the real value of any mortgage held at the end of 2011 has in the spring of 2015 become about 6.5 percent larger than if inflation had equaled the inflation target of 2 percent. This is a much larger effect on real debt than the ones discussed above. Given this effect, Riksbank policy has almost certainly increased real debt and actually been counterproductive; the Riksbank has consequently made any problems and risks with household indebtedness worse. A more complete analysis of the costs and benefits of leaning against the wind should also increase the effects of this "Fisherian" effect on the real debt burden of an inflation rate below inflation expectations (Svensson 2013a).

Conclusion

According to this simple cost-benefit analysis of the Riksbank's policy of leaning against the wind for financial stability purposes, the benefits are tiny, less than 1 percent of the cost, so the cost is two orders of magnitude larger than the benefits. The reason for this result is that the policy rate has a very small and indirect effect on the probability and severity of a crisis but a sizable more direct effect on the unemployment rate during the next few years. Furthermore, because leaning against the wind has led to an inflation rate much below households' inflation expectations over the past few years, the real value of household debt has become substantially higher than expected and planned for. The net effect of the policy has almost certainly been to increase real debt and actually been counterproductive; the policy has most likely made any problems and risks with household indebtedness worse.

If the purpose is to limit the probability and severity of a financial crisis, this cost-benefit analysis indicates that tighter monetary policy is not the right tool (Bernanke 2015). The possible impact on the probability and severity of a financial crisis is simply far too weak compared to the sizable negative impact on inflation and unemployment. Macroprudential policy has much more direct and targeted effects on the probability and severity of a crisis, at apparently much lower costs. Macroprudential policy should, of course, also be subject to a cost-benefit analysis, but it seems very unlikely to me that such an analysis would not in most cases be quite favorable to it. In Sweden, the Financial Supervisory Authority (FSA) has taken several macroprudential actions that should reduce the probability and severity of a future crisis. These include a loan-to-value (LTV) cap of 85 percent, introduced in 2010, after which the average LTV ratio of new mortgages stabilized at around 70 percent, leaving a substantial 30 percent of average equity for new mortgages. The FSA has also increased banks' risk weights on mortgages to 25 percent and systemically important banks' capital requirements to 16 percent of risk-weighted assets. In this context, it is of interest that preliminary results by an IMF team indicate that, with 15–20 percent bank capital relative to risk-weighted assets, about 85 percent of the banking crises in advanced countries since 1970 might have been avoided. It is hard to see that these policy actions by the FSA would have any costs in Sweden comparable to those of a tight monetary policy.

Generally, the Swedish experience points to the importance of doing a thorough cost-benefit analysis before monetary policy is tightened for financial stability purposes, especially in a weak economy, but also with more balanced initial conditions. Even if the Swedish economy had not been weak in June 2010 but the unemployment gap had been closed, the simple cost-benefit analysis presented here indicates that the expected benefits of leaning against the wind would still have been much smaller than the costs. It remains to be seen whether such a cost-benefit analysis for other countries would give the same clear result as in the Swedish case. To me, it seems rather unlikely that conditions in other countries would be so different that a higher policy rate would be a cost-effective measure to affect the probability and severity of a financial crisis. These issues are pursued further in Svensson (2015a).

Notes

1. The Riksbank's inflation target is 2 percent for annual inflation measured by the CPI, the Consumer Price Index. The Riksbank uses forecasts of inflation measured by the CPIF as a guide to achieve the inflation target for the CPI. CPIF inflation differs from CPI inflation in that homeowners' housing costs are calculated with mortgage rates held constant.

2. I served as a deputy governor and member of the executive board of the Riksbank during May 2007–May 2013. My colleague Karolina Ekholm and I consistently dissented against the Riksbank policy, first against the policy tightening of 2010–2011 and then in favor of a rapid lowering of the policy rate. We argued that easier policy would improve target achievement for inflation and resource utilization and that the effects of the policy rate on any risks associated with household debt were too small to justify the tight policy. See, for instance, my speech in November 2010 (Svensson 2010). My lessons from six years of practical policymaking are discussed more extensively in Svensson (2013b).

3. In more recent *Monetary Policy Reports*, the Riksbank has stopped showing the effect of alternative policy rate paths.

4. This number is constructed from the numerical data for Sveriges Riksbank (2014b, figures 2:13 and 2:15). The effect on the unemployment rate of a 0.25-percentage-point higher policy rate during four quarters has been multiplied by 4 to correspond to the effect of a one-percentage-point higher policy rate during four quarters.

5. See Schularick and Taylor (2012, table 3, "Sum of Lag Coefficients," columns 1 to 3). I believe the coefficient 0.4 might be too high, because data for a number of reasonable control variables are not available. This means that "good" credit growth and "bad" credit growth cannot be distinguished. A lower coefficient would result in an even less effect of the policy rate on the probability of a crisis. Preliminary estimates by an IMF team on data for advanced countries since 1970 result in a corresponding coefficient equal to 0.11, only about a fourth of the Schularick and Taylor coefficient.

6. The source of this number is the numerical data for Sveriges Riksbank (2014a, figure A20) with the opposite sign. Figure A20 in the same publication also reveals that the effect on real debt is not statistically significantly different from zero and may be of the opposite sign.

7. Sveriges Riksbank (2014a, figure A22) and Svensson (2015c, figure 6) also reveal that the change in the DTI ratio is not statistically significant from zero and may be of the opposite sign.

8. In June 2010, the Swedish unemployment rate was about 8.5 percent and, according to Sveriges Riksbank (2010, figure B23), the Riksbank's estimate of the long-run sustainable rate was 6.5 percent.

9. With a two-percentage-point initial unemployment gap, the quadratic cost for a one-percentage-point increase in the policy rate is $(2 + 0.5)^2 - 2^2 = 2.25$. The expected benefit is $0.0002 \times 5^2 + 0.04 \times (5^2 - (5 - 0.009)^2) = 0.005 + 0.00352 = 0.00852$ (where I have used Schularick and Taylor's average crisis probability, 4 percent, in the calculation of the expected benefit from a 0.01-basis-points lower increase in unemployment rate in a crisis).

10. With a zero initial unemployment gap, the quadratic cost for a one-percentage-point increase in the policy rate is instead $(0.5)^2 - 0^2 = 0.25$, one-ninth of the loss with a 2 percent unemployment gap, with the same expected benefit. Then the benefit is $0.00852/0.25 = 0.034 = 0.34$ percent of the cost.

11. Ajello, Laubach, López-Salido, and Nakata (2015) examine optimal interest rate policy in a model with the probability of a crisis depending on credit conditions. In a conference discussion of that paper, I found that a cost-benefit analysis using the numbers and estimates from that paper gave similar results as those reported here (Svensson 2015b).

References

Ajello, Andrea, Thomas Laubach, David López-Salido, and Taisuke Nakata. 2015. Financial Stability and Optimal Interest-Rate Policy." Paper presented at the conference "The New Normal for Monetary Policy," Federal Reserve Bank of

San Francisco, March 27, 2015. http://www.frbsf.org/economic-research/files/1A-Ajello-Laubach-Lopez_Salido-Nakata.pdf.

Bank for International Settlements. 2014. *84th Annual Report*. Basel, Bank for International Settlements. http://www.bis.org/publ/arpdf/ar2014e.pdf.

Bernanke, Ben S. 2015. "Should Monetary Policy Take into Account Risks to Financial Stability?" Blog post, *Ben Bernanke's Blog,* April 7. http://www.brookings.edu/blogs/ben-bernanke/posts/2015/04/07-monetary-policy-risks-to-financial-stability.

Flodén, Martin. 2014. "Did Household Debt Matter in the Great Recession?" Supplement to blog post on *Ekonomistas* . http://martinfloden.net/files/hhdebt_supplement_2014.pdf.

Schularick, Moritz, and Alan M. Taylor. 2012. "Credit Booms Gone Bust: Monetary Policy, Leverage Cycles, and Financial Crises, 1870–2008." *American Economic Review* 102:1029–1061.

Stein, Jeremy C. 2013. "Overheating in Credit Markets: Origins, Measurement, and Policy Responses." Speech at the "Restoring Household Financial Stability after the Great Recession: Why Household Balance Sheets Matter" research symposium, St. Louis, February 7. http://www.federalreserve.gov/newsevents/speech/stein20130207a.htm.

Svensson, Lars E. O. 2010. "Some Problems with Swedish Monetary Policy and Possible Solutions." Speech, Stockholm, November 24. http://larseosvensson.se/files/papers/101124e.pdf.

Svensson, Lars E. O. 2013 a. "The Riksbank Causes 'Debt Deflation.'" Blog post, September 30. http://larseosvensson.se/2013/09/30/ekonomistas-the-riksbank-causes-debt-deflation.

Svensson, Lars E. O. 2013 b. "Some Lessons from Six Years of Practical Inflation Targeting." *Sveriges Riksbank Economic Review* 3:29–80. http://larseosvensson.se/files/papers/Svensson-paper--Some-lessons-from-six-years-of-practical-inflation-targeting.pdf.

Svensson, Lars E. O. 2015 a. "Cost-Benefit Analysis of Leaning Against the Wind: Are Costs Larger Also with Less Effective Macroprudential Policy?" Working Paper. http://larseosvensson.se/files/papers/cost-benefit-analysis-of-leaning-against-the-wind-are-costs-larger.pdf.

Svensson, Lars E. O. 2015 b. Discussion of Ajello, Laubach, López-Salido, and Nakata, "Financial Stability and Optimal Interest-Rate Policy," presented at the conference "The New Normal for Monetary Policy," Federal Reserve Bank of San Francisco, March 27, 2015. http://larseosvensson.se/files/papers/svensson-on-ajello-laubach-lopez-salido-nakata.pdf.

Svensson, Lars E. O. 2015 c. "Inflation Targeting and Leaning against the Wind." In *Fourteen Years of Inflation Targeting in South Africa and the Challenge of a Changing Mandate: South African Reserve Bank Conference Proceedings 2014.* South African Reserve Bank, Pretoria. http://larseosvensson.se/files/papers/inflation-targeting-and-leaning-against-the-wind-paper-sarb.pdf.

Sveriges Riksbank. 2010. *Monetary Policy Report October 2010*. Stockholm, Sveriges Riksbank. http://www.riksbank.se/Upload/Dokument_riksbank/Kat_ publicerat/Rapporter/2010/mpr_oct_2010.pdf.

Sveriges Riksbank. 2013. "Financial Imbalances in the Monetary Policy Assessment." Box in *Monetary Policy Report July 2013*. Stockholm, Sveriges Riksbank. http:// www.riksbank.se/Documents/Rapporter/PPR/2013/130703/rap_ppr_130703 _eng.pdf.

Sveriges Riksbank. 2014 a. "The Effects of Monetary Policy on Household Debt." Box in *Monetary Policy Report February 2014*. Stockholm, Sveriges Riksbank. http://www.riksbank.se/Documents/Rapporter/PPR/2014/140213/rap_ppr _140213_eng.pdf.

Sveriges Riksbank. 2014 b. *Monetary Policy Report February 2014*. Stockholm, Sveriges Riksbank. http://www.riksbank.se/Documents/Rapporter/PPR/ 2014/140213/rap_ppr_140213_eng.pdf.

Monetary Policy in the Future

12

Introduction to the Monetary Policy Section

José Viñals

One of the most remarkable features of the last seven years, since the beginning of the global financial crisis, has been the tremendous innovation and experimentation in the field of monetary policy. Pressed by circumstances, central bankers had to take bold and unprecedented actions. Some, of course, continue to do so.

With the passage of time, the question is how this experience has modified our view about the way monetary policy should be conducted in the future, once the crisis is behind us.

These introductory remarks focus on five areas where this question applies very starkly. First, should monetary policy be used to support financial stability? Second, how should monetary policy respond to the increasing risk of hitting the zero lower bound in an environment of persistently low interest rates? Third, how should monetary policy in emerging market economies (EMEs) and small open economies cope with the significant spillovers from monetary policy in their larger neighbors? Fourth, how should monetary policy communication evolve? And finally, what features of the unconventional monetary policy (UMP) toolkit should be maintained in more tranquil times? As these remarks are intended to introduce this chapter, they mostly aim to raise and motivate questions, instead of providing concrete answers.

Should Monetary Policy Be Used to Support Financial Stability?

This may be the quintessential question arising from the crisis, as it brings together the two big themes of the last seven years: monetary policy and financial stability.

We learned from the crisis that price and output stability do not ensure financial stability. During the Great Moderation, inflation expectations were well anchored in many advanced economies, inflation was stable, and output gaps were small, yet very significant risks to financial stability built up in the form of leverage, credit growth, fragile funding structures, common exposures, and loose lending standards. The natural question is thus whether the crisis might have been avoided had monetary policy followed a different course.

Tighter and more effective micro- and macroprudential policy and supervision would have been, no doubt, the preferred response. And indeed, looking ahead, these policies promise to be more effective at containing financial stability risks.

Initial evidence suggests that macroprudential policies can be relatively effective, at least in targeted areas. Korea was able to reduce banks' short-term external debt by half, to 27 percent, between 2008 and 2013. Australia limited the growth of uninsured "low-doc" mortgage loans by imposing higher risk weights (from 50 to 100 percent) on banks. In Brazil, higher capital requirements on new vehicle loans with high loan-to-value ratios decreased the growth of such loans. However, in some countries, such as Switzerland and the U.K., it is still too early to say whether macroprudential measures taken so far have been sufficiently strong to fully arrest housing-related risks. More evidence from around the world is needed to authoritatively gauge the effectiveness of macroprudential policies.

Thus the question is still worth asking: what if prudential policies are not sufficiently effective? Specifically, what if these policies are easily circumvented or arbitraged, slow to adapt to changing circumstances, overly targeted—in the sense of missing new sources of risks—or associated with negative side effects? Should monetary policy then come to the rescue of financial stability?

There are essentially three schools of thought. The first suggests that monetary policy can be used, but only as a second line of defense, after prudential policies have been fully exploited. The second argues that monetary policy should not be used to address financial imbalances, even as a second line of defense. Interest rates are too coarse a tool and thus impose too high a cost on the economy. The contribution of Lars Svensson to this volume espouses a similar view. The third school of thought would disagree. It argues that monetary policy should always accompany prudential policies and thus continuously lean against financial imbalances. By virtue of being a coarse instrument, interest rates permeate all areas of the financial system.

But the discussion should now go beyond mere disagreement, often based on principle, relative to these schools of thought. In order to provide concrete policy advice to central banks, it is essential to undertake a detailed cost-benefit analysis of the general equilibrium effects of using monetary policy to support financial stability. The analysis has three legs: the benefits of monetary policy for financial stability, the costs from deviating from inflation and output objectives in the pursuit of financial stability, and the feedback to financial stability from inflation and output deviations. Only one of these legs, the second, is well known and accurately calibrated. But until more work is done to estimate the other two legs, policymakers will not be able to safely stand on this stool.

How Should Monetary Policy Respond to the Increasing Risk of Hitting the Zero Lower Bound?

Before the crisis, this risk was briskly set aside as improbable. The crisis was a stark reminder that the zero lower bound can occur and is costly. While UMPs in the form of asset purchases were successful at providing additional policy accommodation, their drawbacks do not make them close substitutes for conventional interest rate policy. In particular, asset purchases cannot be easily calibrated or adapted to changing economic conditions. They also entail substantial spillovers to other countries and may—if rates are kept low for an extended period—breed financial stability risks.

But even once economies recover and rates rise above the zero lower bound, the probability of returning to this constraint remains significant. This is because of the secular decline in real long-term interest rates, which hints at an equal pattern in the natural real rate of interest (real rates did not decrease because of higher inflation, or lower nominal yields, which eventually would have bred inflation had the natural rate not also declined). Low real rates and low inflation targets will translate into low nominal rates, and thus a persistent likelihood of hitting the zero lower bound when shocks materialize.

How should monetary policy avoid being constrained by the zero lower bound again in the future? One solution would be a higher inflation target. But this comes with costs. On the one hand, there are costs to central bank credibility, given the potential difficulties of anchoring expectations if the inflation objective is deemed movable, to hit a higher inflation target in an environment of low inflation and to convince markets that a higher target was not chosen to alleviate sovereign debt burdens. On the other hand, there are social welfare costs as higher inflation will complicate planning and price-setting decisions, and is usually accompanied by higher inflation volatility.

An alternative (or, for some, at least a complementary) solution exists: bolstering financial stability. In OECD countries outside the euro area, a third of zero lower bound episodes have followed the start of a systemic banking crisis by a year or less. The proportion rises if we allow for a longer lag. A more solid financial system would (1) decrease the size of financial shocks, (2) reduce the scope for amplifying shocks, and (3) allow monetary policy to respond more freely to shocks. As a result, the probability of hitting the zero lower bound would diminish, as would the expected duration of remaining at the zero lower bound following a particularly severe aggregate demand shock.

How Should Monetary Policy in Emerging Market Economies and Small Open Economies Cope with the Significant Spillovers from Monetary Policy in Their Larger Neighbors?

We live in an interconnected world. Small open economies—including many EMEs—may be significantly affected by capital flows unleashed by monetary policies in major economies. Rapid capital inflows can cause in recipient countries a surge in leverage, debt, asset prices, short-term funding, and balance sheet mismatches, exposing the financial system to large losses in the case of sudden stops and related market volatility.

The crisis highlighted the extent to which capital flows can affect asset prices in emerging markets. Between 2009 and the end of 2012, emerging markets received about US $4.5 trillion of gross capital inflows, representing roughly one-half of global capital flows. More specifically, the example of South Africa, discussed later by Gill Marcus, is telling. Ten-year government bond yields decreased by nearly 250 basis points in the four years of especially accommodative monetary policies in advanced economies following the Lehman bankruptcy (from 8.8 percent in September 2009 to 6.4 percent in May 2013), only to bounce back by almost the same amount in the three months between May and August 2013, during the so-called taper tantrum.

How should monetary policy respond in the countries receiving large capital inflows, and exposed to the risk of sudden outflows? As discussed earlier, prudential policies and supervision will be paramount to support the resilience of the financial sector. But these steps may not be sufficient, and monetary policy will face difficult trade-offs. For instance, capital inflows can lead to overheating. But to what extent will higher rates attract more foreign capital and encourage liabilities to shift into foreign currency? Capital flows can equally lead to a decrease in domestic inflation as the domestic currency appreciates. If the pattern persists, a cut in interest rates could be appropriate; but to what extent would this measure further stoke credit growth and leverage? Central banks may thus be tempted to resort to other means to slow capital inflows more directly, such as foreign exchange interventions or capital flow management measures. But to what extent would these measures be effective, and how should they be designed?

These questions go beyond the goal of containing short-term market volatility. A more fundamental question is, can EMEs and small open economies maintain monetary policy independence? There are two ways to pursue this question. First, can these economies set interest rates independently of foreign interest rate dynamics, even under floating exchange rates? While it is natural for countries to take foreign economic conditions into account, not all countries will take the additional step of shadowing foreign interest rates in order to manage pressures on the exchange rate and capital flows. Second, and perhaps a deeper issue, has the transmission mechanism of monetary policy lost its effectiveness in EMEs and small open economies? In other words, to what extent do output and inflation, but also credit growth and financial stability, depend on foreign, as opposed to domestic, monetary policy? And if the transmission mechanism has lost its effectiveness, what would it take to regain monetary policy independence?

How Should Monetary Policy Communication Evolve?

The crisis has shined a spotlight on signaling, and especially on the role of communication for signaling. Deprived of short-term interest rates, central bankers had to resort to words—in addition to concrete UMP measures—to signal their future policy intentions to the public. At least two areas are worth exploring in an attempt to draw lessons from experience. The first is communication about policy expectations (the modal policy response), and the second is communication about uncertainty (higher moments of the policy response).

Communication should be geared toward supporting the predictability of policy responses. This entails clarifying policy intentions and their justification. But these change in ways that depend on the economic environment. For instance, the relationship between unemployment and wage inflation has been erratic in the United States, undermining the intentions of the Fed to provide guidance on the timing of rate normalization by communicating thresholds related to unemployment. This sort of situation leads to the debate captured in the contributions by Ben Bernanke and John Taylor, about targets-based, versus rules-based, frameworks. In the first, the role of central bank communication is to elucidate the strategy to bring the forecasts of key variables back to their objectives. In the second, it is to explain deviations from immutable and simple instrument rules.

The balancing act that communication must play is even more complex. Communication should not just inform the public's expectations of future policy action; it should convey a sense of existing uncertainty about economic prospects, and possibly about policy responses themselves. The danger is that communication focused on clarifying a modal policy path conveys a false sense of economic and policy predictability, which in turn could prompt an undervaluation of risks. More information—even if about uncertainty—is always better, at least on paper.

But in practice, can communication be used to convey an accurate sense of uncertainty, without creating undue uncertainty itself? Clearly, central banks should not artificially inject uncertainty by clouding their intentions in vague language or, worse, by randomizing their policy actions. But could central banks educate the market as to existing uncertainty, perhaps by publishing stress tests or contingency plans for monetary policy, instead of focusing mostly on modal outcomes? A lot depends on how well the public understands the nature of conditional statements. On this basis, the experience of the crisis has not been especially encouraging, as illustrated by the summer 2013 "taper tantrum" episode.

What Features of the Unconventional Monetary Policy Toolkit Should Be Maintained in More Tranquil Times?

During the crisis, central banks introduced a variety of new instruments. These included longer-term liquidity provision to a wide range of financial entities and markets, price backstops in certain highly volatile markets (such as done by the Term Asset-Backed Securities Loan Facility, or TALF, in the United States), private and public asset purchases, conditional funding operations to encourage bank lending, and policy rate cuts into negative territory.

While some of these measures are clearly aimed at restoring market functioning and banking intermediation under extreme economic conditions, others could still be used in more tranquil times. Asset purchases in particular could become a more standard tool. One purpose might be to enhance signaling, and more finely manage the yield curve by targeting long-term bond yields. But this would come at the cost of volatility in shorter-term bond yields and some loss in the efficiency of monetary policy transmission, given the difficulty of calibrating asset purchases to target specific longer-term interest rates.

More generally, though, central banks might wish to keep larger balance sheets than before the crisis. If excess reserves remained substantial, market interest rates could be managed by setting interest rates on excess reserves or short-term reverse repo operations. A larger balance sheet would also provide a liquidity buffer to the banking sector, and could provide the wider private sector with an elastic supply of safe and liquid assets. Ultimately, the question is how much central banks should make use of their balance sheets in the future, and what their optimal balance sheet size is.

Many of these questions are investigated in the remainder of this part of the volume, but it will take more time—and solid analysis—before final verdicts can be advanced. For now, monetary policy will continue being more art than science.

13

Monetary Policy in the Future

Ben Bernanke

In the few minutes that I have, I'll offer some thoughts on the Fed's monetary policy framework, its tools for implementing monetary policy, and how both are likely to evolve as we return to a more historically normal economic and policy environment.

In January 2012 the Federal Open Market Committee (FOMC) issued for the first time a formal description of its policy framework, which has been reapproved each January since then.[1] The framework document emphasizes the FOMC's commitment to a balanced approach in the pursuit of the Fed's two statutory objectives, price stability and maximum employment. The FOMC has given the public extensive guidance about how it defines those objectives, setting a symmetric inflation target of 2 percent and reporting each quarter FOMC participants' estimates of the sustainable rate of unemployment. This policy framework is backed by substantial explanation and analysis, via the chairman's press conferences, FOMC meeting minutes, FOMC economic projections (including projections of the federal funds rate), testimony, and speeches.

The FOMC's policy framework corresponds to what Lars Svensson has called a targeting rule (see my 2004 speech "The Logic of Monetary Policy" for further discussion).[2] In a targets-based framework, the central bank forecasts its goal variables—inflation and employment, in the case of the Fed—and describes its policy strategy for bringing the forecasts in line with its stated objectives. Although targeting rules are not mechanical, they do provide a transparent framework that is robust to changes in the structure of the economy or the effectiveness of monetary policy, so long as those changes can be incorporated into forecasts. Targeting rules also conform to the basic economic dictum that principals (in this case, Congress and the public) are better off monitoring their agents' outputs (in the case of the FOMC, the outcomes of policy choices) rather than their inputs (the specific settings of policy instruments).

The policy framework has improved the FOMC's communication, I believe. Today, for example, the Fed's commitment to 2 percent inflation is providing the public useful information about the FOMC's likely approach to policy in the year ahead. Moreover, the anchoring of inflation expectations that began under Volcker and Greenspan, and which I believe was further strengthened by the setting of a numerical definition of price stability, gave the Fed more scope to ease monetary policy in response to the global recession than it otherwise would have had.

Of course, no policy framework is without drawbacks, as attested by the difficulties the FOMC has faced in dealing with the zero lower bound on interest rates. If the committee were to contemplate changing its framework, there are two directions it might consider.

The first would be to adopt what Svensson calls an instrument rule, which specifies how the policy instrument, in the Fed's case the federal funds rate, will be set as a relatively simple function of a few variables. I am perfectly fine using such rules as one of many guides for thinking about policy, and I agree that policy should be as transparent and systematic as possible. But I am also sure that, in a complex, ever-changing economy, monetary policymaking cannot be trusted to a simple instrument rule. I was going to elaborate on this point, but I found a nice statement of the argument in a classic piece of research, which I'll quote in its entirety:

Even with many such modifications, it is difficult to see how ... algebraic policy rules could be sufficiently encompassing. For example, interpreting whether a rise in the price level is temporary or permanent is likely to require looking at several measures of prices (such as the consumer price index, the producer price index, or the employment cost index). Looking at expectations of inflation as measured by futures markets, the term structure of interest rates, surveys, or forecasts from other analysts is also likely to be helpful. Interpreting the level and the growth rate of the economy's potential output—which frequently is a factor in policy rules—involves predictions about productivity, labor-force participation, and changes in the natural rate of unemployment. While the analysis of these issues can be aided by quantitative methods, it is difficult to formulate them into a precise algebraic formula. Moreover, there will be episodes where monetary policy will need to be adjusted to deal with special factors. For example, the Federal Reserve provided additional reserves to the banking system after the stock-market break of October 19, 1987 and helped to prevent a contraction of liquidity and to restore confidence. The Fed would need more than a simple policy rule as a guide in such cases.

As some might have guessed, the quotation is from John Taylor's classic 1993 paper introducing the Taylor rule, "Discretion versus Policy Rules in Practice."[3]

The second possible direction of change for the monetary policy framework would be to keep the targets-based approach that I favor but to change the target. Suggestions that have been made include raising the inflation target, targeting the price level, or targeting some function of nominal GDP. Some of these approaches have the advantage of helping deal with the zero-lower-bound problem, at least in principle. My colleagues at the Fed and I spent a good deal of time during the period after the financial crisis considering these and other alternatives, and I think I am familiar with the relevant theoretical arguments. Although we did not adopt one of these alternatives, I will say that I don't see anything magical about targeting 2 percent inflation. My advocacy of inflation targets as an academic and a Fed governor was based much more on the transparency and communication advantages of the approach and not as much on the specific choice of target. Continued research on alternative intermediate targets for monetary policy would certainly be worthwhile.

That said, I want to raise a few practical concerns about the feasibility of changing the FOMC's target, at least in the near term. First, whatever its strengths and weaknesses, the current policy framework, with its two explicit targets and balanced approach, has the advantage of being closely and transparently connected to the Fed's mandate from Congress to promote price stability and maximum employment. It may be that having the Fed target other variables could lead to better results, but the linkages are complex and indirect, and there would be times when the pursuit of an alternative intermediate target might appear inconsistent with the mandate. For example, any of the leading alternative approaches could involve the Fed aiming for a relatively high inflation rate at times. Explaining the consistency of that with the statutory objective of price stability would be a communication challenge, and concerns about the public or congressional reaction would reduce the credibility of the FOMC's commitment to the alternative target.

Second, proponents of alternative targets have to accept the fact that, for better or worse, we are not starting with a blank slate. For several decades now the Fed and other central banks have worked to anchor inflation expectations in the vicinity of 2 percent and to explain the associated policy approach. A change in target would face the hurdles of reanchoring expectations and reestablishing long-term credibility, even though the very fact that the target is being changed could sow some doubts. At a minimum, Congress would have to be consulted, and broad buy-in would have to be achieved.

Finally, a principal motivation that proponents offer for changing the monetary policy target is to deal more effectively with the zero lower bound on interest rates. But economically, it would be preferable to have more proactive fiscal policies and a more balanced monetary-fiscal mix when interest rates are close to zero. Greater reliance on fiscal policy would probably give better results, and would certainly be easier to explain, than changing the target for monetary policy. I think, though, that the probability of getting Congress to accept larger automatic stabilizers and the probability of its endorsing an alternative intermediate target for monetary policy are equally low.

A few words on policy tools: the depth of the global recession, together with the zero lower bound on interest rates, forced the Fed to devise new tools to make monetary policy more accommodative, including large-scale asset purchases and communication about the contingent future path of rates. Under more historically normal circumstances, when the zero lower bound is no longer a constraint, I expect that these tools will go back on the shelf. The operating instrument will once again be the federal funds rate and the communication framework will be the targets-oriented policy framework I described earlier. Of special note, the return to the use of the federal funds rate as the main policy instrument should be feasible even if the Fed's balance sheet remains quite large for a time.

Although reserves in the banking system are not expected to return to precrisis levels for some years, the Fed has a number of instruments—including its authority to pay interest to banks on their excess reserves, as well as the ability to offer reverse repurchase agreements that effectively allow nonbanks to deposit at the Fed at a fixed interest rate—that should allow it to manage short-term interest rates effectively. Concerns about unwinding quantitative easing are therefore misplaced, in that the Fed's ability to tighten monetary policy at the appropriate time will not require that it sell assets or rapidly reduce the size of its balance sheet. To the extent that the large balance sheet has some residual effect on longer-term yields, the effects on the economy can be compensated for by changes in the federal funds rate.

The FOMC has indicated that it intends to let the Fed's portfolio run off over time, so that excess reserves in the banking system eventually return to levels comparable to those before the crisis. Of course, I have not been privy to the internal discussions, having left the Fed more than fourteen months ago, but I wonder if the case for keeping the balance sheet somewhat larger than before the crisis has been adequately explored. As I mentioned, a larger balance sheet should not affect the ability of the FOMC to change the stance of monetary policy as needed. Indeed, most other major central banks have permanently large balance sheets and are able to implement monetary policy without problems. Moreover, the fed funds market is small and idiosyncratic. Monetary control might be more rather than less effective if the Fed changed its operating instrument to the repo rate or another money market rate and managed that rate by its setting of the interest rate paid on excess reserves and the overnight reverse repo rate, analogous to the procedures used by other central banks.

Another potential advantage of a large balance sheet is that it facilitates the creation of an elastically supplied, safe, short-term asset for the private sector, in a world in which such assets seem to be in short supply. On the margin, the Fed's balance sheet is financed by bank reserves and by reverse repos, which can be thought of as reserves held at the Fed by nonbank institutions. From the private sector's point of view, Fed liabilities are safe, overnight assets that could be useful for cash management or as a form of reserve liquidity. In a system of so-called full allotments, these assets would be supplied by the Fed at a fixed interest rate. The Federal Reserve was created, in part, to provide "an elastic currency," so this provision of a liquid asset at a fixed rate seems consistent with the central bank's mission.

The principal objection to a permanently large balance sheet financed in part by a reverse repo program appears to be a concern about financial stability. The worry is that the availability of reverse repos would facilitate runs. For example, in a period of stress, money market funds might dump commercial paper in favor of Fed liabilities. I take that concern seriously but offer a few observations. First, the overall increase in liquidity in the financial system that would be the result of a larger Fed balance sheet would probably itself be a stabilizing factor, so that the net effect on stability is uncertain. Second, if private-sector entities ran to Fed liabilities, there are actions the Fed could take after the fact to mitigate the problem, including not only capping access to reverse repos but also recycling liquidity, for example, by increasing lending to banks (through the discount window) or to dealers (through repo operations). Finally, runs can occur even in the absence of a reverse repo program, as we saw during the crisis. Regulatory action to minimize the risk of or incentives for runs would seem to be the more direct way to deal with the issue. Put another way, if runs really are a major concern, getting rid of the Fed's repo program alone seems an inadequate response.

To be clear, I am not making a recommendation today about the ultimate size of the Fed's balance sheet. It's a complex issue that deserves more discussion. My aim in these few pages is to contribute to that discussion and encourage further public debate.

Notes

1. The January 2012 framework in turn built on earlier FOMC communication. An important step toward greater transparency was the fall 2007 inclusion of three-year-ahead forecasts of inflation and unemployment in the committee's quarterly economic projections. As FOMC participants' projections assume optimal monetary policy, and because three years is normally enough time for monetary policy actions to have their full effects, the long-term projections were appropriately interpreted by the public as policy targets rather than as literal forecasts.

2. Ben Bernanke, "The Logic of Monetary Policy," remarks by Governor Ben S. Bernanke before the National Economists Club, Washington, D.C., December 2, 2004, http://www.federalreserve.gov/boarddocs/speeches/2004/20041202/default.htm.

3. John Taylor, "Discretion versus Policy Rules in Practice," *Carnegie-Rochester Conference Series on Public Policy* 39, no. 1 (1993): 195–214, at 196–197.

14

A Monetary Policy for the Future

John B. Taylor

A year ago at another IMF conference, "Monetary Policy in the New Normal," I argued that central banks should renormalize monetary policy, not new-normalize it to some new normal as some had suggested.[1] I want now to elaborate on that theme, outline an implied monetary policy for the future, and consider some objections that have been raised.

Let me begin with a mini-history of monetary policy in the United States during the past fifty years. When I first started doing monetary economics in the late 1960s and 1970s, monetary policy was highly discretionary and interventionist. It went from boom to bust and back again, repeatedly falling behind the curve and then overreacting. The Fed had lofty goals but no consistent strategy. If you measure macroeconomic performance as I do, by both price stability and output stability, the results were terrible. Unemployment and inflation both rose.

Then, in the early 1980s, policy changed. It became more focused, more systematic, and more rules-based, and it stayed that way through the 1990s and into the start of the twenty-first century. Using the same performance measures, the results were excellent. Inflation and unemployment both came down. We got the Great Moderation, or the NICE period (noninflationary, consistently expansionary), as Mervyn King put it.[2] Researchers like John Judd and Glenn Rudebush at the San Francisco Fed and Richard Clarida, Mark Gertler, and Jordi Gali showed that this improved performance was closely associated with a more rules-based policy, which they defined as systematic changes in the instrument of policy—the federal funds rate—in response to developments in the economy.[3]

Researchers found the same results in other countries. Stephen Cecchetti, Peter Hooper, Bruce Kasman, Kermit Schoenholtz, and Mark

Watson showed that as policy became more rulelike in Germany, the UK, and Japan, economic performance improved.[4]

Few complained about spillovers or beggar-thy-neighbor policies during the Great Moderation. The developed economies were effectively operating in what I call a nearly international cooperative equilibrium, another NICE to join Mervyn King's. This was also a prediction of monetary theory, which implied that if each country followed a good rules-based monetary policy, then the international system would operate in a NICE way.[5]

But then there was a setback. The Fed decided to hold the interest rate very low during 2003–2005, thereby deviating from the rules-based policy that worked well during the Great Moderation. You do not need policy rules to see the change: With the inflation rate around 2 percent, the federal funds rate was only 1 percent in 2003, compared with 5.5 percent in 1997, when the inflation rate was also about 2 percent. The results were not good. In my view this policy change brought on a search for yield, excesses in the housing market, and, along with a regulatory process that broke rules for safety and soundness, was a key factor in the financial crisis and the global recession.

During the ensuing panic in the fall of 2008 the Fed did a good job of providing liquidity through loans to financial firms and swaps to foreign central banks. Reserve balances at the Fed expanded sharply as a result of these temporary liquidity provisions. They would have declined after the panic were it not for the Fed's initiation of its unconventional monetary policy, the large-scale purchases of securities now called quantitative easing (QE). Regardless of what you think of the impact of QE, it was not rulelike or predictable, and my research shows that it was not effective.[6] It did not deliver the economic growth that the Fed had forecasted, and it did not lead to a good recovery. And yet another deviation from rules-based policy was the continuation of a near zero interest rate through the present, long after Great Moderation rules would have called for its end.

This deviation from rules-based monetary policy went beyond the United States, as first pointed out by researchers at the OECD, and is now obvious to any observer.[7] Central banks followed each other down through extra-low interest rates in 2003–2005 and more recently through QE. QE in the United States was followed by QE in Japan and by QE in the euro zone, with exchange rates moving as expected in each case.

Researchers at the Bank for International Settlements[8] showed the deviation went beyond OECD and called it the Global Great Deviation. Rich Clarida[9] commented that "QE begets QE!" Complaints about spillover and pleas for coordination grew. NICE ended in both senses of the word. World monetary policy now seems to have moved into a strategy-free zone.

This short history demonstrates that shifts toward and away from steady predictable monetary policy have made a great deal of difference for the performance of the economy, just as basic macroeconomic theory tells us. This history has now been corroborated by Alex Nikolsko-Rzhevskyy, David H. Papell, and Ruxandra Prodan using modern statistical methods.[10] Allan Meltzer found nearly the same thing in his more detailed monetary history of the Fed.[11]

The implication of this experience is clear: monetary policy should renormalize in the sense of transitioning to a predictable rulelike strategy for the instruments of policy. Of course, it is possible technically for the Fed to move to and stick to such a policy, but the long departures from rules-based policy show that it is difficult.

These departures suggest that some legislative backing might help. Such legislation could simply require the Fed to describe its strategy or rule for adjusting its policy instruments. It would be the Fed's job to choose the strategy and how to describe it. The Fed could change its strategy or deviate from it if circumstances called for a change, but the Fed would have to explain why.

There is precedent for such legislation. The Federal Reserve Act used to require the Fed to report ranges of the monetary and credit aggregates. The requirements were repealed in 2000. In many ways the proposed reform would simply replace them. It would provide responsible oversight without micro-managing. It would not chain the Fed to a mechanical rule. It would not threaten the Fed's independence. Indeed, it would give the Fed more independence from the executive branch of government.

Now let me consider some of the objections to such a monetary policy, whether it is backed by legislation or not.

Some argue that the historical evidence in favor of rules is simply correlation, not causation. But this ignores the crucial timing of events: in each case, the changes in policy occurred before the changes in performance, clear evidence for causality. The decisions taken by Paul Volcker came before the Great Moderation. The decisions to keep interest rates very low in 2003–2005 came before the global recession. And there are clear causal mechanisms, such as the search for yield, risk taking, and the boom and bust in the housing market, which were factors in the financial crisis.

Another point relates to the zero lower bound. Wasn't that the reason that the central banks had to deviate from rules in recent years? Well, it was certainly not a reason in 2003–2005 and it is not a reason now, because the zero lower bound is not binding. It appears that there was a short period in 2009 when zero was clearly binding. But the zero lower bound is not a new thing in economics research. Policy rule design research took that into account long ago.[12] The default was to move to a stable money growth regime, not to massive asset purchases.[13]

Some argue that a rules-based policy is not enough anymore and that we need more international coordination. I believe the current spillovers are largely the result of these policy deviations and of unconventional monetary policy. We heard complaints about the spillovers during the stop-and-go monetary policy in the 1970s. But during the 1980s and 1990s and until recently there were few such complaints. The evidence and theory are that rules-based policy brings about NICE results in both senses of the word.

Some argue that rules-based policy for the instruments is not needed if you have goals for the inflation rate or other variables. They say that all you really need for effective policymaking is a goal, such as an inflation target and an employment target. The rest of policymaking is doing whatever the policymakers think needs to be done with the policy instruments. You do not need to articulate or describe a strategy, a decision rule, or a contingency plan for the instruments. If you want to hold the interest rate well below the rules-based strategy that worked well during the Great Moderation, as the Fed did in 2003–2005, then it's OK as long as you can justify it at the moment in terms of the goal.

This approach has been called "constrained discretion" by Ben Bernanke,[14] and it may be constraining discretion in some sense, but it is not inducing or encouraging a rule as a "rules versus discretion" dichotomy might suggest. Simply having a specific numerical goal or objective is not a rule for the instruments of policy; it is not a strategy; it ends up being all tactics. I think the evidence shows that relying solely on constrained discretion has not worked for monetary policy.

Some of the recent objections to a rules-based strategy sound like a revival of earlier debates. Larry Summers draws analogies with medicine, saying he would "rather have a doctor who most of the time didn't tell me to take some stuff, and every once in a while said I needed to ingest some stuff into my body in response to the particular problem that I had. That would be a doctor who's [advice], believe me, would be less predictable."[15]

So, much as did the proponents of discretion in earlier rules versus discretion debates (such as between Walter Heller and Milton Friedman), Summers argues in favor of relying on an all-knowing expert, a doctor who does not perceive the need for, and does not use, a set of guidelines.

But much of the progress in medicine over the years has been the result of doctors using checklists. Experience shows that checklists are invaluable for preventing mistakes, making good diagnoses, and prescribing appropriate treatments.[16] Of course, doctors need to exercise judgment in implementing checklists, but if they start winging it or skipping steps, the patients usually suffer. Checklist-free medicine is as bad as rules-free monetary policy.

Many say that macroprudential policy of the countercyclical variety is an essential part of a monetary policy for the future. In my view, it is more important to get required levels of capital and liquidity sufficiently high. We do not know enough about the impacts of cyclical movements in capital buffers to engage in fine-tuning, and it puts the central bank in the middle of a very difficult political issue.

Some argue that we should have QE forever, leave the balance sheet bloated, and use interest on reserves or reverse repos to set the short-term interest rate. But the distortions caused by these massive interventions and the impossibility of such policy being rule-like indicate that QE forever should not be part of a monetary policy for the future. The goal should be to get the balance sheet back to levels where the demand and supply of reserves determine the interest rate. Of course, interest rates on reserves and reverse repos could be used during a transition. And a corridor system would work if the market interest rate was in between the upper and lower bands and not hugging one or the other.

Should forward guidance be part of a monetary policy for the future? My answer is yes, but only if it is consistent with the rules-based strategy of the central bank, and then it is simply a way to be transparent.

If forward guidance is used to make promises for the future that will not be appropriate in the future, then it is time-inconsistent and should not be part of monetary policy.

For all these reasons, monetary policy in the future should be centered on a rule or strategy for the policy instruments designed to achieve stated goals with consistent forward guidance but without cyclical macroprudential actions or QE.

Notes

This chapter is a written version of my opening remarks at a panel with Ben Bernanke and Gill Marcus titled "Monetary Policy in the Future" and chaired by José Viñals. It was part of the IMF conference, "Rethinking Macro Policy III: Progress or Confusion?"

1. The presentation was later published as "Re-Normalize, Don't New-Normalize Monetary Policy," *Macroeconomic Review* (Monetary Authority of Singapore) 13 (October 2014): 86–90.

2. Mervyn King, speech delivered at the East Midlands Development Agency/ Bank of England Dinner, Leicester, October 14, 2003.

3. John P. Judd and Glenn D. Rudebusch, "Taylor's Rule and the Fed: 1970– 1997," *FRBSF Economic Review* 3 (1998): 3–16; Clarida Richard, Jordi Gali, and Mark Gertler, "Monetary Policy Rules and Macroeconomic Stability: Evidence and Some Theory," *Quarterly Journal of Economics* 115, no. 1 (2000): 147–180.

4. Stephen G. Cecchetti, Peter Hooper, Bruce C. Kasman, Kermit L. Schoenholtz, and Mark W. Watson, "Understanding the Evolving Inflation Process," paper presented at the US Monetary Policy Forum, Washington, DC, March 9, 2007.

5. See John B. Taylor "International Monetary Policy Coordination: Past, Present and Future," BIS Working Paper 437, Bank for International Settlements, December 2013, for a summary.

6. Johannes C. Stroebel and John B. Taylor "Estimated Impact of the Federal Reserve's Mortgage-Backed Securities Purchase Program," *International Journal of Central Banking* 8, no. 2 (2012): 1–42.

7. Rudiger Ahrend, "Monetary Ease: A Factor behind Financial Crises? Some Evidence from OECD Countries," *Economics: The Open-Access, Open-Assessment E-Journal* 4, no. 2010–12 (April 14, 2010): 1–30.

8. Boris Hofmann and Bilyana Bogdanova, "Taylor Rules and Monetary Policy: A Global 'Great Deviation'?," *BIS Quarterly Review*, September 2012, 37–49.

9. Richard Clarida, "Discussion of 'The Federal Reserve in a Globalized World Economy,'" at the conference, "The Federal Reserve's Role in the Global Economy: A Historical Perspective," Dallas Federal Reserve Bank, September 2014.

10. Alex Nikolsko-Rzhevskyy, David H. Papell, and Ruxandra Prodan, "Deviations from Rules-Based Policy and Their Effects," *Journal of Economic Dynamics and Control* 49 (December 2014): 4–17.

11. Allan Meltzer, "Federal Reserve Policy in the Great Recession," *Cato Journal* 32, no. 2 (2012): 255–263.

12. For example, in my 1993 book, *Macroeconomic Policy in a World Economy: From Econometric Design to Practical Operation* (http://web.stanford.edu/~johntayl/MacroPolicyWorld.htm), in the chapter "Design of Policy Systems," I state that "since negative nominal interest rates are not feasible, Equation (6.1) [for the interest rate] must be truncated below some nonnegative value, which is taken to be 1 percent in this analysis.... In other words, whenever the function in Equation (6.1) calls for a nominal interest rate below 1 percent, the nominal interest rate is set to 1 percent. This truncated form of Equation (6.1) is the policy rule that the monetary authorities are assumed to follow" (pp. 225–226). It is in that zero bound context that we looked for an optimal rule.

13. My general view has been that interest rate rules are best thought of as part of a metarule according to which the instrument switches to money growth in deflationary or hyperinflationary situations. For example, in my 1996 paper "Policy Rules as a Means to a More Effective Monetary Policy" (*Monetary and Economic Studies* [Bank of Japan] 14, no. 1), I state that the "interest rate rule needs to be supplemented by money supply rules in cases of either extended deflation or hyperinflation" (p. 27). I held this same view at the end of 2008 as the Fed's temporary liquidity facilities began to draw down. For example, in a paper I presented at the January 2009 ASSA meetings, "The Need to Return to a Monetary Framework" (subsequently published in *Business Economics* 44, no. 2 [2009]: 63–72), I said that in the region where rates would be negative, "policymakers could use Milton Friedman's famous constant growth rate rule.... Or policymakers could design another procedure for determining the quantity based on economic principles." I also referred there to Lawrence Christiano and Massimo Rostagno's "Money Growth Monitoring and the Taylor Rule" (NBER Working Paper 8539 [Cambridge, MA: National Bureau of Economic Research, 2001]), which had shown how a broader framework could work technically.

14. Ben S. Bernanke, "'Constrained Discretion' and Monetary Policy," remarks by Governor Ben S. Bernanke before the Money Marketeers of New York University, New York, February 3, 2003.

15. Transcript published in the *Journal of Policy Modeling* 36, no. 4 (2013).

16. Atul Gawande, "The Checklist: If Something So Simple Can Transform Intensive Care, What Else Can It Do?," *The New Yorker*, December 19, 2007.

15

The Credit Surface and Monetary Policy

John Geanakoplos

I believe that credit plays a central role in the booms and busts of market economies, and even in milder fluctuations. But I do not believe that the credit conditions influencing booms and busts are driven primarily by fluctuations in riskless interest rates, or by the wrong riskless interest rates. When bankers say credit is tight, they do not simply mean that riskless interest rates are so high they are choking off demand for loans. They mean that many businesses and households that would like to borrow at the current riskless interest rates cannot get a loan. They are referring to the supply side of the credit market, not just the demand side.

The reason some borrowers cannot get a loan at the same (riskless) interest rate that others do is that their lenders are afraid they may default. Risky interest rates (or spreads to riskless interest rates on loans that might default) are often more important indicators of economic conditions than riskless interest rates. Nevertheless, central bankers have paid scant attention to default in their macroeconomic models.[1] In my opinion, central banks should pay attention to, and influence, risky interest rates if they want to preserve financial stability.

When lenders are afraid of default, they often ask for collateral to secure their loans. How much collateral they require is a crucial variable in the economy called the collateral rate or leverage. Lenders also worry about the creditworthiness of the borrowers, which in the case of firms is represented by credit ratings and in the case of households is often represented by a FICO credit score.[2] The credit conditions of the economy cannot be summarized accurately by a single riskless interest rate, but rather by an entire surface, where the offered interest rate from lenders can be thought of as a function of the collateral and the FICO score: $r = f(\text{collateral}, \text{FICO})$.[3] The higher the collateral, or the higher the

FICO score, the lower will be the interest rate. For sufficiently high collateral and FICO score, the interest rate may stabilize at a constant called the riskless interest rate. If we compare two different economic climates, represented by two different surfaces f and g, it might well be the case that both of them give precisely the same riskless interest rate, but nevertheless g depicts much tighter credit conditions than f. For example, in g the riskless interest rate might be attained only with much higher levels of collateral and FICO, or the rate in g might rise much faster above the riskless level as collateral and FICO fall.

In figure 15.1 I present the average interest rate charged on a large sample of Fannie and Freddie thirty-year fixed rate mortgage loans during 2013. One can see that as FICO falls and as collateral falls (loan-to-value ratio, or LTV, rises), the corresponding interest rate rises.[4]

In my opinion, central banks should be trying to estimate the existing credit surfaces on a quarterly basis. They could get the data to do much of this if they looked at individual transactions to see how the rates change as the terms change. They could do even better if they could collect the offers banks make. Part of the surface would have to be estimated by extrapolation, since it covers conditions at which no trades (or only a few trades) are observed. Estimating these surfaces explicitly would bring much clarity to the general credit climate.[5]

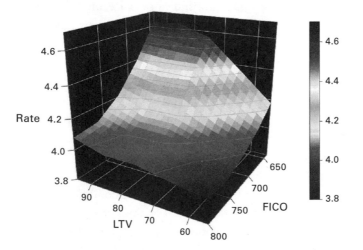

Figure 15.1
Two-Dimensional Credit Surface.

Credit Surface Theory

The riskless interest rate depends on the impatience of the agents in the economy and on the expectations for future growth, among other factors. The rest of the credit surface is driven primarily by the risk tolerance of borrowers and lenders' fears of default, in addition to the conventional determinants like impatience and growth, which apply with or without uncertainty. The probability of default in turn depends on at least two factors: one is the volatility of collateral prices, and the other is the indebtedness of the borrowers.

The higher the volatility of collateral prices (at least in the down tail), the more insecure lenders will feel and the higher the interest rate they will insist on for the same collateral. The higher the indebtedness of the borrowers, the less likely it is that they will be willing or able to repay a new loan. Higher volatility and higher indebtedness make for a tighter credit climate.

The tightness of the credit environment is more related to the steepness of the credit surface than to the level of the riskless interest rate. Borrowers know that if they want to borrow more money with the same collateral, they will pay a higher interest rate, because the LTV of the loan will move up.[6] In traditional macroeconomic theory, any investor can borrow all he wants at the going rate of interest. With an upward-sloping credit surface agents will typically feel constrained, borrowing less than they would like at a constant interest rate.

A stark case of this can be seen from the binomial leverage theorem of Fostel and Geanakoplos (forthcoming). Let's consider the situation in which all loans are entirely no recourse (and there is no reputation to be lost), so borrowers deliver only up to the value of the collateral. The credit surface then depends on LTV but not on the FICO score. In figure 15.2 the interest rate is constant at the riskless rate so long as the LTV is sufficiently low (to make the loan absolutely safe) but rises for higher LTV. Fostel and Geanakoplos (forthcoming) showed that if the collateral gives no direct utility (as would be the case if the collateral were a financial security like an MBS or stock) and has only two possible payoffs, then nobody will ever borrow at higher LTV than at point *A* in the diagram, the maximum LTV at which there will be no default. All the observed loans in the economy will transact at the riskless interest rate, yet many

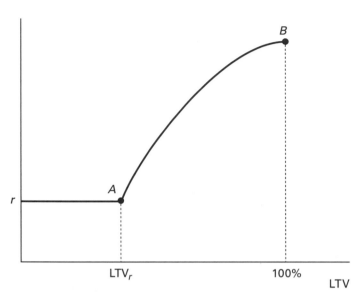

Figure 15.2
One-Dimensional Credit Surface.

borrowers would want to borrow much more if only they could increase their borrowing at the same rate. Credit conditions become looser when point *A* moves to the right. This happens when the volatility of the collateral prices declines, so the maximum LTV at which a loan is still riskless increases.

The Credit Surface and Asset Prices

The theory of asset pricing is one area that would be radically improved by considerations of the credit surface. Economists as far back as Irving Fisher have understood that the riskless interest rate influences the price of an asset by changing the expected present value of its dividends, or its fundamental value. But economists have not sufficiently appreciated that the rest of the credit surface also influences risky asset prices. As I have demonstrated (Geanakoplos 1997, 2003, 2010a), a looser credit surface boosts the demand for the corresponding collateral asset, and thus tends to raise its price.[7]

One can measure the looseness of the credit surface by exploring global measures such as its average slope. Alternatively, one can look at

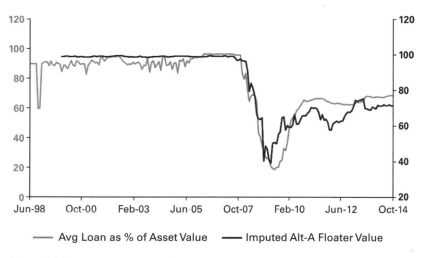

Figure 15.3
Mortgage Bond Leverage Cycle.
Note: The chart represents the average total repo loan as a percentage of asset value available from dealers on a hypothetical portfolio of CMOs originally rated AAA, subject to certain adjustments noted below. The price time series of imputed Alt-A floater prices is based on the Alt-A price drop versus agency collateral time series available from Barclays.

The portfolio evolved over time, and changes in average margin reflect changes in composition as well as changes in margins of particular securities. In the period following August 2008, a substantial part of the increase in margins is due to bonds that could no longer be used as collateral after being downgraded, or for other reasons, and hence count as 100 percent margin.

the distribution (or average or top quartile) of LTVs or FICO scores of loans that have actually been given. These latter numbers reflect demand as well as supply, but, ceteris paribus, the realized LTVs will be higher and the FICO scores lower when the credit surface is looser.

Figure 15.3 illustrates the connection between the price of a portfolio of AAA-rated mortgage securities and how much they could be leveraged over a sixteen-year period before and after the crisis.[8] Before the crisis leverage and prices rose together, during and after the crisis leverage and prices dramatically fell, and then they rose together, in a leverage cycle.

We have seen the same kind of leverage cycle in mortgage loan LTVs and housing prices, in student loan LTVs and school tuition, and in ECB collateral requirements and sovereign bond prices.

The Multidimensional Credit Surface and Volume

As mentioned several times already, the credit surface should really be more than a two-dimensional object, since rates also depend on ratios such as debt servicing to income or debt to wealth, and so on. These numbers are sometimes hard to get. There are often unobserved factors that affect the supply of loans. For example, new regulations may tighten credit supply by requiring increased documentation that some borrowers simply cannot provide. If the credit surface is calibrated against realized loans without taking into account the unobserved factors, it may actually look looser when credit is getting tighter because the restricted group of borrowers in the data is of higher quality, and so would be receiving more favorable interest rate offers for the same collateral. In such a case the drop in volume might reveal the tightening effect of the regulation.

The Credit Surface and Monetary Policy

I argued that monitoring and publishing the credit surface (and volume data) would greatly improve our understanding of evolving credit conditions and provide a framework for discussing monetary policy. It might even encourage policymakers to predict what effect their interventions would have on the whole surface, not just on the riskless interest rate. How clearly did the US Federal Reserve Board of Governors understand that its recent policy of quantitative easing (achieved partly by buying agency mortgages) would dramatically loosen the credit surface for high-yield bonds, but provide very little loosening of the credit surface for mortgage borrowers with average credit scores? In my opinion, policymaking would be enormously sharpened if it were disciplined by the question of the whole credit surface.

If a very tight credit climate is unhealthy for the economic environment, then we are led by considerations of the credit surface to two radical-sounding conclusions. First, central banks could intervene not only by influencing the riskless interest rate (fully cognizant of the indirect effects on the rest of the credit surface, as I mentioned earlier) but also by directly influencing risky debt. In one direction, central banks could tighten overly hot credit markets by, for example, prohibiting loans at LTV exceeding some threshold, as the Bank of Israel did in 2010 by banning mortgage loans at LTV ratios above 60 percent. In the other direction, a central bank could extend credit to borrowers at terms that no private investor would provide, as the Fed did in 2009, lending 95 cents against a dollar's worth of credit card collateral, and student loan collateral, and car loan collateral.[9] The ECB has done the same with sovereign debt.

Second, in extreme environments, such as the United States faced in 2007–2009 and Europe faces now, debt forgiveness could also figure into the policy mix of central banks. Once it is admitted that there may be defaults against the central bank, one can consider the idea of partial forgiveness as a policy tool. Properly implemented, forgiveness can actually recover more money for the lender, without creating any moral hazard for present or future borrowers. The stigma against default is so strong that it has stymied rational discussion about forgiveness.[10]

The Current Environment

Several commentators have remarked that in the United States, and especially in Europe, we have seen several years of low growth and extraordinarily low interest rates. Some have concluded that we must be entering a period of secular stagnation in which there are very few projects with high expected returns. An alternative view, one that can only be understood in terms of the credit surface, is that even though the riskless rate may have declined, the full credit surface may have become steeper, and thus for many or most potential borrowers the credit environment might be tighter than before.

In the United States the credit surface for corporate loans is quite different from the credit surface for consumer (or small business) loans. We are witnessing a tale of two different leverage cycles. Corporate borrowers with mediocre credit ratings and high debt-to-equity ratios are able to issue bonds at extraordinarily low interest rates. But homeowners with average credit scores cannot easily get loans. One reason is that banks holding AAA-rated mortgage securities now incur capital charges they did not bear before. This lowers the price of the AAA-rated piece and lowers the profitability of nonagency securitizations. Without a vehicle into which to sell their loans, banks offer far fewer loans. Second, the banks are terrified of putbacks, which oblige them to buy back loans at

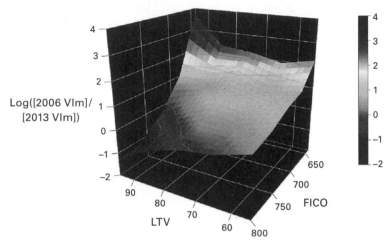

Figure 15.4
Change in Origination Volumes, 2006 versus 2013.

par that were not properly vetted. To temper that fear, regulators created a safe harbor of qualified mortgages that could not be put back, but this has only served to convince banks that non-QM loans are in graver danger of putbacks. Figure 15.4 shows that there were vastly more loans made to borrowers with below 725 FICO scores securitized by Fannie Mae and Freddie Mac in 2006 than in 2013. The only category of loans that was more prevalent in 2013 consisted of very high FICO score loans.

Default and Forgiveness

The American crisis began over eight years ago in February 2007 when the BBB subprime mortgage index collapsed. The economy has finally picked up, but I believe our biggest mistake after the crisis began was not taking effective measures to ameliorate the massive foreclosure problem, or to confront the problems of debt overhang for homeowners, small businesses, and government. We did save our banks. What we should have done is partially forgive subprime debt.

Between four and seven million homes were foreclosed on as a result of the American mortgage crisis, involving more defaulters in the households than the number of people in Greece. In a *New York Times* op-ed with Susan Koniak in October 2008, I warned of the impending foreclosure disaster and predicted that government efforts to help homeowners by temporarily reducing their interest payments would fail. We argued that subprime borrowers, without a good credit rating to protect, who were far underwater and who took a hit in their earnings would default. For subprime loans with an LTV of 140 percent to 160 percent, the rate of new defaults at the time was 7.4 percent *per month*!

In another *New York Times* op-ed in March 2009, Susan Koniak and I advocated reducing principal as the only way to help homeowners and lenders and the country at the same time. Losses from foreclosures of subprime loans have been horrible. The average recovery is under 25 percent. This is understandable once one realizes that in many states, it takes eighteen month to three years to throw somebody out of his house. In that time the mortgage isn't paid, the taxes aren't paid, the house is not repaired, the house is often vandalized, and the realtor must be paid. Consider a $160,000 subprime loan on a house that is now worth only $100,000. If the borrower loses his job or finds his earnings prospects are reduced, he will default.

The lender who forecloses will then end up with about $40,000. But if the loan is forgiven down to $90,000 (perhaps with the added proviso that if the house rises in value and is then sold, half the sale price beyond $100,000 will also be returned to the lender), both the lender and the borrower can be made better off. The borrower might choose to stay in his house and continue to pay the mortgage, or he might decide to sell the house as expeditiously as possible, returning $90,000 to the lender and pocketing the $10,000 himself. Either way the lender makes out much better than with $40,000. And this does not count the boost to the economy and to home prices if a large number of potential foreclosed homes are taken off the market.

Partially forgiving underwater debt before the homeowner defaults eliminates moral hazard. But it runs the risk that some homeowners who would have paid everything are asked to pay less. Only a careful analysis of what happened loan by loan, couched in a model that takes into account the effect of forgiveness on home prices, can reveal what would have been the effect on losses. I am working on that analysis now.

Notes

1. Of course, central bankers pay a great deal of attention to the solvency of individual banks, but when it comes to their macroeconomic forecasts of demand and growth, it is my impression that default does not figure in.

2. FICO is a private company that provides credit scores to financial institutions to help them in their decision making. The FICO score is not the perfect representation of creditworthiness. Ideally one would like a measure that represented the willingness of the borrower to repay even if there was no collateral, which would depend on the ratio between the internal penalty (in lost reputation and embarrassment, etc.) and the marginal utility of consumption or wealth.

3. There should be a different credit surface for each maturity and each type of collateral. One could also imagine adding more variables beyond LTV and creditworthiness, such as debt-to-income or debt-to-wealth ratios.

4. The full credit surface for mortgages should include nonagency loans. This would give a much greater variation in interest rates. The difficulty is that these loans are often of a different type (say, variable rate), so that it is not so easy to assign a comparable rate to them. But this difficulty could probably be overcome by using a so-called option-adjusted spread.

5. The credit surface or credit menu was introduced in an equilibrium model in Geanakoplos (1997), and the recommendation that central banks should monitor it appears in Geanakoplos (2014).

6. If we added more axes to the credit surface to reflect ratios such as credit servicing to income, or credit to income, or credit to wealth, then it would be still more obvious that bigger loans would involve higher interest rates.

7. Retailers who find ingenious ways to extend credit to their customers have understood this principle for decades (if not centuries). Consider the binomial case illustrated in figure 15.2. A looser credit surface pushes point A to the right. Any borrower who felt credit constrained would naturally borrow more on his existing collateral. But where would he spend the extra cash? All his other choices have unchanged marginal utility. But the next unit of collateral brings higher marginal utility than before, because now its purchase can be accompanied by a bigger loan.

8. Think of the leverage as the LTV corresponding to point A in figure 15.2. The price on the portfolio is measured by Barclays by looking at the price difference from a similar mortgage that is guaranteed against default, and then subtracting this difference from 100. A floater (which pays a current coupon equal to the going interest rate) that was guaranteed not to default would always be priced at 100, so the vertical axis is the implied price of a floater that defaults like the AAA tranche of Alt-A bonds in the portfolio.

9. This might lead to a whole new kind of policy, tailored to specific kinds of borrowers.

10. If central banks are not allowed to consider the possibility that there may be defaults on their loans, then they cannot be allowed to calculate that losses might

be reduced by partial forgiveness. In my view it is impossible to fully separate the central bank from a fiscal authority such as the Treasury. There needs to be a well-defined mechanism for the central banks to lose money as well as make money. When private lenders are pooled, as was the case with bondholders of subprime securitizations, there may be no coordination mechanism for them to partially forgive debt. In my view, in extreme situations policymakers should consider imposing debt forgiveness on private lenders, as well as extending debt forgiveness themselves. See Geanakoplos (2010b).

References

Fostel, Ana, and John Geanakoplos. Forthcoming. "Leverage and Default in Binomial Economies: A Complete Characterization." *Econometrica*.

Geanakoplos, John. 1997. "Promises, Promises." In *The Economy as an Evolving Complex System II*, ed. W. Brian Arthur, Steven Durlauf, and David Lane, 285–320. Reading, MA: Addison-Wesley.

Geanakoplos, John. 2003. "Liquidity, Default, and Crashes: Endogenous Contracts in General Equilibrium." In *Advances in Economics and Econometrics: Theory and Applications, Eighth World Conference, Vol. 2*, 170–205. Econometric Society Monographs. Cambridge: Cambridge University Press.

Geanakoplos, John. 2010 a. "The Leverage Cycle." *NBER Macro-Annual* 2009:1–64.

Geanakoplos, John, 2010 b. "Solving the Present Crisis and Managing the Leverage Cycle." *FRBNY Economic Policy Review*, August, 101–131.

Geanakoplos, John, 2014. "Leverage Default, and Forgiveness: Lessons from the American and European Crises." *Journal of Macroeconomics* 39, Pt. B (March): 313–333.

Geanakoplos, John, and Susan Koniak. 2008. "Mortgage Justice Is Blind." Op-ed. *New York Times*, October 30.

Geanakoplos, John, and Susan Koniak. 2009. "Principal Matters." Op-ed. *New York Times*, March 5.

16

Remarks on the Future of Monetary Policy

Gill Marcus

During the precrisis period, monetary policy appeared to be relatively predictable and straightforward. The Great Moderation saw low inflation rates around the world, with inflation targeting, either formal or informal, prevailing as the dominant framework. Interest rate policy was focused on maintaining price stability, central banks generally had almost undisputed independence in this regard, and emerging risks to financial stability from low interest rates were not generally regarded as a concern for monetary policy. In the words of Mervyn King, monetary policy had in fact reached its objective, with its indicator of success being "boring." However, since the onset of the global financial crisis, monetary policy has become anything but boring, and, as was later said, "Bring back boring!"

Little did we know at that time that, in the wake of the global financial crisis, we would be asking whether inflation targeting was enough, and if not, how should the framework be modified or augmented, and should central bank mandates be expanded. And if so, by whom and against what expectations? The global financial crisis was a salutary reminder that nothing is static, that central banks at the best of times largely deal with the unknown future, and that we have to adapt to changing and unexpected circumstances. However, there is still an intense debate about whether monetary policy should change, and if so, how it should change. My comments touch briefly on three issues: first, the challenges to central bank independence; second, the relationship between monetary policy and financial stability; and third, how to deal with spillover effects from advanced economy monetary policies, and the implications for exchange rate policies in emerging market economies (EMEs) in particular.

Challenges to Central Bank Independence

At the previous IMF conference, "Rethinking Macro Policy II," the IMF's managing director, Christine Lagarde, suggested that central banks have emerged as the heroes of the crisis. In her view, one that is also widely held, the extraordinary actions undertaken by central banks, particularly in the advanced economies, probably saved the global economy from a far worse fate than what transpired. But this view of central banks as the heroes places inordinate pressures on them, not least because it leads to unrealistic expectations combined with an ever-expanding mandate, as well as a perception that they have become too powerful. This could ultimately lead to a backlash, with serious implications for both the independence and the mandates of central banks. While price stability remains a core objective of central banks, the persistence of the global crisis has raised expectations about what central banks can and should do and, in particular, how their expanding mandates regarding economic growth and financial stability should interact with their price stability objective. There seems to be little awareness of what central banks cannot do, as well as what they should in fact not do.

That central banks in some instances are presently regarded as the only game in town, or that they were in effect forced into taking unconventional measures, has resulted in a blurring of the boundaries between monetary and fiscal policies in some instances. Although monetary policy always has distributional effects, balance sheet policies probably have more consequences, in that choices often are made with respect to different market segments. In effect, monetary policy has become highly politicized as central bank balance sheets have expanded. This not only increases scrutiny of central banks, there is also the requirement for greater public accountability of central banks. More important, the increased scrutiny may have implications for central bank and monetary policy independence.

Eichengreen and Weder di Mauro (2015) have argued that central banks should not be concerned about incurring losses, and a paper by David Archer and Paul Moser-Boehm (2013) at the Bank for International Settlements has also argued that central banks are not profit-making organizations; they do not have a profit motive, and therefore their decisions should not be dictated by these considerations. Rather, the central bank balance sheet should be seen as part of the broader government budget constraint.

However, in reality, central bank balance sheets can at times take on a direct political dimension. In a number of advanced and EM economies this has come through intervention in the foreign exchange markets. Losses incurred in such instances result in potential pressure on central banks, for example the Swiss National Bank. In the United States the Fed is under increased political scrutiny with the proposed Audit the Fed bill, which, according to Janet Yellen, in her testimony to the Senate Banking Committee in February, "is a bill that would politicize monetary policy, putting short-term political pressures to bear on the Fed."

In a number of EMEs, including South Africa, losses have been incurred in undertaking sterilization activities following large inflows during the US quantitative easing. This was due to the significant interest rate differentials that exist between many EMEs and the advanced economies, which are at or close to the zero bound. How these losses are dealt with or perceived will vary from country to country and depend on accounting conventions and institutional structures. But they could result, and in some instances have resulted, in conflicts between central banks and the fiscal authorities

It does not help to try and avoid risks to independence by narrowly focusing on monetary policy. Most central bankers recognize that independence and credibility can also be undermined if they focus too narrowly on inflation. In the same way that a central bank's legitimacy may be undermined if it ignores growth and employment issues (in other words, a strict inflation targeter), it will similarly be undermined if it ignores financial stability issues. And in reality, a central bank will have responsibilities imposed on it in the event of a crisis arising from financial instability. Similarly, unconventional monetary policies (UMPs) may allow much-needed fiscal or structural reforms to be postponed, and ultimately may end up being harmful and undermine credibility.

Central banks therefore have to face the challenge of being seen to be doing too little or too much. There is a general lack of understanding of the complexity of these issues, and a key task ahead is how to broaden public knowledge and appreciation of what the challenges are. So an important role for monetary policy and central banking in general will be communicating about the role of the central bank and monetary policy, and its limitations. This is not new, but sustained outreach programs, not just with the markets, are increasingly important.

Relationship between Monetary Policy and Financial Stability

My second theme relates to whether financial stability should be incorporated into monetary policy frameworks. There is no doubt that a focus on financial stability is essential, although how to incorporate it into monetary policy remains a subject of debate. Should we extend the time horizon for monetary policy to account for the financial cycle, as Claudio Borio (2013) and others have suggested? In a recent speech, in answer to the question as to whether monetary policy should be responsible for financial stability *and* price stability, Christine Lagarde said, "The short answer is 'No'" (Lagarde 2015). I am of the view that the amount of monetary policy tightening that would have been needed to avoid the buildup of leverage before the crisis would have been on such a scale that it would have had severe growth repercussions. However, while I agree that in general, monetary policy should focus on price stability and macro- and microprudential policies should focus on financial stability, I am not sure that we can be dogmatic about it, or that it is an absolute. In practice, there may be instances in which monetary policy will be needed to lean against incipient asset bubbles, or it may be necessary to loosen monetary policy for financial stability reasons, as interest rates also affect financial stability and macroprudential tools may also have implications for price stability. This is particularly the case where the source of the financial stability risks relates to interest rates being too low, in which case there may be excessive leverage, or too high. Coordination will be required whatever the institutional arrangements are, as both sets of policies have an impact on each other. This will be the case whether or not macroprudential policy is located in the central bank. For coordination to work optimally, a deep understanding of both policy arenas will be required, and to allow for flexibility in the mix of policies in differing circumstances.

Furthermore, the distinction between what is monetary policy and what is macroprudential policy may not be that clear-cut. A good example is foreign exchange market intervention. The basic inflation-targeting model with a purely flexible exchange rate regime is no longer seen as ideal. Some form of exchange rate intervention has become increasingly acceptable. But the motivations may differ, and it is not clear whether such interventions are macroprudential policy, or monetary policy, or indeed industrial policy. Often the lines may be blurred. Are interventions in the face of strong capital inflows an attempt at leaning against possible impacts on asset or credit markets and excessive leverage, in which case they may be seen as macroprudential? Or is the concern rather that credit market implications could have an impact on inflation, or with the pass-through to inflation, in which case it is a monetary policy reaction? Or are we concerned about the impact on the country's competitiveness? Although this is an issue of particular concern to many EMEs, this is not exclusively the case. Much of the postcrisis monetary policy debates are about currency wars: the Swiss attempt to cap the Swiss franc appreciation and, some would argue, the recent quantitative easing by the ECB, which could be interpreted as competitiveness issues.

Dealing with Spillovers from Monetary Policy in Advanced Economies

The issue of spillovers from advanced economy monetary policy therefore has important implications for monetary policy going forward, particularly in EMEs, where the impact of UMPs has been felt most strongly. The sizable capital inflows to these countries, with attendant currency appreciation, misalignment, and credit and asset market booms; the volatility and reversal of capital flows when tapering began; and again the recent speculation regarding the timing and extent of US monetary policy normalization saw an appreciating dollar and significant depreciation and volatility in the currencies of many EM countries.

Some of the debate assumes that this is a temporary issue, and that once monetary policies have normalized, "normal" flows will follow. However, we have seen that UMP in the advanced economies can persist for some time; we have not seen the end of it yet, with the ECB only starting down this road and the effectiveness of such policies in Japan yet to be determined; and we have no idea how the normalization in the US economy will unfold. Furthermore, we do not know whether we are in for a period of secular stagnation, and if so, what the longer-term implications for flows to EMEs are likely to be. So we could be in for a protracted period of uncertainty and volatile capital flows.

How should EMEs adjust to these developments? Simply respond-
ing with monetary policy in an inflation-targeting context (interest rate
response and exchange rate flexibility) has been shown to be inadequate.
EM countries are, and should be, concerned about financial stability and
competitiveness issues. In a world where not all currencies float, currencies that do float find themselves taking on an even greater burden of
adjustment. Even the IMF has moved away from the perfect capital mobility approach and now sees a place for sterilized intervention and capital
flow management. However, we have noted that sterilized intervention is
costly, and the efficacy of capital flow management polices differs from
country to country, depending on structural features of domestic financial
markets. But even so, there is much disagreement and debate on this issue.
For example, did controls on inflows work in Chile in the 1990s? Did
they work recently in Brazil? Despite much research on the subject, there
are no definitive answers.

EM nations are often told that they can reduce their vulnerability to
these flows by liberalizing and developing their financial markets. Yet it is
precisely those countries with deep and liquid financial markets that are
more likely to attract inflows and more likely to experience the reversals,
because of ease of entry and exit. This conclusion has been confirmed in
a number of studies (e.g., Eichengreen and Gupta 2014). These inflows
and outflows have significant implications for monetary policy through
the inflation pressures from exchange rate changes. That is not to say that
financial market development should not be encouraged, but the limitations and vulnerabilities associated with it should be recognized. This is
particularly the case when these countries face sizable flows in response
to monetary policy actions in the advanced economies.

I agree with Raghuram Rajan, who has argued that recipient countries
are not being irrational when they lament the fact that the timing and
speed of implementation of and exit from unconventional policies are
driven solely by conditions in the source country. As he argues, "Having become more vulnerable because of leverage and crowding, recipient
countries may call for an exit whose pace and timing is responsive, at
least in part, to conditions they face" (Rajan 2014).

This implies that there is a strong case for more coordinated monetary policy globally. Although it is not only the EM countries that are
vulnerable to monetary policy decisions made in advanced economies,

they are the most affected. This is a reality that they have been living with for some time, but it does not mean that there cannot or should not be more serious effort in this regard. At the very least, monetary policy in advanced economies has to be sensitive to the impact of the actions on other countries. Immediate attention should be given to the establishment of bilateral credit lines beyond those countries that have been granted them. There also needs to be clear international coordination of lender of last resort function among central banks (e.g., currency swaps among central banks) when liquidity is required. Both of these measures should be considered a priority in the appropriate forums, and preferably have a decision made in principle and when there is no immediate need or request on the table.

While recent communication by the US Fed has attempted to recognize the possible spillover effects of its actions, the ultimate test will be in the actions of the advanced economies and their willingness to go beyond talking.

The future remains uncertain, with numerous political flash points that have erupted into localized or regional conflict adding to the dangers that lie ahead. It is a time for cool heads, clear thinking, and enhanced interaction among central bankers. It is also not a time for dogmatism. Central banks have been innovative, thoughtful, and courageous in tackling the financial crisis. But significant new challenges lie ahead that will require all of our collective wisdom. We cannot underestimate the level of interconnectedness. After all, we have yet to find out what the "new normal" will be. And behind all the numbers and statistics lie the tens of millions of people whose lives have been deeply affected.

Confidence and trust matter!

References

Archer, David, and Paul Moser-Boehm. 2013. "Central Bank Finances." BIS Paper 71. Bank for International Settlements, April. http://www.bis.org/publ/bppdf/bispap71.pdf.

Borio, Claudio. 2013. "The Financial Cycle and Macroeconomics: What Have We Learnt?" BIS Working Paper 395. Bank for International Settlements, December. http://www.bis.org/publ/work395.pdf.

Eichengreen, Barry J., and Poonam Gupta. 2014. "Tapering Talk: The Impact of Expectations of Reduced Federal Reserve Security Purchases on Emerging

Markets." Policy Research Working Paper WPS6754. World Bank, Washington, DC, January 1. http://documents.worldbank.org/curated/en/2014/01/18832605/tapering-talk-impact-expectations-reduced-federal-reserve-security-purchases-emerging-markets.

Eichengreen, Barry, and Beatrice Weder di Mauro. 2015. "Central Banks and the Bottom Line." ProjectSyndicate.org, February 12. http://www.project-syndicate .org/commentary/central-bank-balance-sheet-losses-by-barry-eichengreen-and-beatrice-weder-di-mauro-2015-02.

Lagarde, Christine. 2015. "Monetary Policy in the New Normal." Remarks at the 2015 China Development Forum Panel Discussion, Beijing, March 22. https://www.imf.org/external/np/speeches/2015/032215a.htm.

Rajan, Raghuram. 2014. Concerns about Competitive Monetary Easing." Remarks at the Policy Panel Discussion, the 2014 BOJ-IMES "Conference on Monetary Policy in a Post-Financial Crisis Era," organized by the Institute of Monetary and Economic Studies, Bank of Japan, Tokyo, May 28.

Fiscal Policy in the Future

17

Fiscal Policy for the Twenty-First Century: Testing the Limits of the Tax State?

Vitor Gaspar

Public finance and fiscal policy are in search of a new paradigm.Richard Musgrave's threefold classification of public finance functions—allocation, distribution, and stabilization—is showing signs of wear and tear, after a half century. Similarly, the later paradigm whereby government intervention is justified on the basis of market failure is also showing signs of fatigue. Assumptions necessary for market efficiency are unlikely to hold in the real world. We now know that market failure is pervasive and so does not provide much clarity about when governments should or should not intervene. Clearly, full symmetric information, complete markets, an absence of externalities, perfect competition, and an absence of transaction costs do not prevail in the real world. And this list does not include human behavioral flaws, which further contribute to market failures: limited computation capacity, myopia, envy, greed, fear, and much else. From Immanuel Kant's famous saying, "Out of the crooked timber of mankind no straight thing was ever made," it follows that possible failures of government intervention must be taken into account as well. As Brad DeLong put it in his contribution, "We know that as bad as market failures can be, government failures can often be little if any less immense."

But conceptual questions run deeper. What are the areas where government intervention serves the interests of society better than private arrangements? How can public-sector organizations be designed so that they provide public-sector agents with the means and incentives to deliver what they are set up to do? How can accountability be pursued? How can governments and markets co-evolve so as to serve the interests of the people? These are only a few of the many questions that remain unanswered.

At this point, there does not seem to be an alternative emerging paradigm. The public finance field has been prolific in looking at a number of areas where the state does or should intervene:

- macroeconomic stability and growth,
- the provision of basic public services,
- the provision of a social safety net,
- equitable distribution,
- market regulation and competition, and
- insurance against catastrophic risks.

This list oversimplifies the field. For example, I have not mentioned international aspects. To assess the importance of the omission, we need only recall global warming and the euro area.

A critical dimension in the analysis of public finances, however, is the means that the state uses to finance such interventions. Max Weber famously defined the state as any human community that has successfully ensured a monopoly over the legitimate use of violence. Schumpeter underscored another crucial characteristic of the modern state: its reliance on taxation. The tax state can be analogously defined as a political organization that relies on compulsory mobilization of private-sector resources to finance its multiple activities.

However, the state's ability to tax in order to sustain expanding budgets is increasingly under pressure in the twenty-first century. Public finances are being shaped by evolutionary dynamics such as globalization, technological change, demographic transitions, regional integration, and much else. Shocks expose further limits to the state's ability to react. Hence, a big encompassing question was asked by Schumpeter almost one hundred years ago: *What are the limits of the tax state?*

Answering such a profound question is beyond the scope of this chapter. Going forward, the IMF's Fiscal Affairs Department will certainly be tackling aspects of this question as part of its work agenda. This will include, for example, an IMF policy paper on fiscal anchors and policy frameworks to be issued in 2016.

In the remainder of this chapter I will focus on aspects related to public finance and macroeconomic stability and growth, the first issue listed above. I will center my discussion on two questions. First, how can fiscal policy be designed to minimize the likelihood and the effects of possible future economic and financial disasters? Second, how can fiscal policy, following a rules-like course of action, contribute to macroeconomic stability and economic growth?

Managing Public Finance Risks

Government debt is, in advanced economies, at unprecedented levels in peacetime. Moreover, it is clear that government debt affords only a partial view of public finances. In isolation it can be misleading. Wider risks to public finances are today sizable and manifold. Clear and present risks arise from low growth and inflation in some advanced economies. Developing economies face pressures from adverse changes in exchange rates and financing conditions. Volatile commodity prices hurt commodity exporters. In the context of diverging monetary policies across major economies, there is the risk of sudden jumps in interest rate growth differentials, which could jeopardize debt sustainability. Furthermore, shifting demographic trends pose serious challenges for fiscal policymakers in all countries. Contingent liabilities arising from struggling banks and troubled public enterprises pose additional sources of risk, often materializing when macro fundamentals are weak. Moreover, when an adequate institutional setup is lacking, these contingent liabilities can be difficult to limit ex ante because the state typically serves as the insurer of last resort whenever something goes wrong in the economy. Once realized, these risks can quickly spill over into regional and even global crises.[1]

In this context of high debt and latent risks, several key policy questions come to the fore. How can public finances be made safe in a world full of risks? How can these risks be usefully estimated and analyzed? How can fiscal policy contribute to mitigating those risks and promoting more sustainable and inclusive growth?

Most frameworks used to analyze fiscal risks rely, explicitly or implicitly, on a number of unexamined assumptions concerning the behavior and relevance of those risks. Specifically, they assume that fiscal risks are *independent* (the realization of one risk does not make the realization of any other risk more or less likely), *symmetric* (positive and negative shocks to the public finances are equally likely and equally beneficial or costly), and *linear* (the costs and benefits increase in proportion with the size of the underlying disturbance).

The global crisis provided a costly lesson on the limitations of such assumptions. It reminded us that, in fact:

1. *Fiscal risks are highly correlated.* When it comes to public finances, bad news really does "come in threes." Figure 17.1 illustrates the perfect storm of fiscal shocks for the ten countries hardest hit by the crisis. Not only were there multiple sources of increases in debt, these were also systematically linked: undisclosed general government deficits; adverse macroeconomic developments; contingent liabilities to the financial sector, state-owned enterprises, and private-public partnerships; and the government's own discretionary policy response to the crisis.

2. *Fiscal risks are asymmetric.* Politicians are quick to "bank" upside risks to their fiscal forecasts and are prone to downplay or overlook downside risks. Nowhere is this more evident than in the way

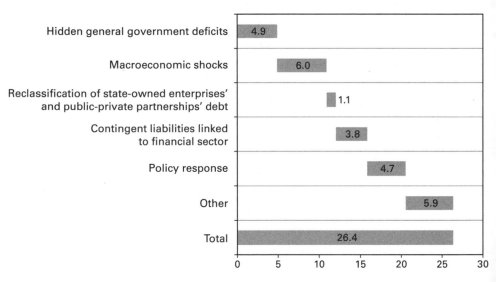

Figure 17.1
Unexpected Increase in General Government Debt in Selected Countries (2007–2010, percent of 2010 GDP).
Note: PPP-GDP weighted average across ten countries with largest increase in general government gross debt–to-GDP ratio during 2007–2010. Includes France, Germany, Greece, Iceland, Ireland, Netherlands, Spain, Portugal, UK, and the United States. *Source:* International Monetary Fund, "Fiscal Transparency, Accountability, and Risk," IMF Policy Paper, Washington, DC, 2012.

countries treat contingent assets and liabilities. Government forecasts often include revenues from future asset sales to reduce borrowing requirements, even though the precise amount or timing of the sale is uncertain. By contrast, governments typically exclude contingent liabilities, such as guarantees, because it is uncertain whether or when they will be called. The result is a forecast in which the balance of risks is skewed, with downside risks consistently understated. Figure 17.2 illustrates the optimistic bias by EU countries in forecasting government debt over the last twelve years. Positive skewness and kurtosis in the distribution of fiscal shocks justify prudent fiscal policy in "normal" times.

3.   *Fiscal risks are nonlinear.* For small disturbances it is reasonable to assume that costs increase in proportion to the size of the disturbance. However, in extreme events, the associated financial, economic, social, and political consequences can be much greater. Once markets

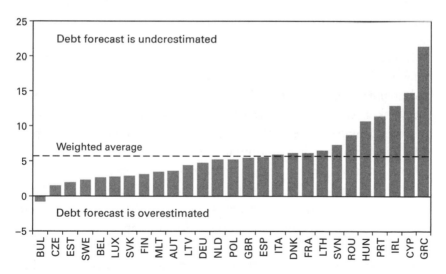

Figure 17.2
Forecast Error for General Government Debt (actual minus forecast for year *t* + 2, 2001–2013 average as percent of GDP).
Note: The chart presents annual forecast errors averaged between 2001 and 2013. Forecast errors are calculated as the actual outcome for debt-to-GDP ratio minus the forecast for the debt-to-GDP ratio prepared two years earlier. Includes all EU member-states except Croatia because of data availability. *Sources:* EU Stability and Convergence Programmes; IMF staff estimates.

perceive government debt to be unsustainable, spiraling interest rates and depreciating exchange rates can ensue. In some cases, countries may suffer a "sudden stop," simply cut off from market access. This nonlinear relationship between economic shocks and their consequences can give rise to what Olivier Blanchard calls "dark corners," situations in which the economy can malfunction badly.[2] Specifically in this context, important nonlinearities may be associated with public debt overhangs and the possibility of multiple equilibria. Both examples are well illustrated by recent examples in the euro area.

The combination of high debt levels with fiscal risks that are highly correlated, asymmetric, and nonlinear demands a new approach to fiscal policymaking, one in which fiscal risk analysis actively informs the most important fiscal decisions.

The IMF has already taken some important steps to improve and inform fiscal risk analysis among its members. A number of tools are already in place, including the fan charts in the IMF's debt sustainability analyses,[3] heat maps in fiscal transparency evaluations,[4] and work on future liabilities from age-related spending.

Going forward, we will consider how to better measure, prevent, and minimize fiscal risks by taking into account their correlated, asymmetric, and nonlinear characteristics. We will also explore how to mainstream fiscal risk assessments into fiscal decision making. This analysis will be part of a comprehensive approach to fiscal policymaking that also provides guidance on setting appropriate medium-term fiscal objectives that balance inclusive growth, stability, and risk management—a balancing act especially important in a monetary union, as underscored by Marco Buti in his contribution to the symposium. It will also take into account the role of fiscal policy in building resilience and supporting growth, in both the short and the medium term. As emphasized by Martin Feldstein in his contribution, fiscal policy plays a crucial role, particularly when economic downturns are expected to be deep and longlasting, as fiscal incentives can support private investment with lower associated risks than unconventional monetary policy. For policy authorities facing binding constraints, Feldstein also considers the possibility of revenue-neutral tax policy as an effective alternative to support investment.

Automatic Stabilization, Macroeconomic Stability, and Growth: The Power of FISCO

Does fiscal policy respond systematically to economic activity? Can fiscal policy promote macroeconomic stability? Does greater stability support stronger growth? The answer is yes on all counts, as suggested by our recent analysis in the April 2015 *Fiscal Monitor.*[5]

To measure whether fiscal policy contributes to stability, we introduce the novel concept of the fiscal stabilization coefficient (FISCO). FISCO measures how much a country's overall budget balance changes in response to a change in economic slack (as measured by the output gap). If FISCO is equal to 1, it means that when output falls below potential by 1 percent of GDP, the overall balance worsens by the same percentage of GDP. The higher FISCO, the more countercyclical is the conduct of fiscal policy, whereby governments build fiscal buffers in good times that they can then rely on during bad times. The average FISCO is 0.7 among advanced economies and 0.3 among emerging and developing economies (figure 17.3), with considerable cross-country differences (figure 17.4).

FISCO takes into account the fact that many revenue and expenditure items respond to the state of the economy even though the underlying

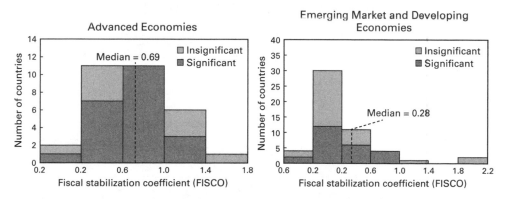

Figure 17.3
Distribution of Fiscal Stabilization Coefficients.
Note: "Significant" is defined as a coefficient with a *P* value less than 0.10.*Source:* IMF, *Fiscal Monitor,* "Now is the Time: Fiscal Policies for Sustainable Growth," April 2015.

provisions or programs were primarily designed for other reasons. Monitoring the relationship between the budget balance and the output gap would help policymakers understand how much their action contributes to output stability, including in comparison to other countries.

With FISCO, we assess the effect that fiscal policy can have on medium-term growth through its support of macroeconomic stability. Findings suggest that countries that can improve their FISCO would be able to significantly reduce macroeconomic volatility (figure 17.5).

Why is this important? First, lower macroeconomic volatility helps avoid wasteful fluctuations in employment and growth. Second, lower macroeconomic uncertainty provides a favorable environment for physical and social capital accumulation, thereby boosting medium-term growth.

The results further suggest that making fiscal policy more stabilizing would support growth, as illustrated in figure 17.5. The effect can be significant. Take, for example, the case of an advanced economy that raises

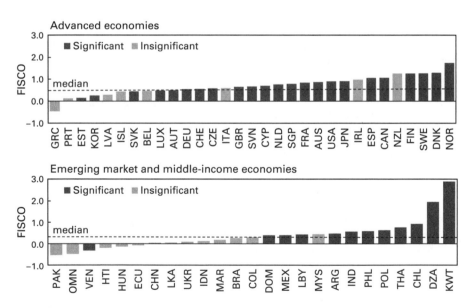

Figure 17.4
Selected Fiscal Stabilization Coefficients (FISCO).
Note: "Significant" is defined as a coefficient with a *P* value less than 0.10. *Source:* IMF, *Fiscal Monitor*, "Now is the Time: Fiscal Policies for Sustainable Growth," April 2015.

its FISCO from the average level (0.7) to that in the top third of countries (about 0.8). This would reduce output volatility by about 15 percent, which in turn would bring about a growth dividend of 0.3 percentage points annually. Note, however, that a 0.1 improvement in FISCO implies considerable reform efforts.

The effects on growth come from growth regressions. As is well known in the economic literature, growth regressions need to address the problems of joint endogeneity. The April 2015 *Fiscal Monitor* provides greater details of the methodology underlying this estimate, which attempts to address these well-known challenges. Still, as with all econometric findings, these results must be interpreted with caution.

We also find evidence that fiscal stabilization policies are asymmetric through the business cycle. Countries tend to deliver fiscal stabilization during cyclical downturns. But during expansions, fiscal policy changes seem to (partially) offset the work of automatic stabilizers. The simulation in figure 17.6 illustrates that a systematic asymmetric response whereby half of cyclical revenues windfalls is spent during good times, while the deficit fully absorbs the shortfalls in bad times, would be associated with a visible upward drift in the debt-to-GDP ratio.

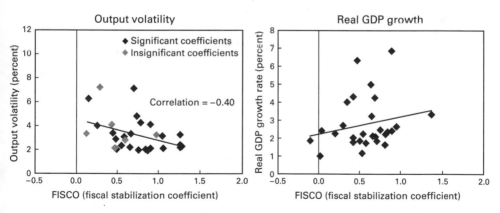

Figure 17.5
Advanced Economies: FISCO, Output Volatility and Real GDP Growth, 1980–2013.
Note: Output volatility is defined as the standard deviation of the real GDP growth rate over the sample period. *Source:* IMF, *Fiscal Monitor,* "Now Is the Time: Fiscal Policies for Sustainable Growth," April 2015.

What can countries do to improve fiscal stabilization? As argued above, it is crucial to have in place a fiscal framework to manage public finance risks. Well-designed fiscal rules and medium-term frameworks can also help by enabling uninterrupted access to borrowing at favorable conditions, ensuring expenditure control over the entire cycle and leaving flexibility to respond to output shocks.

Another important aspect of fiscal frameworks is to induce ruleslike, automatic stabilizing responses to economic developments. I will outline a few for illustration.

- Tax payments that move in sync with income, and social transfers, such as unemployment benefits, can automatically boost aggregate demand during downturns and moderate it during upswings. They

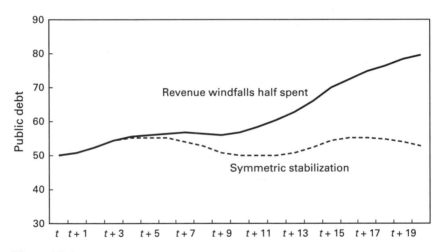

Figure 17.6
Asymmetric Stabilization: Unpleasant Public Debt Arithmetic (percent of GDP).
Note: The simulations are based on the stock flow identity between debt and the overall balance. Other assumptions are nominal potential growth of 4 percent, an automatic stabilization coefficient of 0.5, an implicit interest rate on public debt of 5 percent, and symmetric cycles, with the output gap smoothly oscillating between −2 and 2 percent. No fiscal adjustment is built into the scenario. The *t* denotes the initial year of the simulation. *Source*: IMF staff estimates.

are a very effective way to make fiscal policy stabilizing because they operate in real time, without political approval or implementation lags.

• Automatic tax deductions during recessions can be stabilizing because they reduce the cost of capital and ease credit constraints. This in turn helps stimulate investment. In Sweden, these served as countercyclical fiscal measures between the mid-1950s and the mid-1970s.

• Cyclical loss-carry backward is a measure that allows the deduction of corporate tax losses against past profits and provides companies immediate tax refunds during recessions. It has been applied in Canada, France, Germany, the UK, and the United States.

Although the peak of the global financial crisis now seems distant, we are left with its difficult legacies, namely, the disappointing growth outlook across most regions and fragile fiscal positions in many countries. The main challenge for public finances in the twenty-first century is therefore to support sustainable and inclusive growth, mindful of the limits to the tax state, in order to avoid sowing the seeds of the next crisis.

Notes

1. This section draws on joint work with Richard Hughes and Laura Jaramillo that appeared on the blog *Dams and Dykes for Public Finances*, March 18, 2015, http://blog-imfdirect.imf.org/2015/03/18/dams-and-dikes-for-public-finances.

2. See Olivier Blanchard, "Where Danger Lurks," *Finance & Development* 51, no. 3 (2014).

3. See the template for the IMF's "Debt Sustainability Analysis for Market-Access Countries," IMF, June 15, 2015, https://www.imf.org/external/pubs/ft/dsa/mac.htm.

4. See the IMF's published fiscal transparency evaluations at http://www.imf.org/external/np/fad/trans.

5. The IMF's April 2015 *Fiscal Monitor*, "Now is the Time: Fiscal Policies for Sustainable Growth," is available at http://www.imf.org/external/pubs/ft/fm/2015/01/fmindex.htm.

18

The Future of Fiscal Policy

Martin Feldstein

There are of course many important issues about the future of fiscal policy, especially long-term issues about the size of the national debt and the structure of taxes. But, leaving broader issues to other times and places, I am going to focus on the following question: At the zero lower bound, can fiscal policy be more effective than monetary policy in stimulating investment without the potential risks associated with quantitative easing (QE)?

I think it is useful to separate the question into two parts:

First, can fiscal policy be more effective than monetary policy in stimulating investment?

Second, can fiscal policy stimulate investment without the financial risks associated with QE?

Financial Sector Risks Associated with Quantitative Easing

I'll start with the second of these questions, which is also the easier one to answer. The answer is clear: fiscal policy does not entail the financial risks associated with QE.

Experience in the United States and Europe shows that QE—the combination of large-scale asset purchases and a long period of low short-term interest rates—leads investors and lenders to strategies of reaching for yield that involve substantial risk.

For investors, we see a bidding up of equity prices, as well as low yields on long-term bonds and a narrowing of yields between high-risk bonds and Treasuries. There has also been a large increase in the supply of junk bonds that now carry much lower interest rates than traditionally prevailed.

Banks and other lenders are extending credit to lower-quality borrowers, they are increasing their portfolios of leveraged loans to borrowers with large amounts of preexisting debt, and they are extending credit with fewer conditions, so called covenant-light loans.

In principle, the resulting financial risks could be limited by macroprudential policies. But in practice we are not seeing the introduction of such policies in the United States except for the increased capital requirements that have been placed on commercial banks. There are essentially no new macroprudential policies targeted at insurance companies, shadow banking firms, and others.

The Financial Stability Oversight Council (FSOC), the US interagency group charged with the responsibility for macroprudential policies, has done very little to reduce financial sector risks. In contrast, it has actually moved to increase financial instability by recommending that money market funds be allowed to "gate" their deposits—that is, to limit withdrawals—when they fear that market conditions will lead to investor runs. The Securities and Exchange Commission accepted this recommendation to allow gating, thereby increasing the probability that such runs will occur.

In addition, the increased capital requirements imposed by the Dodd-Frank legislation reduces the willingness of banks to hold inventories of corporate bonds and to purchase those bonds when there is selling pressure in those markets. The risk of such selling pressure has increased because the low interest rates have induced a very large increase in the issuance of corporate bonds, which have been purchased by mutual funds. Investors in the funds have essentially immediate liquidity, but when investors exercise that liquidity option, the funds must sell the bonds in order to raise cash to meet the demands of their investors. It is not clear who would step forward to buy those bonds.

Risks were also increased in the housing market when Fannie Mae and Freddy Mac dropped the requirement that mortgage originators keep 5 percent of the value of the mortgages that they originate in order to increase their caution in lending. And it is now again possible for some borrowers to get a mortgage with a 97 percent loan-to-value ratio. Fannie Mae and Freddy Mac have shifted some of the resulting risk to private investors by issuing bonds that finance different tranches of the 3 percent down payment. If house prices fall, some of the homeowners who will then have negative equity may choose to default on their mortgages, leading to foreclosures and house sales, which drive down house prices more generally.

In short, the QE policies involve financial risks that have not been offset by macroprudential policies.

In contrast, fiscal policies aimed at stimulating investment would not carry such financial sector risks.

Effectiveness of Fiscal Policy in Stimulating Investment

That brings me to the first part of the overall question: can fiscal policy be more effective than monetary policy in stimulating investment?

It's not clear why the attractiveness of fiscal policy should require it to be *more* effective than monetary policy. Wouldn't fiscal policy be attractive in this context if it were just *as* effective as QE without creating financial risks? In any case, the impact of fiscal incentives depends on the magnitude of the fiscal incentive policy.

Before discussing the impact of fiscal policy on private investment, let me summarize my view about the impact that QE has had on the US recovery. I believe that QE did succeed in stimulating GDP and bringing about the stronger recovery that we observed in the second half of 2013 and since then.

I think Ben Bernanke was correct in his prediction that the QE policy would raise the value of equities and the prices of owner-occupied homes. The increase in these values raised household wealth by more than $10 trillion in 2013. That led to an increase in consumer spending, which then contributed to a strong increase in nonresidential fixed investment. The lower interest rates produced by QE also appear to have increased nonresidential fixed investment in 2011 and the first half of 2012.

So I am not disputing that QE can and did contribute to increased investment. But I believe that fiscal policy can also stimulate investment and can do so without the accompanying financial sector risks.

It is useful to distinguish two types of fiscal stimulus. The first is tax cuts that increase fiscal deficits and raise GDP through traditional Keynesian channels. These could be cuts in personal income taxes, payroll taxes, or corporate taxes. By raising GDP they stimulate investment through higher-capacity utilization and higher profits.

The second type of fiscal stimulus includes specific investment incentives, such as the investment tax credit or accelerated depreciation, that increase the profitability of investment. A large body of research confirms that such targeted incentives have been effective in raising business investment.

There is, of course, a potential concern about using such investment incentives at a time when the economy already has a large fiscal deficit or national debt. In that context, it would be possible to pay for these fiscal incentives with a concurrent increase in the corporate tax. More specifically, a revenue neutral fiscal incentive would combine an investment tax credit for (say) the next two years with a temporary increase in the corporate tax rate during those same two years that would raise enough revenue to pay for the investment tax credit.

The key point is that the investment tax credit would reduce the tax on new investment while the higher corporate tax rate would fall on existing capital. Businesses would have an increased incentive to invest during the two years when the investment tax credits were available. The higher corporate tax rate would also increase the tax value of depreciation, further stimulating investment.

The Issue of Timing

There is, of course, an issue of timing in the effect of both fiscal and monetary policies. I have long believed and continue to believe that the problem of timing makes it unwise to use fiscal policy to stimulate demand in a *traditional* recession and that it is better to use monetary policy in those circumstances.

The traditional recession in the past half century lasted only an average of ten months from peak to trough. This is almost certainly less than the time it takes for the political process to recognize the need for a significant stimulus, to enact the changes in tax rates or tax rules, to then implement those tax changes, and to experience the impact of the changes on the economy. The impact of the fiscal change can therefore come well after the economy has passed the trough of the cycle and is expanding.

I have therefore believed that expansionary fiscal policy should be used only when the economic downturn is expected to be deep and long so that timing is not important. Those conditions prevailed in the recession that began at the end of 2007.

The problem of timing also affects monetary policy. The experience in 2006 through 2008 shows the difficulty of moving quickly to ease monetary policy. The minutes of the Federal Reserve show that it took considerable time to recognize the seriousness of the downturn and to decide how large the stimulus should be. That continued to be true after the interest rate reached the zero lower bound and the Fed shifted to a variety of different QE formulations. And even after those policies were put in place, it inevitably took time before they caused the desired increase in demand.

My basic conclusion, therefore, is that although fiscal incentives do involve problems of timing, they can be used effectively in the context of deep and longlasting downturns to stimulate investment, without the adverse effects on financial stability that result from QE.

19

What Future for Rules-Based Fiscal Policy?

Marco Buti*

In this chapter, I wish to address the issue of rules-based fiscal policy. Specifically, the question I wish to put forward is, what is the future of rules-based fiscal policy?

Fiscal rules are now widespread, in both advanced and emerging economies (EMEs), which is a testament to their increasing popularity. Yet, as before in the monetary field, the growing experience with rules-based fiscal policy has illuminated potential pitfalls. And there has always been a view that rules are at best an "unnecessary ornament," if not positively harmful.

The reflection has been continually active with regard to the European set of rules, where a specific context is additionally created by the monetary union of member states that still enjoy fiscal sovereignty. The European rule book has been amended several times in response to problems that have been identified. This is a rich experience already.

The judgment over European fiscal rules is occasionally dismissive—as if the successive revisions, together with disappointing macroeconomic performance, sufficed to demonstrate an inherent failure. As one might expect, I will adopt a more nuanced and positive assessment. While not hiding the challenges of operating fiscal rules, including our present toolbox in Europe, I argue that there has been an impressive number of lessons learned, paving the way for smarter and more effective rules-based frameworks.

Let me outline the three specific take-home messages from my intervention:

1. From a purely macroeconomic perspective, the fiscal stance was at times too restrictive during the crisis, but this reflected more the

incompleteness of the architecture of the European Monetary Union (EMU) rather than inherent flaws in the EU's fiscal framework.

2. Fiscal rules should anchor public debt ratios to long-term prudent levels while helping to stabilize the economy. Achieving such a double act is even more important in a currency union than in independent jurisdictions. In the present juncture, in achieving this double act, a broadly neutral fiscal stance appears appropriate for the euro area as a whole, but its distribution is suboptimal. If an expansionary policy proves desirable, it would be better pursued at the central level than at the national level.

3. A prudent debt anchor and a stabilization goal are consistent with the present EU fiscal rules, but are "hidden" in a framework that is overly complicated and suffers from an "authority gap" at the center. The latter two features are two faces of the same coin and can be traced back to lack of trust.

As a final word of introduction, let me note the importance of this debate, especially from the perspective of Europeans. Deep fiscal union among members of the EMU might be on the long-term agenda, but the foreseeable future largely hinges on a stepped-up coordination of national fiscal entities. This coordination can hardly be organized without some elaborated underpinning framework. And one must also recognize, as a political reality, the attachment within influential constituencies to ordo-liberal settings.

These joint contextual features have crucial implications. They point to the vital need to forge intellectual common ground, to a greater degree than currently obtains, with regard to the merits, limitations, and above all the proper attributes of rules-based fiscal frameworks. It is to this endeavor that I wish to contribute here. I would also like to add as a disclaimer that these views are my own.

An Existential Crisis: Fiscal Rules in an Incomplete EMU

The fiscal rules in Europe have been submitted to a severe "stress test" in recent years. Debt levels have risen to unprecedented levels in a depressed environment shaped by the balance sheet downturn combined with permanent stagnation features that predated the crisis. In this unusually challenging situation, it has been difficult to credibly apply fiscal rules all along in a sensible manner.

Have the EU fiscal rules made things better or worse? From a purely macroeconomic perspective, the fiscal stance was at times excessively tight and procyclical, especially at the height of the sovereign crisis, for example from mid-2011 to early 2013. For the euro area as a whole, structural balances improved by 1 percent of GDP per year in the three years 2011–2013, a significant contraction against large negative output gaps. There are indications that the underlying policy effort was in fact even a bit higher, given the significant revenue shortfalls compared with ordinary tax elasticities.

In some countries, mainly those under financial market pressure, the effort has been more impressive still. To take just one example, in Spain the underlying budgetary adjustment was about double the average in those years, although the stance has now been relaxed. At the same time, the few countries arguably benefiting from some fiscal space, such as Germany, advanced faster on consolidation than they might have, taking a macroeconomic perspective.

At the same time, one must stress that these developments occurred in the highly unusual economic environment that I mentioned above, doubled by the incomplete institutional setting of a monetary union still very much in the making:

- On the financial side, several EU member states were on the verge of or had effectively lost market access.

- Meanwhile, the institutional foundations that could have supported a more balanced fiscal strategy were not there ex ante. They had to be devised as the crisis developed.

In particular, the setting up of European firewalls (the European Financial Stability Facility and the European Financial Stabilisation Mechanism, and later the European Stability Mechanism), the decision to launch a banking union, and the crucial actions of the European Central Bank (ECB), including the announcement of Outright Monetary Transactions (OMT), were decisive in turning the corner of acute financial stress.

Once these elements were in place, a more gradual fiscal adjustment policy could effectively be deployed.

The take-away, from my perspective, is not that fiscal rules per se proved their inadequacy with the crisis. Rather, the main lesson is that fiscal rules operate in a certain institutional and political environment, which has to be conducive to sensible implementation. The fiscal rules *stricto sensu* could in fact have been applied in a less procyclical fashion.

In addition, the "excessive procyclicality" should not be overdone. Given very large initial sustainability gaps, most EU countries had to embark on sustained consolidation, if more gradual and better composed. Even Germany arguably faced dilemmas, as it also had to shoulder the credibility of the overall European framework much on its own.

That said, this difficult experience from the crisis has also led to renewed questions over the design of our fiscal rules. This is the topic to which I turn now.

Fiscal Rules: The "Double Act" of Anchoring Discipline while Helping Stabilization

There are several desirable features of fiscal rules. More than fifteen years ago an influential IMF paper (Kopits and Symansky 1998) encapsulated these in eight criteria, such as adequacy, simplicity, efficiency, and others. It was concurrently recognized that jointly fulfilling all the relevant criteria would be no easy feat, as there are apparent trade-offs between them.

While all criteria from Kopits and Symansky or similar grids deserve attention, there is one aspect that, although not absent, was not emphasized enough in the light of subsequent experience. This "focal point," which I wish to stress now, is the ability to preserve, or even to empower, the macroeconomic role of fiscal policy in stabilizing the economy, within the framework set by the rules.

I wish to emphasize the stabilization role of fiscal policy without forgetting, of course, the classic motivations for fiscal rules. Broadly speaking, fiscal rules are expected to discipline budgetary policymaking and confer credibility. A rich literature has expounded a ubiquitous deficit bias, from informational problems to electoral competition and the tragedy of the commons. Together with unprecedented levels of public indebtedness, this explains the attraction for rules bolstering the commitment to time-consistent policies.

However, while committing to long-run budgetary discipline is the key motivation for fiscal rules, my view is that allowing fiscal policy to help stabilize the economy in the short run is also important.

Achieving this "double act" is the central issue in designing a rules-based framework. Let me emphasize that this is symmetric: good times should be accompanied by tight policies in order to build buffers for the less good times.

There is a view that fiscal rules should only be about forcing fiscal discipline, that is, constraining the deficit bias that policymakers are prone to. This one-sided approach is vulnerable in practice to a double criticism, as we have learned. In real time, some observers will consider the rules too restrictive, while others argue that they are too lax. Indeed, this is precisely what we see in European discussions, where the European Commission's advice on an appropriate fiscal stance is typically met with skepticism running in opposite directions.

The way out of this double bind is to actively make the case that the rules deliver a sensible stance, if not optimal.

Integrating countercyclical properties in fiscal rules is all the more important in the EMU. Countries sharing the euro cannot benefit from tailored monetary policy and nominal exchange rate adjustments in response to asymmetric developments, with fiscal policy remaining the main macroeconomic tool at a national level. Besides, in a more general manner, the experience of the past years has inflected views on the effectiveness of fiscal policy, partially giving it back its earlier Keynesian legitimacy.

Another reason why we need cyclically friendly rules in the euro zone is to avoid putting an excessive burden on monetary policy for managing the overall *policy mix*. This concern has been illuminated in the recent past, when deflationary threats have led the president of the ECB himself (Draghi 2014) to call for a better consideration of the aggregate fiscal stance within the rules of the Stability and Growth Pact. In the absence of a central fiscal capacity, that equates with the sum of country policies.

The important implication is that rules for national budgets cannot be conceived as only forbidding profligate behavior. Again, rules should be conceived also to prescribe, not just proscribe.

In sum, fiscal rules in a currency union should ensure no overburdening of monetary policy both in the long run—thereby avoiding the unpleasant monetary arithmetic (Sargent and Wallace 1981)—and in the short run, by helping deliver an appropriate policy mix in good and bad times while catering for asymmetric shocks.

Prudent Public Debt Objectives as Long-Run Anchors

Expanding on matters of rules design, I wish to also stress the importance of the details. There as well we have learned and continue to learn.

When designing a rules-based fiscal framework, the first step is to establish an operational notion of sustainability that can serve as a long-run anchor.

From this perspective, there is an important discussion to be held on the effective limits to public indebtedness. This debate is being revived in a world presenting features of secular stagnation. That is because in principle, persistent excess private saving could be countered by persistent fiscal expansion, implying a growing stock of public debt that agents are only too happy to buy.

However, economists have generally agreed that keeping public debt at prudent levels is a sensible long-term objective. Indeed, high debt levels are empirically associated with risks of lower growth, intergenerational equity issues, and threats of reaching fiscal limits, as well as compromising the ability to use fiscal policy in downturns.

A significant prerequisite for devising fiscal rules is thus to pin down the order of magnitude of what constitutes prudent debt levels, and this is an important topic for empirical research.

Recent research, however, lends support to the view that several advanced economies have already exceeded the range of prudent indebtedness. This holds true in particular for members of the EMU, where, interestingly, the levels of prudent public indebtedness may be lower insofar as each individual member does not have a native central bank underpinning its public debt exposure (Fall et al. 2015).

Therefore, I think that moving toward moderate levels of public debt as a long-run objective remains a sensible approach for a country participating in the euro area. Accordingly, the achievement of prudent debt levels is and should remain a key anchor of a rules-based framework.

Designing Subtle Rules

We have encountered the issue that rules are exposed as being either too lax or too restrictive, or both, depending on circumstances. This circumstance has led to a quest for smarter rules. For example, the European Commission has recently introduced a matrix that differentiates fiscal policies according to the twin dimensions of sustainability needs and economic conditions (European Commission 2015).

Progress in designing "second-generation" rules also has occurred, if sometimes below the radar screen, though perceivable in experts' discussions. One thing we have learned something about is the choice of operational target, by which I mean a variable that is effectively targeted through annual budgets. Here, the experience is that both debt and deficit objectives raise questions.

Of course, public debt ratios should act as a long-run anchor, as I explained. However, they are too exposed to uncontrollable factors to serve as annual targets. We have seen this firsthand in Europe, where the so-called debt rule has become temporarily unrealistic in an environment of very low nominal GDP growth. This happened despite the sophisticated features embedded in the rule (such as three-year smoothing and cyclical correction).

Yet budget balance rules also suffer significant shortcomings in this regard. Headline balances usually reflect cyclical developments through the working of automatic stabilizers. In principle, the solution is to rely on cyclically adjusted balances, as has long been recognized in the EU framework. But structural deficits are weakened by large measurement uncertainties, especially in level terms, but also to some extent in first differences.

These methodological concerns are truly first-order problems in practice. One implication is that changes in the structural balances cannot be equated with policy-driven impulses. It has become evident, for example, that changes in structural balances have differed by more than 1.5 percent of GDP on average over the past decade in EU countries from a competing measure of the discretionary fiscal effort. These are major gaps when it comes to implementing continued surveillance. Correcting at least partly for these methodological problems is possible, and that is what we often do when implementing the Stability and Growth Pact (such as in the assessment of effective action in the context of the Excessive Deficit Procedure). However, such corrections make the system very complex (more on complexity below).

These empirical features also explain the attraction of rules that use as operational targets a quantum that is more evidently linked to government actions at the frequency of annual budgets, such as expenditure rules in conjunction with a bottom-up assessment of revenue measures.

Putting all these threads together, we see the broad contours of a robust and economically based rule. Such a rule would prescribe a proper notion of the fiscal effort, as just evoked, against the two objectives I have discussed, debt sustainability and cyclical stabilization (Carnot 2014). In practice, such an economically robust rule can be used as a benchmark to evaluate the fiscal stance. For example, it was used to show that in the conditions of a slow recovery and large debt legacy, a close to neutral stance struck an appropriate balance for the euro zone as a whole in 2015, although the distribution across countries could be improved (Buti and Carnot 2015).

Lack of Authority and Complexity Are Hampering a Sound Application of EU Fiscal Framework

Good Design Helps but Doesn't Guarantee Implementation

All this is very well, you might say, but the true weakness with fiscal rules does not lie so much with design as with effective implementation. It is commonly agreed that enforcing the rules is the Achilles' heel of EMU surveillance.

Before going into this issue in more depth, I wish to note that matters of "political ownership" and effective implementation are also partly connected to design issues. Good design, recognized as such, is more conducive to subsequent effective implementation. This is not only because the policy is better but also because it can be more legitimately enforced, by coercive means, if needed, since there is an ex ante broader acceptance by policymakers and the public at large. Conversely, an insufficiently adequate rule will not be implemented, not just because policymakers are sinners but simply because it would really be stupid to insist on it. *Lex mala, lex nulla.*

But while good design is necessary and conducive to implementation, it will not always be sufficient. This is where the topic of rules meets the question of institutions.

Lack of "Authority," Excessive Complexity

In this regard, it is fair to admit that the European fiscal framework suffers from two interlinked issues: an overly complicated set of rules and an insufficient "authority" from the center.

The complexity is most visible not so much in the subtlety of a given rule—that is partly necessary to meet the criterion of adequacy—as in the plurality of rules and subrules. While most federations impose limits on the borrowings of subgovernments, the EU is unique in the number of rules it imposes on member states and in the size of its rule book (Eyraud and Wu 2015).

At the same time, the incomplete authority is seen in the lingering doubts over the ability to effectively impose the discipline of agreed-on rules on recalcitrant member states.

In principle, the rules are enshrined in legal texts, which have to be enforced through a quasi-judicial approach, including with the possible use of financial sanctions. The legal apparatus has been strengthened in recent years as part of EU law, as well as by the Fiscal Compact, the intergovernmental agreement of quasi-constitutional provisions in national legislations.

Yet in practice, the implementation of the Stability and Growth Pact can be seen as closer to a political model of peer pressure. The decisions on fiscal policies essentially reflect a mix of circumstantial judgments and political compromises, far from the mechanical application of fixed norms. This system tends to foster a perception that the application of rules is exposed to a degree of arbitrariness or insufficient consistency of treatment. The perception is also there that the coercive means for enforcing the rules remain incomplete.

What is important to note is that the two issues of complexity and insufficient authority are truly two faces of a single problem. Any rules-based setting, however smart in design, requires an authoritative enforcer to provide firm guidance and ultimately to call the shots. However, if you suspect that you miss this authority, the temptation is to substitute with additional fine print in the contract. Rules are complemented by subrules and subprovisions to try to take into account all kinds of circumstances, in the hope of increasing predictability and preventing risks of abuse.

This lack of trust, together with incomplete consensus over proper design, seems to be the driving force behind the growing complexity of the EU fiscal framework. An added factor is the incremental nature of changes over the past twenty years (whereby secondary legislation is gradually made "fatter" while primary legislation, enshrined in the Maastricht Treaty, stays unchanged).

However, the "complete contract" approach is far from an ideal or even a viable setting. This is most easily seen by drawing a comparison with modern monetary policy settings.

Reconciling Credibility with Flexibility: The Need for "Institutions"
In the monetary sphere, a double move was apparent some time ago. First the focus was put on rules to address the inflation bias; then the emphasis moved on to institutions.

This occurred as it became clear that even though simple rules, such as the Taylor rule, could offer a reasonably sensible benchmark (other early rules, such as monetary aggregates, were soon dismissed as inadequate), they might not be adequate in each and every circumstance. Institutions, specifically an independent central bank with a clear mandate, have taken the upper role.

Such an arrangement has been understood as a superior way of marrying flexibility and credibility. And indeed, in the fiscal realm too, the case has recently been made by the president of the ECB that fiscal institutions may ultimately offer a superior alternative to fiscal rules when it comes to the EMU governance architecture.

There are two complementary reasons why an institutional center carrying more authority would be useful in the European fiscal framework (Draghi 2015):

- One, as laid out before, is to ensure the full enforcement of the fiscal agreements. The current enforcement gap is what explains the attraction of an authority with the legitimacy and accountability to transcend the national polities.

- The other reason is to allow a move from purely proscribing rules to a more prescriptive approach, where the case is positively made that the recommended policies are economically sound.

Recent initiatives taken by the European Commission have to be seen in this double light. We can see that in particular in the Communication over making the best use of flexibility within the Stability and Growth Pact that the new commission issued earlier this year (European Commission 2015).

From a political angle, the Communication might be seen as a small step toward a more authoritative center. This should be kept in proportion, of course: the European Commission's formal powers remain unchanged. And significant changes toward stronger European institutions would require deep legal (i.e., treaty) changes and more political appetite than is currently encountered in national capitals.

In terms of substance, the Communication takes a number of small steps while not amending the legal rules: it charts a clear differentiation of the fiscal stance according to sustainability risks and cyclical conditions in the preventive arm of the pact. It also makes uses of the existing flexibility to foster investment and structural reforms. This is important to provide incentives for growth-oriented policies, without which public finances cannot be sustained in the long run.

Conclusion

The need for stronger institutions comes from two separate angles in the EMU. One is the possibility of enforcing the common rules; the other is the ability to exert the necessary discretion to depart from the quantitative parameters enshrined in the rules under specific circumstances.

It should be clear from what I have said, however, that I see a complementary relationship between rules and institutions, not a relation of substitutes.

In this regard, the limits to comparing monetary and fiscal settings must also be acknowledged. The sustainability objective cannot be defined as clearly as an inflation mandate. And while the macroeconomic direction of fiscal policy, as opposed to its composition, is not necessarily more redistributive than interest rate policy, parliamentary control of the public finances has always been at the heart of democratic arrangements.

These reasons make it less likely that fiscal policy can be delegated in the same manner as monetary policy has been.

They also mean that pure discretion is less appealing in the fiscal realm, even within a sound institutional framework. Pure discretion, where the policy is determined from scratch at the beginning of each period, would impose too great a risk that the discipline objective would be overlooked in favor of short-term results.

By contrast, a fiscal rule that is referred to on a steady basis will help underwrite consistent policies, even if there is some freedom to depart from the rule on occasions.

In fact, once the proper institutional framework is in place, one would be in a better position to use economically sensible rules as a broad compass. The EU member states could keep it simple by limiting the agreed-upon code to one "rule of thumb" reconciling smartness and simplicity.

I have outlined such a possible robust rule (prescribing a proper idea of the fiscal effort against the two objectives of debt sustainability and cyclical stabilization). This would give a useful benchmark for assessing the fiscal policies and frame the recommendations, while leaving room for judgment in their application.

In a nutshell, a fruitful long-term approach would involve a framework in which a simple and smart rule acts as the basis and permanent anchor for authoritative discretionary policymaking.

Note

*I would like to thank Nicolas Carnot for his contribution in the preparation of this intervention.

References

Buti, Marco, and Nicolas Carnot. 2015. "What Is a Responsible Fiscal Policy Today for Europe?" *VoxEU,* Centre for Economic Policy and Research, February 24. http://www.voxeu.org/article/defining-responsible-fiscal-policy-europe.

Carnot, Nicolas. 2014. "Evaluating Fiscal Policy: A Rule of Thumb." European Commission, Economic Papers 526. EC, Directorate-General for Economic and Financial Affairs, August. http://ec.europa.eu/economy_finance/publications/economic_paper/2014/pdf/ecp526_en.pdf.

Draghi, Mario. 2014. "Unemployment in the Euro Area." Speech at the Annual Central Bank Symposium, Jackson Hole, WY, August 22. https://www.ecb.europa.eu/press/key/date/2014/html/sp140822.en.html.

Draghi, Mario. 2015. "Speech by the President at SZ Finance Day." Frankfurt am Main, March 16. https://www.ecb.europa.eu/press/key/date/2015/html/sp150316.en.html.

Eyraud, Luc, and Tao Wu. 2015. "Playing by the Rules: Reforming Fiscal Governance in Europe." IMF Working Paper WP/15/67. IMF, March. https://www.imf.org/external/pubs/ft/wp/2015/wp1567.pdf.

European Commission. 2015. "Making the Best Use of the Flexibility within the Existing Rules of the Stability and Growth Pact." Communication from the Commission to the European Parliament …, COM 2015(12), Strasbourg, January 13.

Fall, Falilou, Debra Bloch, Jean-Marc Fournier, and Peter Hoeller. 2015. "Prudent Debt Targets and Fiscal Frameworks." *OECD Economic Policy Papers* 15. OECD Publishing, July 1. http://www.oecd-ilibrary.org/docserver/download/5jrxtjmmt9f7.pdf?expires=1442697237&id=id&accname=guest&checksum=B02AC8EB1924F7E13D53FAADD2702BB1.

Kopits, George, and Steven A. Symansky. 1998. "Fiscal Policy Rules." IMF Occasional Paper 162. IMF, July 22.

Sargent, Thomas J., and Neil Wallace. 1981. "Some Unpleasant Monetarist Arithmetic." *Federal Reserve Bank of Minneapolis Quarterly Review* 5 (3): 1–19. https://www.minneapolisfed.org/research/qr/qr531.pdf.

20

On the Proper Size of the Public Sector and the Level of Public Debt in the Twenty-First Century

J. Bradford DeLong

Olivier Blanchard, when he parachuted me into the panel, asked me to "be provocative."

So let me provoke:

My assigned focus on "fiscal policy in the medium term" has implications. It requires me to assume that things are or will be true that are not now or may not be true in the future, at least not for the rest of this decade and into the next. It makes sense to distinguish the medium from the short term only if the North Atlantic economies will relatively soon enter a regime in which the economy is not at the zero lower bound on safe nominal interest rates. The medium term is at a horizon at which monetary policy can adequately handle all of the demand-stabilization role.

The focus on a medium run thus assumes that answers have been found and policies implemented for three of the most important macroeconomic questions facing us right now, here in the short run, today. Those three are:

- What role does fiscal policy have to play as a cyclical stabilization policy?
- What is the proper level of the inflation target so that open-market operation-driven normal monetary policy has sufficient purchase?
- Should truly extraordinary measures that could be classified as "social credit" policies—mixed monetary and fiscal expansion via direct assignment of seigniorage to households, money-financed government purchases, central bank–undertaken large-scale public lending programs, and other such—be on the table?

Those three are still the most urgent questions facing us today. But I will drop them, and leave them to others. I will presume that satisfactory answers have been found to them, and that they have thus been answered.

As I see it, there are three major medium-run questions that then remain, even further confining my scope to the North Atlantic alone, and to the major sovereigns of the North Atlantic. (Extending the focus to emerging markets, to the links between the North Atlantic and the rest of the world, and to Japan would raise additional important questions, which I would also drop on the floor.) These three remaining medium-run questions are:

- What is the proper size of the twenty-first-century public sector?
- What is the proper level of the twenty-first-century public debt for growth and prosperity?
- What are the systemic risks caused by government debt, and what adjustment to the proper level of twenty-first-century public debt is advisable because of systemic risk considerations?

To me, at least, the answer to the first question—what is the proper size of the twenty-first-century public sector?—appears very clear.

The optimal size of the twenty-first-century public sector will be significantly larger than the optimal size of the twentieth-century public sector. Changes in technology and social organization are moving us away from a "Smithian" economy, one in which the presumption is that the free market or the Pigovian-adjusted market does well, to one that requires more economic activity to be regulated by differently tuned social and economic arrangements (see DeLong and Froomkin 2000). One such is the government. Thus, there should be more public sector and less private sector in the twenty-first century than there was in the twentieth.

Similarly, the answer to the second question appears clear, to me at least.

The proper level of the twenty-first-century public debt should be significantly higher than typical debt levels we have seen in the twentieth century. Looking back at economic history reveals that it has been generations since the intertemporal budget constraint tightly bound peacetime or victorious reserve-currency-issuing sovereigns possessing exorbitant privilege (see DeLong 2014; Kogan et al. 2015).

Thus, at the margin, additional government debt has not required a greater primary surplus but rather has allowed a greater primary deficit—a consideration that strongly militates for higher debt levels *unless interest rates in the twenty-first century reverse the pattern we have seen in the twentieth century, and mount to levels greater than economic growth rates.*

This consideration is strengthened by observing that the North Atlantic economies have now moved into a regime in which the opposite has taken place. Real interest rates on government debt are not higher but even lower relative to growth rates than they were in the past century. Financial market participants now appear to expect this now ultra-low interest rate regime to continue indefinitely (see Summers 2014).

The answer to the third question—what are the systemic risks caused by government debt?—is much more murky.

To be clear: the point is not that additional government debt imposes an undue burden in the form of distortionary taxation and inequitable income distribution on the future. When current and projected interest rates are low, they do not do so. The point is not that additional government debt crowds out productive investment and slows growth. When interest rates are unresponsive or minimally responsive to deficits, they do not do so. Were either of those to fail to hold, we would have exited the current regime of ultra-low interest rates, and the answer to the second question immediately above would become different.

The question, instead, is this: in a world of low current and projected future interest rates—and thus also one in which interest rates are not responsive to deficits—without much expected crowding out or expected burdens on the future, what happens in the lower tail, and how should that lower tail move policies away from those optimal on certainty equivalence? And that question has four subquestions: How much more likely does higher debt make it that interest rates will spike in the absence of fundamental reasons? How much would they spike? What would government policy be in response to such a spike? And what would be the effect on the economy?

The answer thus hinges on:

- the risk of a large sudden upward shift in the willingness to hold government debt, even absent substantial fundamental news, and
- the ability of governments to deal with such a risk that threatens to push economies far enough up the Laffer curve to turn a sustainable into an unsustainable debt.

I believe the risk in such a panicked flight from an otherwise sustainable debt is small. I hold, along with Reinhart and Rogoff (2013), that the government's legal tools to finance its debt through financial repression are very powerful. Thus I think this consideration has little weight. I believe that little adjustment to one's view of the proper level of twenty-first-century public debt of *reserve-currency-issuing sovereigns with exorbitant privilege* is called for because of systemic risk considerations.

But my belief here is fragile. And my comprehension of the issues is inadequate.

Let me expand on these three answers.

The Proper Size of Twenty-First-Century Government

Suppose commodities produced and distributed are properly rival and excludible:

- Access to them needs to be cheaply and easily controlled.
- They need to be scarce.
- They need to be produced under roughly constant-returns-to-scale conditions.

Suppose, further, that information about what is being bought and sold is equally present on both sides of the marketplace—that is, limited adverse selection and moral hazard.

Suppose, last, that the distribution of wealth is such as to accord fairly with utility and desert.

If all these hold, then the competitive Smithian market has its standard powerful advantages. And so the role of the public sector should then be confined to:

1. antitrust policy, to reduce market power and microeconomic price and contract stickinesses,
2. demand-stabilization policy, to offset the macroeconomic damage caused by macroeconomic price and contract stickinesses,
3. financial regulation, to try to neutralize the effect on asset prices of the correlation of current wealth with biases toward optimism or pessimism, along with

4. largely fruitless public-sector attempts to deal with other behavioral economics-psychological market failures—envy, spite, myopia, salience, etc.

The problem, however, is that as we move into the twenty-first century, the commodities we will be producing are becoming:

- less rival,
- less excludible,
- more subject to adverse selection and moral hazard, and
- more subject to myopia and other behavioral-psychological market failures.

The twenty-first century sees more knowledge to be learned, and thus a greater role for education. If there is a single sector in which behavioral economics and adverse selection have major roles to play, it is education. Deciding to fund education through very long-term loan financing, and thus to leave the cost-benefit investment calculations to be undertaken by adolescents, shows every sign of having been a disaster when it has been tried (see Goldin and Katz 2009).

The twenty-first century will see longer life expectancy, and thus a greater role for pensions. Yet here in the United States the privatization of pensions via 401(k)s has been, in my assessment, an equally great disaster (Munnell 2015).

The twenty-first century will see health care spending as a share of total income cross 25 percent if not 33 percent, or even higher. The skewed distribution across potential patients of health care expenditures, the vulnerability of health insurance markets to adverse selection and moral hazard, and simple arithmetic mandate either that social insurance will have to cover a greater share of health care costs or that enormous utilitarian benefits from health care will be left on the sidewalk.

Moreover, the twenty-first century will see information goods a much larger part of the total pie than in the twentieth. And if we know one thing, it is that it is not efficient to try to provide information goods by means of a competitive market for they are neither rival nor excludible. It makes no microeconomic sense at all for services like those provided by Google to be funded and incentivized by how much money can be raised not fromthe value of the services but fromthe fumes rising from

Google's ability to sell the eyeballs of the users to advertisers as an intermediate good.

And then there are the standard public goods, like infrastructure and basic research.

Enough said.

The only major category of potential government spending that both should not—and to an important degree cannot—be provided by a competitive price-taking market, and that *might* be a smaller share of total income in the twenty-first century than it was in the twentieth? Defense.

We thus face a pronounced secular shift away from commodities that have the characteristics—rivalry, excludability, and enough repetition in purchasing and value of reputation to limit myopia—needed for the Smithian market to function well as a societal coordinating mechanism. This raises enormous problems: We know that as bad as market failures can be, government failures can often be little if any less immense.

We will badly need to develop new effective institutional forms for the twenty-first century.

But, meanwhile, it is clear that the increasing salience of these market failures has powerful implications for the relative sizes of the private market and the public administrative spheres in the twenty-first century. The decreasing salience of "Smithian" commodities in the twenty-first century means that rational governance would expect the private-market sphere to shrink relative to the public. This is very elementary micro- and behavioral economics. And we need to think hard about what its implications for public finance are.

The Proper Size of the Twenty-First-Century Public Debt

Back in the Clinton administration—back when the US government's debt really did look like it was on an unsustainable course—we noted that the correlation between shocks to US interest rates and the value of the dollar appeared to be shifting from positive to zero, and we were scared that the United States was alarmingly close to its debt capacity and needed major, radical policy changes to reduce the deficit (see Blinder and Yellen 2000).

Whether we were starting at shadows then, or whether we were right then and the world has changed since, or whether the current world is in an unstable configuration and we will return to normal within a decade is unclear to me.

But right now, financial markets are telling us very strange things about the debt capacity of reserve-currency-issuing sovereigns.

Since 2005, the interest rate on US ten-year Treasury bonds has fallen from roughly the growth rate of nominal GDP—5 percent/year—to 250 basis points below the growth rate of nominal GDP. Because the duration of the debt is short, the average interest rate on Treasury securities has gone from 100 basis points below the economy's trend growth rate to nearly 350 basis points below. Maybe you can convince yourself that the market expects the ten-year rate over the next generation to average 50 basis points higher than it is now. Maybe.

Taking a longer run view, Richard Kogan and co-workers (2015) of the Center on Budget and Policy Priorities have been cleaning the data from the Office of Management and Budget. Over the past two hundred years, for the United States, the government's borrowing rate has averaged 100 basis points lower than the economy's growth rate. Over the past one hundred years, 170 basis points lower. Over the past fifty years, 30 basis points lower. Over the past twenty years, the Treasury's borrowing rate

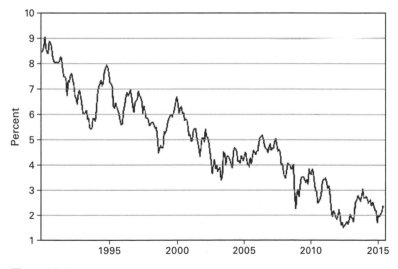

Figure 20.1
Ten-year Constant Maturity U.S. Treasury Nominal Rate. *Source: Federal Reserve Economic Data,* Federal Reserve Bank of St. Louis.

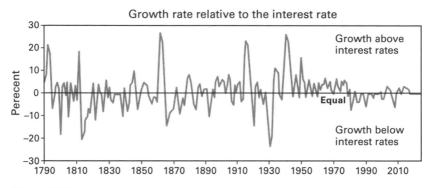

Figure 20.2
Economic Growth and Interest Rates Have Become More Closely Aligned. *Source*:
Center on Budget and Policy Priorities, CBPP.org.

has been on average greater than g by 20 basis points. And over the past ten years, it has been 70 basis points lower.

When we examine the public finance history of major North Atlantic industrial powers, we find that the last time that the average over any decade of government debt service as a percentage of outstanding principal was higher than the average growth rate of its economy was during the Great Depression. And before that, in1890.

Since then, over any extended time period for the major North Atlantic reserve-currency-issuing economies, $g > r$, for government debt.

Only those who see a very large and I believe exaggerated chance of global thermonuclear war or environmental collapse see the North Atlantic economies as dynamically inefficient from the standpoint of our past investments in private physical, knowledge, and organizational capital: $r > g$ by a very comfortable margin. Investments in wealth in the form of private capital are, comfortably, a cash flow source for savers.

But the fact that $g > r$ with respect to the investments we have made in our governments raises deep and troubling questions. Since 1890, a North Atlantic government that borrows more at the margin benefits its current citizens, increases economic growth, and increases the well-being of its bondholders (for they do buy the paper voluntarily): it is win-win-win.

That fact strongly suggests that North Atlantic economies throughout the entire twentieth century suffered from excessive accumulation of societal wealth in the form of net government capital—in other words, government debt has been too low.

The North Atlantic economies of major sovereigns throughout the entire twentieth century have thus suffered from a peculiar and particular form of dynamic inefficiency. Over the past one hundred years, in the United States, at the margin, each extra stock 10 percent of annual GDP's worth of debt has provided a flow of 0.1 percent of GDP of services to taxpayers, either in increased primary expenditures, reduced taxes, or both.

What is the elementary macroeconomics of dynamic inefficiency? If a class of investment—in this case, investment by taxpayers in the form of wealth held by the government through amortizing the debt—is dynamically inefficient, do less of it. Do less of it until you get to the Golden Rule, and do even less if you are impatient. How do taxpayers move away from dynamic inefficiency toward the Golden Rule? By not amortizing the debt, but rather by borrowing more.

Now we resist this logic. I resist this logic.

Debt secured by government-held social wealth ought to be a close substitute in investors' portfolios with debt secured by private capital formation. So it is difficult to understand how economies can be dynamically efficient with respect to private capital and yet "dynamically inefficient" with respect to government-held societal wealth. But it appears to be the case that it is so.

But there is this outsized risk premium, outsized equity and low-quality debt premium, outsized wedge. And that means that while investments in wealth in the form of private capital are a dynamically efficient cash flow source for savers, investments by taxpayers in the form of paying down debt are a cash flow sink.

I tend to say that we have a huge underlying market failure here that we see in the form of the equity return premium—a failure of financial markets to mobilize society's risk-bearing capacity—and that pushes down the value of risky investments and pushes up the value of assets perceived as safe, in this case the debt of sovereigns possessing exorbitant privilege. But how do we fix this risk-bearing capacity mobilization market failure? And isn't the point of the market economy to make things that are valuable? And isn't the debt of reserve-currency-issuing sovereigns an extraordinarily valuable thing that is very cheap to make? So shouldn't we be making more of it? Looking out the yield curve, such government debt looks to be incredibly valuable for the next half century, at least.

These considerations militate strongly for higher public debts in the twenty-first century then we saw in the twentieth century. Investors want to hold more government debt: the extraordinary prices at which it has sold since 1890 tell us that. Market economies are supposed to be in the business of producing things that households want whenever that can be done cheaply. Government debt fits the bill, especially now. And looking out the yield curve, government debt looks to fit the bill for the next half century at least.

Systemic Risks and Public Debt Accumulation

One very important question remains very live: Would levels of government debt issue large enough to drive $r > g$ for government bonds create significant systemic risks? Yes, the prices of the government debt of major North Atlantic industrial economies are very high now. But what if there is a sudden downward shock to the willingness of investors to hold this debt? What if the next generation born and coming to the market is much more impatient? Governments might then have to roll over their debt on terms that require high debt-amortization taxes, and if the debt is high enough, those taxes could push economies far enough up a debt Laffer curve. That might render the debt unsustainable in the aftermath of such a preference shift.

Two considerations make me think that this is a relatively small danger.

First, when I look back in history, I cannot see any such strong fundamental news-free negative preference shock to the willingness to hold the government debt of the North Atlantic's major industrial powers since the advent of parliamentary government. The fiscal crises we see—of the Weimar Republic, Louis XIV Bourbon, Charles II Stuart, Felipe IV Habsburg, and so forth—were all driven by fundamental news.

Second, as Reinhart and Rogoff (2013) have pointed out at substantial length, twentieth- and nineteenth-century North Atlantic governments proved able to tax their financial sectors through financial repression with great ease. The amount of real wealth for debt amortization raised by financial repression scales roughly with the value of outstanding government debt. And such taxes are painful for those taxed. But only when even semi-major industrial countries have allowed large-scale borrowing in potentially harder currencies than their own—and thus have written unhedged puts on their currencies in large volume—is there any substantial likelihood of major additional difficulty or disruption.

Now, Kenneth Rogoff (2015) disagrees with drawing this lesson from Reinhart and Rogoff (2013). And one always disagrees analytically with Kenneth Rogoff at one's great intellectual peril. He sees the profoundly depressed level of interest rates on the debt of major North Atlantic sovereigns as a temporary and disequilibrium phenomenon that will soon be rectified. He believes that excessive debt issue and overleverage are at the roots of our problems—call it secular stagnation, the global savings glut, the safe asset shortage, the balance sheet recession, whatever.

In Rogoff's view:

> Unlike secular stagnation, a debt supercycle is not forever.... Modern macroeconomics has been slow to get to grips with the analytics of how to incorporate debt supercycles.... There has been far too much focus on orthodox policy responses and not enough on heterodox responses.... In a world where regulation has sharply curtailed access for many smaller and riskier borrowers, low sovereign bond yields do not necessarily capture the broader "credit surface" the global economy faces.... The elevated credit surface is partly due to inherent riskiness and slow growth in the post-Crisis economy, but policy has also played a large role.

The key here is Rogoff's assertion that the low borrowing rate faced by major North Atlantic sovereigns "do[es] not necessarily capture the broader 'credit surface'"—that the proper shadow price of government debt issue is far in excess of the sovereign borrowing rate. Why? Apparently because future states of the world in which private bondholders would default are also those in which it would be very costly in social utility terms for the government to raise money through taxes.

I do not see this. A major North Atlantic sovereign's potential tax base is immensely wide and deep. The instruments at its disposal to raise revenue are varied and powerful. The correlation between the government's taxing capacity and the operating cash flow of private borrowers is not that high. A shock like that of 2008–2009 temporarily destroyed the American corporate sector's ability to generate operating cash flows to repay debt at the same time that it greatly raised the cost of rolling over debt. But the US government's financial opportunities became much more favorable during that episode.

Moreover, Rogoff also says:

> When it comes to government spending that productively and efficiently enhances future growth, the differences are not first order. With low real interest rates,

and large numbers of unemployed (or underemployed) construction workers, good infrastructure projects should offer a much higher rate of return than usual.

and thus with sensible financing and recapture of the economic benefits of government spending, have little or no impact on debt-to-income ratios.

Conclusion

Looking forward, I draw the following conclusions:

1.   North Atlantic public sectors for major sovereigns ought, technocrat-ically, to be larger than they have been in the past century.
2.   North Atlantic relative public debt levels for major sovereigns ought, technocratically, to be higher than they have been in the past century.
3.   With prudent regulation—that is, the effective limitation of the bank-ing sector's ability to write unhedged puts on the currency—the power major sovereigns possess to tax the financial sector through financial repression provides sufficient insurance against an adverse preference shock to the desire for government debt.

The first two of these conclusions appear to me to be close to rock-solid. The third is, I think, considerably less secure.

Nevertheless, in my view, if the argument against a larger public sector and more public debt in the twenty-first century than in the twentieth for major North Atlantic sovereigns is going to be made successfully, it seems to me that it needs to be made on a political-economy government-failure basis.

The argument needs to be not that larger government spending and a higher government debt issued by a functional government would dimin-ish utility but rather that government itself will be highly dysfunctional.

Government needs to be viewed not as one of several instrumentalities we possess and can deploy to manage and coordinate our societal divi-sion of labor but rather as the equivalent of a loss-making industry under really existing socialism. Government spending must be viewed as worse than useless. Therefore relaxing any constraints that limit the size of the government needs to be viewed as an evil.

Now the public choice school has gone there. As Lawrence Summers (2011) said, they have taken the insights on government failure and "driven it relentlessly towards nihilism in a way that isn't actually helpful for those charged with designing regulatory institutions," or, indeed, making public policy in general. In my opinion, if this argument is to be made, it needs a helpful public choice foundation before it can be properly built.

References

Blinder, Alan, and Janet Yellen. 2000. *The Fabulous Decade: Macroeconomic Lessons from the 1990s*. New York: Century Foundation.

DeLong, J. Bradford. 2014. "Notes on Fiscal Policy in a Depressed Interest-Rate Environment." Faculty blog, Department of Economics, University of California, Berkeley, March 16. http://delong.typepad.com/delong_long_form/2014/03/talk-preliminary-notes-on-fiscal-policy-in-a-depressed-interest-rate-environment-the-honest-broker-for-the-week-of-february.html.

DeLong, J. Bradford, and A. Michael Froomkin. 2000. "Speculative Microeconomics for Tomorrow's Economy." *First Monday* 5 (2), February 7. http://firstmonday.org/ojs/index.php/fm/article/view/726.

Goldin, Claudia, and Lawrence Katz. 2009. *The Race between Education and Technology*. Cambridge, MA: Harvard University Press.

Kogan, Richard, Chad Stone, Bryann Dasilva, and Jan Rezeski. 2015. "Difference between Economic Growth Rates and Treasury Interest Rates Significantly Affects Long-Term Budget Outlook." Washington, DC: Center on Budget and Policy Priorities, February 27. http://www.cbpp.org/research/federal-budget/difference-between-economic-growth-rates-and-treasury-interest-rates.

Munnell, Alicia. 2015. "Falling Short: The Coming Retirement Crisis and What to Do About It." Brief 15-7. Center for Retirement and Research, Boston College, April. http://crr.bc.edu/briefs/falling-short-the-coming-retirement-crisis-and-what-to-do-about-it-2.

Reinhart, Carmen M., and Kenneth S. Rogoff. 2013. "Financial and Sovereign Debt Crises: Some Lessons Learned and Those Forgotten." Working Paper 266. IMF, Washington, DC, December 24. https://www.imf.org/external/pubs/cat/longres.aspx?sk=41173.0.

Rogoff, Kenneth. 2015. "Debt Supercycle, Not Secular Stagnation." *VoxEU*. Centre for Economic Policy and Research, April 22. http://www.voxeu.org/article/debt-supercycle-not-secular-stagnation.

Summers, Lawrence. 2011. "A Conversation on New Economic Thinking." LarrySummers.com, April 8. http://larrysummers.com/commentary/speeches/brenton-woods-speech.

Summers, Lawrence. 2014. "U.S. Economic Prospects: Secular Stagnation, Hysteresis, and the Zero Lower Bound." *Business Economics* 49 (2): 65–73.

Capital Flows, Exchange Rate Management, and Capital Controls

21

Floating Exchange Rates, Self-Oriented Policies, and Limits to Economic Integration

Maurice Obstfeld

I will frame my discussion by asking a time-honored question: Are floating exchange rates working? My answer is a qualified yes.

Over the past twenty years, many emerging market economies (EMEs) moved to more flexible exchange rate regimes. These have been widely credited with helping them navigate the 2008–2009 crisis. But the system comes under stress when exchange rates move sharply, especially in a context, such as the period since the summer, when projected turning points in monetary policy and growth drive sudden large exchange-rate readjustments. Those movements are driven by portfolio shifts in international financial markets that have become more extensive and interconnected than ever before in history.

None of this is totally new. The 1980s, for example, featured big swings in the dollar that culminated both in a failed attempt to implement "target zones" for major exchange rates (the Louvre Accord) and the US Omnibus Trade Bill of 1988, from which the annual US Treasury report on foreign exchange is inherited. Past decades also saw multiple episodes of monetary policy transmission, leading to large capital inflows and sometimes to sharp reversals in the form of crises.

When Milton Friedman and Harry Johnson famously argued their cases for floating exchange rates in the 1950s and 1960s, they saw governments' attempts to maintain disequilibrium fixed parities as sources of official restrictions both on international trade and on international capital movements. To some extent, they initially appeared right, in that floating rates promoted international financial liberalization while allowing a continuing expansion of world trade, as well as greater production efficiency through the development of more finely articulated international supply chains.

But the very success of floating rates in promoting expanded real and especially financial integration has increased the scope for international macroeconomic and financial spillovers, thereby spurring a contrary dynamic in the form of political or economic arguments to reintroduce elements of market segmentation in several dimensions.

In the trade dimension, talk of "currency wars" in the immediate post-crisis years exemplified the political limits of domestic stimulus measures that sharply appreciate foreign countries' currencies; in some countries the response was to limit capital inflows. Currently the shoe is on the other foot, and the erstwhile alleged currency aggressor, the United States, faces depreciating foreign currencies, including the euro. The result is more serious support for bills in both houses of the US Congress to discipline foreign currency undervaluation or manipulation through automatic sanctions, for example, countervailing duties. Such measures raise the real risk of retaliation by US trading partners and a subsequent disruption of the multilateral global trading system. Unilateral currency sanctions could be open to challenge in the WTO, while WTO decisions reversing national legislative actions could themselves be even more broadly destabilizing.

With the demise of the Bretton Woods system and the adoption of floating exchange rates, countries made a decisive move toward sovereignty over monetary policy. However, the strength of the spillovers from those sovereign policies to other economies was hardly recognized at the time. Countries have been willing to give up some sovereignty through the WTO process because trade policy instruments are comparatively easy to identify and the gains from coordinated agreement to forgo their use are so clear-cut. Countries may also welcome a "commitment mechanism" that helps them withstand political pressure from vested trade interests. This is all less so in the area of monetary policy—countries simply will not commit to constraining their monetary policy tools, even if all other countries make similar commitments, because those tools are too central to macroeconomic stability and growth, and past experience with exchange rate commitments (as under the gold standard) has, on the whole, not been favorable.

At the same time, the potential for competitive currency practices has long been recognized, and avoiding them has been one of the goals of the IMF as well as the G-7 and G-20 processes. Those processes have made gradual progress, but evidently not rapidly enough to head off domestic political reactions when exchange rates move strongly and abruptly. Are those reactions something the system must simply continue to live with? Or is there any scope for a more robust multilateral approach that would command a widespread perception of legitimacy among domestic electorates? Of course, another goal of the IMF and G-20 is to maintain internationally balanced growth and economically justifiable payments patterns, which themselves would help contain big exchange rate movements. But divergences in national performance are bound to arise despite the best efforts. So, somehow finding ways to strengthen the multilateral approach to exchange rate and macroeconomic surveillance will have to remain high on the agenda.

Another area of serious policy spillovers, not envisaged in the debates of the first two postwar decades, is through interest rates, balance sheets, and capital flows. Long-term nominal interest rates are now tightly linked across major economies, and liquidity conditions in major economies spill over to EMEs through multiple channels.[1] Indeed, some go so far as to argue that this international transmission process must inevitably overwhelm domestic policy measures in EM countries, notwithstanding the nature of the exchange rate regime.[2] There certainly is strong evidence of a global financial cycle—such as the one that drove global credit expansion and housing appreciation in the run-up to the global financial crisis.

EM countries awash with global credit are advised to let their currencies appreciate, but this can be painful, just as it can be for advanced economies, but probably more so for countries whose firms lack the market power of larger firms in highly developed economies. Moreover, even appreciation does not insulate the financial sector completely, for example, from the easing of quantitative credit constraints and from balance sheet effects. Thus, liquidity conditions abroad may still be transmitted, potentially fueling bubbles and excessive credit growth—and these effects are stronger if the recipient central bank intervenes (as it typically will) to dampen appreciation, and cannot fully sterilize the resulting monetary effects. On the other hand, depreciation in the face of potential financial outflows could be perilous if there are foreign currency liabilities, either onshore or (as the Bank for International Settlements has warned) on the books of offshore corporates.

These dilemmas—and especially the well-founded concern that capital inflows can lead to financial stability problems if the resulting domestic credit is not channeled efficiently—have led to a second-best argument for capital controls: macroprudential policy is preferred in principle, but if it cannot be deployed effectively (and frankly, we have little practical idea how to do that beyond housing market interventions, nor is the evidence on what actually works very strong), capital inflow control may be next best. In the current environment of US interest rates being prepared for liftoff, capital *outflow* controls may next receive more attention, even though they seem much harder to make effective. The hope has been that adequate *inflow* controls may reduce the volume of footloose capital seeking an exit when economic conditions turn, thereby reducing the desire for *outflow* controls. But theoretical justifications for capital controls—for example, the paper by Farhi and Werning given at the IMF's 2013 Annual Research Conference—tend to ignore enforcement issues and yield symmetric prescriptions about inflow and outflow controls.[3]

A persuasive argument for some form of segmentation between domestic and international capital markets is that national sovereignty over financial stability policy makes macroprudential policy much harder, if not impossible, to execute with fully open capital markets. This is the "financial trilemma" argument that has been elaborated by Schoenmaker (2013). According to the financial trilemma, countries cannot simultaneous enjoy all three of:

1. internationally open financial markets,
2. national sovereignty over financial policy, and
3. financial stability.

For example, nationalistically motivated decisions about supervision or resolution are likely to take inadequate account of repercussions abroad, thereby weakening resilience of the entire interconnected global financial system. Domestic surveillance and regulation stricter than what prevails abroad could draw in foreign intermediaries able to circumvent local rules. These types of problem became painfully obvious in the euro area in the early part of this decade, and have motivated the drive toward banking union in the EU—embodying a sacrifice of national sovereignty in the financial policy sphere—but the general issue extends even to financially linked economies that do not have a common currency.

Therefore, despite floating exchange rates—indeed, coincident with floating and the expanding international capital market that floating encouraged—central bankers in the richer countries recognized the growing importance of financial spillovers and initiated the Basel process of international coordination in 1974. This forum for information exchange and regulatory best practice has grown to encompass many countries and is one of the most shining examples of successful international policy coordination. It recognizes the severe limitations of nationally oriented financial policies in an era of globalized capital markets, but it still does not solve all problems, for example those in the sphere of bank resolution of global systemically important financial institutions, or the possible inability of countries to make macroprudential levers effective when substantial credit originates abroad. This has led regulators in several countries to ring-fence, as exemplified by the US Federal Reserve's requirement that foreign banking organizations with US nonbranch assets above $50 billion set up holding companies subject to Fed regulation.[4]

Is ring-fencing a capital control or a macroprudential measure? Arguably it is the latter, when there is no discrimination in the treatment of domestic and foreign residents. On the other hand, such rules segment international capital markets—they can impede the free flow of liquidity among components of a banking organization located in multiple jurisdictions—thereby potentially sacrificing some efficiencies and synergies by segmenting the banking firm's internal capital market.[5] Those synergies, however, come partly at the expense of hidden social costs to the financial stability of host, and indeed parent, countries, and some ring-fencing strikes me as a worthwhile price to pay. But it does represent a departure from the state of unfettered mobility of financial resources that would maximize banking profits. I would argue that this is very much in line with Schoenmaker's financial trilemma.

In cases where actual capital controls are needed, perhaps because of nonbank channels of intermediation and a weaker regulatory infrastructure, there probably still need to be international rules of the road on their deployment, to discourage financial protectionism, to limit externalities for other countries, and to prevent the use of controls in currency manipulation. This is yet one more coordination challenge for today's floating exchange rate system. To invoke the old Churchillian cliché, the system certainly has problem areas where reform is needed, but it still appears to be the best possible arrangement in a world of sovereign actors and largely free global trade in goods and assets.

Notes

1. For example, see Blanchard, Furceri, and Pescatori (2014) and Obstfeld (2015).
2. See, for example, Rey (2013).
3. See Farhi and Werning (2014).
4. See Tarullo (2014).
5. See Goldberg and Cetorelli (2011).

References

Blanchard, Olivier J., Davide Furceri, and Andrea Pescatori. 2014. "A Prolonged Period of Low Real Interest Rates?" In *Secular Stagnation: Facts, Causes and Cures*, ed. Coen Teulings and Richard Baldwin. London: CEPR Press.

Farhi, Emmanuel, and Iván Werning. 2014. "Dilemma Not Trilemma? Capital Controls and Exchange Rates with Volatile Capital Flows." *IMF Economic Review* 62 (4): 569–605.

Goldberg, Linda S., and Nicola Cetorelli. 2011. "Global Banks and International Shock Transmission: Evidence from the Crisis." *IMF Economic Review* 59 (1): 41–76.

Obstfeld, Maurice. 2015. "Trilemmas and Tradeoffs: Living with Financial Globalization." In *Global Liquidity, Spillovers in Emerging Markets and Policy Responses*, ed. Claudio Raddatz, Diego Saravia and Jaume Ventura. Santiago: Central Bank of Chile.

Rey, Hélène. 2013. "Dilemma Not Trilemma: The Global Financial Cycle and Monetary Policy Independence." In *Proceedings, 2013 Economic Policy Symposium: Global Dimensions of Unconventional Monetary Policy*, 285–333. Jackson Hole, WY. Federal Reserve Bank of Kansas City.

Schoenmaker, Dirk. 2013. *Governance of International Banking: The Financial Trilemma*. London: Oxford University Press.

Tarullo, Daniel K. 2014. "Regulating Large Foreign Banking Organizations." Speech at the Harvard Law School Symposium, "Building the Financial System of the Twenty-First Century: An Agenda for Europe and the United States," Armonk, NY, March 27.

22

Some Lessons of the Global Financial Crisis from an EME and a Brazilian Perspective

Luiz Awazu Pereira da Silva

Introduction: Progress and Conundrums after the Global Financial Crisis

I would like to give an emerging market economy (EME) perspective for this session on capital flows, exchange rate management, and capital controls, or, to use current terminology, capital flow management.[1] I don't want to oversimplify, but let me suggest that, for many of us, the global financial crisis incited feelings of déjà vu: what was happening with the advanced economies was very much what we had experienced and learned about large debt-financial crises, putting aside size and scope.

From this angle, I see some progress in many ways. The global financial crisis had a lax regulatory component at its origin,[2] which we in EMEs were quite familiar with from our past experiences with bad origination, high debt, and currency mismatches. To some extent the crisis validated many aspects of the pragmatic policy framework that EMEs in general and Brazil in particular had been using to ensure macroeconomic and financial stability in our countries. This framework allowed us to conduct monetary policy with independence even in an increasingly financially globalized and interdependent world. The crisis also showed the importance of quickly unleashing countercyclical policies to respond to a severe collapse in confidence, using extreme, though necessary, versions of highly expansionary policies (e.g., including fiscal and unconventional monetary policy [UMP] actions). In EMEs in particular, we knew that too, and for the first time we had some (fiscal and monetary) room to join the collective G-20 countercyclical effort. And we also understood how to pragmatically manage the spillover effects of UMP while maintaining our macrofinancial frameworks (through an inflation-targeting and flexible exchange rate regime) and preserving our stability.

Having said that, I do not necessarily see confusion but conundrums. Why did such massive stimuli deliver so little growth in advanced economies? Why are we debating whether we are just on a "plateau," waiting for a new growth cycle, or are in in a "secular stagnation" desert? Did we underestimate (1) the "balance sheet" effect of a high-debt crisis, with its effect of weakening both credit multipliers and financial accelerators; (2) the political economy, which can complicate (to say the least) any coordination between monetary and fiscal policies; (3) a "structural change" in labor markets, which affects traditional Phillips curves; or (4) changes in the postcrisis value of key parameters of central bank reaction functions, such as the nonaccelerating inflation rate of employment and the neutral interest rate?

I do not try to solve these puzzles and will concentrate my remarks on lessons to be drawn from the crisis from an EME and more specifically Brazilian perspective for capital flows, exchange rate management, and capital flow management. I will deal essentially with how we developed a pragmatic policy framework to address sudden stops and sudden floods of foreign capital while maintaining an independent monetary policy aimed at macro and financial stability.

How Did EMEs End Up with a Pragmatic Policy Framework? Learning from Our Typical Crises of the 1990s

The global financial crisis exhibited many familiar analytical features for EMEs and for Brazil in particular, because of our currency-financial crises of the 1990s. These crises spawned a large body of literature that pointed regularly to a perennial problem of policy inconsistency. In many cases, the local political economy leaned toward macropopulist policies[3] that expanded domestic absorption to unsustainable levels in order to grow faster or accommodate conflicting demands over the budget and resources in general. Whether the component of aggregate demand driving the excess was consumption (Latin America) or investment (Asia), both cases ended in a debt crisis, a banking crisis, a currency crisis, and high or even hyperinflation. The severity of the ensuing crisis naturally depended on other features, such as fiscal profligacy, financial fragility, available reserves vis-à-vis forex liabilities under the chosen exchange rate regime, and other institutional characteristics, such as various forms of indexation, monetization of deficits, and different ways of conducting monetary policy. Despite significant differences between emerging and advanced economies in governance, institutions and income per capita, from a macroeconomic perspective there are some resemblances (e.g., financial exuberance and intra-euro-zone bank credit flows in the wake of interest rate convergence, neglect of self-imposed fiscal thresholds and debt ceilings, quasi-fiscal guarantees for the housing sector to enhance social inclusion).

In the case of EMEs, naturally the first step after the 1990 crises was to limit fiscal and parafiscal excesses, especially in countries with several layers of government (and thus of debt). That step implied, first, prohibiting monetization of deficits, privatizing, and relying on rules (of law) and less on discretion. In parallel, monetary policy lessons were learned,[4] and most EMEs moved their policy frameworks from money targeting to exchange rate targeting and then to inflation targeting. An important part of the lesson was also to understand the macrofinancial dangers of destabilizing external shocks for fixed or even pegged exchange rate arrangements for EMEs and progressively adopting a flexible exchange rate regime.[5] That went, pari passu, with understanding that capital flows to EMEs are essentially procyclical, and therefore that prevention is better than cure: to avoid the typical confidence-crisis triggering à la Calvo "sudden stops,"[6] we came to the logical conclusion that we needed stronger fundamentals, sound macrofinancial policies, and buffers of self-insurance to pursue our own development strategies in a stable and sustainable way if we wanted to make good use of foreign savings. Naturally, in some EMEs, there were various idiosyncratic contributing factors, some related to the significant improvement in our terms of trade owing to the commodity supercycle. That allowed some EMEs (Brazil is a case in point) to accumulate reserves, become net creditors, and significantly reduce their risk premia to the point of becoming investment grade and a destination of sizable portfolio and direct investment flows.

But when facing distrust and crisis, many EMEs came out of these episodes with a sobering and pragmatic way to face the challenges of the new global world or, in other words, to "manage the impossible trinity." In essence, the pragmatic option was to: adopt a floating exchange rate

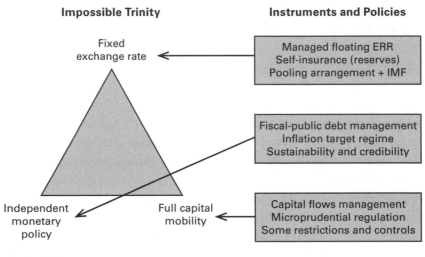

Figure 22.1
The Impossible Trinity, and Instruments and Policies to Manage It.

as a first line of defense against external shocks; to keep debt, especially public debt, within reasonable limits—if possible—through legal explicit rules; and to control inflation by implementing a credible monetary rule, in many cases using an inflation-targeting framework. The "pragmatism" consisted in building (some) self-insurance and/or using multilateral liquidity when need be, and, if foreign exchange global markets were excessively jittery, to smooth volatility in local foreign exchange markets. The combination of these textbook plus pragmatic policies and regimes proved adequate to build policy credibility and maintain fiscal and external sustainability.

Why, Like Almost Everybody Else, Did We Underestimate the Gobal Financial Crisis? What Have We Learned from It?

Well, we underestimated because the gray area in this pragmatic framework was how to combine financial stability with the "divine coincidence" of output-price stability.

It was assumed that, as a complement to using the pragmatic framework outlined above, using a set of microprudential regulations, that is, rules that would apply to each individual financial institution, would enable the financial system as a whole to remain stable. Under average financial conditions that might have been true. Another way to explain this underestimation of systemic financial risk is to remember the benign neglect with which we brushed aside some precrisis warning signals of trouble (e.g., "global imbalances," "irrational exuberance," "asset-price booms," etc.).

In any event, major novelties emerged in the last couple of decades that had positive and negative (risky) aspects for exacerbating financial cycles:[7] (1) the financial system became larger in size, much more global and interconnected; (2) financial globalization spread and, while allowing larger local imbalances to get financing globally, it also made it possible to accept pusillanimous attitudes toward debt ("this time [seems always] different" but never is);[8] (3) financial innovation improved risk metrics, created new products, and facilitated financial outreach, but it also allowed more opacity to grow unnoticed in large, interconnected balance sheets of globalized, too-big-to-fail financial institutions; and (4) prolonged periods of very low short-term interest rates and very moderate inflation seemed to confirm our full control of the business cycle but also enticed to take more risk with more leverage and less capital.

In a nutshell, the global financial crisis left all of us with the following questions or lessons:

1. Financial regulation and supervision cannot simply focus on individual firms' conduct and risk and need to adopt a macroprudential perspective to identify weaknesses in the financial system as a whole and mitigate systemic risk.

2. Low and stable inflation does not, by itself, guarantee financial stability. The logical next question is whether central banks need to rethink their role in preventing the buildup of systemic risk and financial imbalances.

3. If central banks do need to rethink their role, should monetary policy respond to (some measure of) financial (in)stability; should we revisit the (old) debate of "leaning against" the financial cycle versus "cleaning up after" asset bubbles burst, and what metric of financial (in)stability should be considered an early warning indicator (e.g., asset prices)?

The postcrisis reflection[9] seems to go in the direction of a "new normal" and another "pragmatic" framework: in order to address macro and financial stability objectives, monetary and macroprudential policy are independent, but can act in a complementary, coordinated way with their respective instruments to achieve price and financial stability. Although a kind of "divine coincidence II" between macro and financial stability objectives does not seem to exist, under a "new normal" regime, either a single unified authority or two different authorities can act, effectively combining demand management policies with macro- or microprudential tools to achieve macrofinancial stability.

In particular, the G-20, the Financial Stability Board (FSB), and the Bank for International Settlements (BIS) made a significant effort to address the excessive procyclicality of bank lending behavior that tends to exacerbate exuberance. This effort led to the idea and implementation of countercyclical regulatory instruments (e.g., countercyclical capital requirements, maximum leverage ratio, minimum liquidity requirements, and more stable medium-term funding ratios) that would prevent or limit global/local financial cycles by making procyclical behavior more costly, owing to the need to raise more capital or to keep more liquid assets on balance sheets, or both.[10]

How EMEs Enhanced Their Pragmatic Policy Framework with Macroprudential Tools: The Brazilian Experience

Therefore, in addition to the behavior of bank lending in general, for EMEs the global financial crisis did pose specific and more complex issues of macrofinancial stability. We were used to managing an "old normal" of "sudden stops" of capital flows. Now we had to learn how to maintain macrofinancial stability under a "new normal" situation of sudden floods of capital flows. In other words, we needed to learn how to avoid the transmission of external exuberance into our local asset and credit markets by combining monetary policy and macroprudential tools and using, when needed, capital flow management instruments?

Indeed, depending on the nature of shocks, the scope for using monetary policy may be limited, with the additional "pulling effect" of monetary policy in the case of sudden floods of capital. That might represent a serious issue for EMEs as these flows are often a cause of macroeconomic and financial instability.[11]

The problem is not capital flows per se, it is their volume and intensity. When volume and intensity are too much, they can lead to excessive credit expansion, lower quality of credit origination, increased financial system exposure to exchange rate risk, asset price distortions (including excessive exchange rate appreciation), and even inflationary pressures (if the inflationary effects from the boom in aggregate demand surpass the opposite effect stemming from exchange rate appreciation). Easy global money can boost domestic demand in whatever policy stance the economy might need to be; it amplifies expansion beyond what you might desire; you might have then to slow down expansion sooner than envisaged; the "party gets too wild too soon." And when you get this "feeling good" mind-set, it complicates even further your domestic political economy (sometimes already complex even without easy money); that means it hampers your capacity to slow down the party with policy instruments that depend on political cycles; this is for all countries, advanced and emerging economies alike. Then, if you tighten monetary policy, it might exacerbate short-term inflows and compound potentially destabilizing forces in domestic asset markets.[12] It is a threat to financial stability; and in particular, the collateral effects of UMP in EMEs was real exchange rate appreciation, a widening of current account deficits, a more rapid credit and monetary expansion, and asset-price pressures, as occurred, for example, in Brazil.[13]

The Brazilian experience might be useful to illustrate how we enhanced our pragmatic policy framework by means of the following measures: (1) keeping an independent monetary policy and acting accordingly to address domestic inflationary pressure; (2) strengthening the robustness of our financial system, that is, making sure it was well capitalized, liquid, and well provisioned; (3) using macroprudential tools to avoid excessive domestic credit growth; (4) using foreign exchange interventions to smooth volatility and provide a foreign exchange hedge to our domestic firms; and (5) now that we approach the full exiting of UMP (with the prospects of a forthcoming rate rise in the United States), strengthening our policies to sail through this last phase of the crisis.

During the phase of large inflows in 2011–2012, corresponding to the beginning of the Federal Reserve's asset-purchase programs or quantitative easing (QE) in the United States[14] and massive capital inflows into Brazil, we used a combination of monetary policy and macroprudential tools to tighten capital rules. These measures aimed at calibrating consumer credit growth (e.g., asking for more capital for some consumer loans, lowering loan-to-value ratios, and hiking reserve requirements).

Hence, our large capital inflows were "managed" through price (dis) incentives and not through typical quantitative controls. It remains, however, an important policy issue for both emerging and advanced economies whether periods of excessive inflows need to be addressed by a combination of monetary, fiscal, and capital flow management policies. As mentioned earlier, in building the European monetary union, perhaps massive intra-euro-zone bank credit flows into peripheral European countries could have been moderated by applying capital flow management instruments and macroprudential tools, given that after the euro, monetary policy was unavailable at the country level, and the fiscal position of some countries was already prudent. It remains to be seen whether it would have produced less debt and avoided the crisis at all. In any event, in Brazil, we also enhanced the monitoring of household indebtedness and raised reserve requirements to reduce excessive bank exposures in foreign exchange. These rules were eventually relaxed when we had to turn to the next phase of the global financial crisis.

The next phase began when the Fed started communicating in May 2013 that it could start moderating its assets repurchase program. Global financial markets became more volatile, and there was a repricing of risks, sometimes leading to a sell-off of EM assets. As usual, market perceptions of EMEs seemed to have shifted more than fundamentals might have warranted: the optimistic view of the immediate postcrisis rebound was replaced by a gloomy pessimism. However, by the end of 2013, and since then, the tapering took place and there was a significant improvement in sentiment and more cautious and detailed communication, including about the next logical steps by the Fed, which would be the timing of the beginning of rate movements. There too, the general sense is that the full exit from UMP with a rate increase, at the appropriate time, is a welcome transition to a more normal global monetary policy condition. Since that would be a result of economic recovery in the world's largest economy, it shall be a net positive for EMEs, which will benefit, including through global trade.

In Brazil, in addition to our experience with sudden stops, sudden floods, and improved fundamentals, we prepared ourselves for this transition. In particular, we designed and implemented a foreign exchange intervention program to provide timely and ample hedge to mitigate financial risks arising from monetary policy normalization in the United States.

The program was adopted in August 2013 and functions essentially by selling currency-derivative swaps that are settled in domestic currency.[15] It was last renewed in December 2014 until March 31, 2015, when it was not extended. However, all swaps expiring after May 1, 2015, will be rolled over. The program was successful in preserving financial stability by providing a foreign exchange hedge to private agents. Approximately 80 percent of the stock of swaps is allocated in nonfinancial companies. The total amount supplied by April 2015, approximately the equivalent of US $114 billion, corresponded to about 30 percent of our foreign exchange reserves.

Finally, we are now entering the (hopefully final) phase of the global financial crisis, where we expect episodes of greater volatility in the wake of normalization of monetary policy rates, especially in and beginning with the United States. Whether one anticipates a Fed rate-hiking scenario similar to that in 1994 (less orderly in terms of how short-term rates transmitted to longer-term rates) or in 2004 (more orderly), and irrespective of efforts by the Federal Open Market Committee to communicate its policy stance and prepare markets as well as it could, the textbook recipe is to strengthen policies. And our framework is precisely being strengthened. Brazil sailed well through the crisis, but the intensity and duration of our fiscal and parafiscal countercyclical responses during the last couple of years resulted in typical twin imbalances (e.g., of current account and fiscal deficits), signaling excessive domestic absorption. That eventually caused public debt ratios to deteriorate, put rating agencies on alert, and affected private-sector confidence. Early in 2015, Brazil addressed these challenges with (1) a double adjustment in relative prices (i.e., a realignment of administered prices vis-à-vis the consumer price index and external prices vis-à-vis domestic prices through the exchange rate) and (2) a consistent set of fiscal tightening measures, which include the reduction of current fiscal and parafiscal expenditures, the elimination of subsidies, realignment of public utility charges, and more structural measures that are being put in place; the measures have the objective of sending public debt on a declining path in the medium term. Last but not least, Brazil's central bank has been tightening monetary policy to ensure the convergence of inflation to target by the end of 2016, as the role and objective of monetary policy is to contain the second-order effects resulting from these relative prices adjustments, circumscribing their impact to 2015 and anchoring inflation expectations going forward in medium- and longer-terms horizons.

Conclusion: A Pragmatic Framework Is at Work in This (Last?) Phase of the Crisis

With the benefit of hindsight, the global financial crisis revealed that both mature and developing countries, advanced and emerging economies, despite obvious differences in institutional maturity, could have crises with similar ingredients: too much financial exuberance, too much debt, inconsistent exchange rate regimes, lax fiscal policy, lax monetary policy, lax regulations, poor governance, a political economy favoring unsustainable expansionist policy stance, and so on.

Like many EMEs, but with a stronger prudential and regulatory differential, we developed in Brazil a pragmatic policy framework, building on our experience with our past crises of the 1990s and strengthening it with standard policies to ensure price stability (an inflation-targeting regime) and fiscal responsibility laws (a set of rules to control public debt). We also adopted a flexible exchange rate as a first line of defense against external shocks.

Our framework sailed well through the various phases of the global financial crisis and proved resilient. We are testing it again in this period of normalization of monetary conditions in the United States. Are there any general lessons?

First, one should keep the "old pragmatic framework" as strong as possible (e.g., the flexible exchange rate regime, the sound fiscal stance generating low levels of indebtedness, a strong inflation-targeting framework). And work as hard as possible against the powerful tendency to accommodate political economy pressure with more debt. It is difficult to ensure financial stability in the absence of confidence in long term fiscal stability. Local political economy factors can create or exacerbate volatility that eventually threatens the overall macroeconomic stance.

Second, a solid financial system is needed, an intrusive supervision with the relevant and timely information (market infrastructure) about vulnerabilities so that the regulator can act preemptively. Indeed, we rely on the robustness of our financial system. The Brazilian financial system is well capitalized and liquid, and provisions are high. Our financial system has a historically low default rate and is very resilient to variations in the exchange rate. There is low reliance on cross-border financing. Foreign currency debt is also low and the bulk of it is hedged through exports, assets held abroad or financially hedged. We had already a number of stringent microprudential regulations and an intrusive supervision of our financial system that ensured its resilience and health (e.g., above Basel minimum capital requirements, a high level of liquidity and provisions, and very detailed market infrastructure with mandatory reporting of financial transactions and trading through CCPs).

Third, it is important to communicate well the separation principle that ensures that each policy objective will be addressed by one policy instrument, even if there could be—and indeed there often is—ex post complementarity between them. Macroprudential tools are geared to address financial stability and monetary policy price stability, but such tools do influence the transmission of monetary policy. Understanding separation with complementarity helps to strengthen the rationale and the credibility of the policy framework as a whole.

It seems that both the practical experience of some EMEs (and Brazil) and the new analytical work that has been testing policy responses to external shocks, simulated by dynamic stochastic general equilibrium modeling with the financial sector, using both monetary policy and macroprudential tools, suggest promising ways to design a consistent approach to achieve macroeconomic and financial stability.[16]

A summary of these features is shown in figure 22.2.

Fourth, while keeping the floating exchange rate regime as a first line of defense, it is useful to smooth excessive exchange rate volatility, which can affect the financial stability of the system. There are many avenues to achieving that, depending on the characteristics of your foreign exchange markets, but using directly or indirectly some combination of self-insurance (e.g., international reserves) and access to multilateral protection seems to be efficient.

Fifth, maintaining macroeconomic and financial stability is necessary, but working on your growth potential through structural reforms is paramount. Not only does it strengthen solvency ratios and fundamentals, it also allows more room to maneuver for social improvement, which in turn affects positively the stability of institutions and social welfare.

	Macroeconomic Stability (Activity / Inflation & Financial)			
Policy Areas	Price Stability	Debt Stability	Financial Stability	
	Monetary Policy	Fiscal Policy	Macroprudential	Exchange Rate
Policy Instruments	Place central bank rate policy under clear arrangement (flex IT, etc.) to manage activity/inflation and anchor expectations	Identify short-term credible fiscal targets to stabilize (gross, net) public debt-to-GDP; medium-long-term public debt management	Reduce excessive procyclicality, i.e., smooth financial accelerator and credit multiplier; reduce "excesses" in prices and quantities	Use floating as first line of defense; reserves accumulation for self-insurance; FX intervention to avoid excessive volatility; FX hedge program to strengthen financial stability, etc.

Figure 22.2
Macroeconomic Stability (Activity/Inflation and Financial).

Notes

1. This session at the 2013 "Rethinking Macro Policy II" conference focused on the importance of the choice of an adequate exchange rate arrangement for EMEs and the role of macroprudential instruments and capital controls in mitigating the effects of global excessive liquidity. See George Akerlof, Olivier Blanchard, David Romer, and Joseph E. Stiglitz, eds., *What Have We Learned? Macroeconomic Policy after the Crisis* (Cambridge, MA: MIT Press, 2014).

2. Alan S. Blinder, *After the Music Stopped* (New York: Penguin Press, 2013).

3. See Rudi Dornbusch and Sebastian Edwards, eds., *The Macroeconomics of Populism in Latin America* (Chicago: University of Chicago Press, 1991).

4. Jeffrey Frankel, "Monetary Policy in Emerging Markets," in *Handbook of Monetary Economics*, vol. 3B (Amsterdam: North-Holland, 2011), 1439–1520.

5. Frederic Mishkin, *Monetary Policy Strategy* (Cambridge, MA: MIT Press, 2007), esp. chap. 17, "The Dangers of Exchange Rate Pegging in Emerging Market Countries," 445–463.

6. Guillermo A. Calvo, "Capital Flows and Capital-Market Crises: The Simple Economics of Sudden Stops," *Journal of Applied Economics*, November 1998.

7. Claudio Borio, "The Financial Cycle and Macroeconomics: What Have We Learnt?," BIS Working Paper 395, Bank for International Settlements, December 2012.

8. Kenneth Rogoff and Carmen M. Reinhart, *This Time Is Different: Eight Centuries of Financial Folly* (Princeton, NJ: Princeton University Press, 2009).

9. See IMF, "Key Aspects of Macroprudential Policy," June 10, 2013, http://www.imf.org/external/np/pp/eng/2013/061013b.pdf, and IMF, "The Interaction between Monetary and Macroprudential Policies," January 29, 2013, http://www.imf.org/external/np/pp/eng/2013/012913.pdf; Olivier Blanchard, David Romer, M. Spence, and Joseph E. Stiglitz, eds., *In the Wake of the Crisis: Leading Economists Reassess Economic Policy* (Washington, DC: IMF; Cambridge, MA: MIT Press, 2012).

10. See, among others, for the CCCB, Mathias Drehmann, Claudio Borio, Leonardo Gambacorta, and Gabriel Jiménez, "Countercyclical Capital Buffers: Exploring Options," BIS Working Paper 317, Bank for International Settlements, July 2010; and Basel Committee on Banking Supervision, Consultative Document: "Countercyclical Capital Buffer Proposal," issued for comment by September 10, 2010, Bank for International Settlements, July 2010.

11. See Rhaguran Rajan, "Competitive Monetary Easing—Is It Yesterday?," speech at the Brookings Institution, Washington, DC, April 10, 2014; Hélène Rey, "The Global Financial Cycle and Monetary Policy Independence," paper presented at the Federal Reserve Bank of Kansas City 2013 Economic Policy Symposium, "Global Dimensions of Unconventional Monetary Policy," Jackson Hole, WY, August 24, 2013; and Pierre-Richard Agénor, Koray Alper, and Luiz A. Pereira da Silva, "Sudden Floods, Macroprudential Regulation and Financial Stability in an Open Economy," *Journal of International Money and Finance* 48 (2014): 68–100.

12. In 2010 alone, EM and developing economies received almost US $225 billion in net portfolio flows. This was more than double the already very strong portfolio flows received in 2007, just before the crisis, and can be compared to an average level of net portfolio flows below US $20 billion earlier in the decade.

13. See M. S. Mohanty, "Overview," in "The Transmission of Unconventional Monetary Policy to the Emerging Markets," BIS Paper 78, Bank for International Settlements, September 2014; or João Barata, Luiz Awazu Pereira da Silva, and Adriana Soares, "Quantitative Easing and Related Capital Flows into Brazil: Measuring Its Effects and Transmission Channels through a Rigorous Counterfactual Evaluation," *Journal of International Money and Finance* 48 (2014): 68–100.

14. See Luiz Awazu Pereira da Silva and Ricardo Eyer Harris, "Sailing through the Global Financial Storm: Brazil's Recent Experience with Monetary and Macroprudential Policies to Lean against the Financial Cycle and Deal with Systemic Risks," in *Managing Capital Flows: Issues in Selected Emerging Market Economies*, ed. Bruno Carrasco, Subir Gokarn, and Hiranya Mukhopadhyay (Mandaluyong City, Philippines: Asian Development Bank; Oxford: Oxford University Press, 2014), chap. 7.

15. Instead of using classic sterilized interventions, we implemented the largest intervention foreign exchange program of any EME not by selling directly US dollars to buy domestic currency (the BRL) but by selling currency-derivative FX forward. These currency-derivative swaps are not settled in US dollars but in BRL.

The contract between the central bank and dealers pays the difference between the BRL/USD foreign exchange rate at the beginning of the contract and the actual foreign exchange rate at the end, plus a dollar-linked on-shore rate of interest. In return, the central bank receives the cumulative overnight interbank rate for the period of the contract, in BRL. Therefore, the central bank is insuring buyers against BRL depreciation with no direct use of USD reserves. The dealer can be either a bank that resells the contract to an end-user or a financial institution itself.

16. For a review of EMEs approaches on this issue, see Pierre-Richard Agénor and Luiz A. Pereira da Silva, "Inflation Targeting and Financial Stability: A Perspective from the Developing World," CEMLA and IDB, 2013. http://idbdocs.iadb.org/wsdocs/getdocument.aspx?docnum=38367231.

23

Capital Inflows, Exchange Rate Management, and Capital Controls

Agustín Carstens

A discussion of the interaction between capital inflows, exchange rate management, and capital controls is quite timely. However, it is by no means a new discussion. The interactions between and among these three items have been extensively analyzed, in particular at the IMF. What makes such interactions a recurrent topic of discussion is that the prevailing situation and perspectives in the global economy and financial markets at different times might modify how countries should adjust their exchange rate management and their position with regard to the use of capital controls in the face of the capital inflows or outflows they might be confronting.

What makes the discussion interesting and relevant now is that we are facing an "abnormal situation" in the global economy. Let me elaborate. Under "normal conditions," most advanced economies have the capacity to reach an adequate combination of growth and financial stability, without implementing unconventional fiscal or monetary policies. Basically, we can define an unconventional policy stance as one that goes beyond its traditional reachto address an unusual circumstance, owing to insufficient space or lack of suitable instruments to address such a circumstance in a given span of time. So, in normal circumstances, for small open economies, whether emerging or advanced, a combination of a freely floating exchange rate regime and no capital controls allows monetary policy independence, which has traditionally contributed to the simultaneous attainment of economic growth with financial stability.

But under a regime of unconventional monetary policies (UMPs) in the main advanced economies (the ones that issue the reserve currencies around the world), major externalities are generated that can make it undesirable for emerging market economies (EMEs) to sustain a position of freely floating exchange rates with free capital mobility. As an additional unintended consequence of UMPs, in their presence the adequate monetary policy stance in EMEs is heavily influenced by the monetary policy stance of advanced economies, that is, by the UMPs implemented by advanced economies. I will illustrate this in what follows.

The starting point of my argument is that in 2008, a financial crisis erupted in the United States, spread rapidly to most of the rest of the advanced economies, and eventually affected the world as a whole.

Even though the most critical aspects of the global financial crisis have been overcome or averted—in particular the possibility of extreme tail-risk events that would have been disastrous had they materialized—the process of recovery has been extremely slow, and is still vulnerable to setbacks. World economic growth continues to be sluggish, and a huge deficit in job creation persists.

Most worrisome about the process of recovery of the world economy is that it still depends heavily on the monetary policy stances in the main advanced economies that are not sustainable over the medium and long term. Let me explain.

Relatively soon after the start of the crisis, it became clear that the feasibility in most advanced economies of stimulating growth through fiscal policy came to an end, as debt-to-GDP ratios grew very fast. Thus, the only stabilization policy instrument left was monetary policy, and therefore the main advanced economies' central banks adopted, at different times and speeds and with varied modalities, unprecedented expansionary monetary policies. The Federal Reserve System led the way, followed by the Bank of England, the Bank of Japan, and the European Central Bank, the last two motivated also by the growing risk of deflation. These policies have engineered sharp declines in interest rates across the yield curve. The zero lower bound in the policy reference rates became binding in all the above-mentioned cases. In addition, forward guidance for the policy rates and quantitative easing (QE) were adopted. As a result, the balance sheets of advanced economies' central banks increased sharply.

The overall objective of implementing UMPs in these advanced economies was to stimulate growth and employment, while inducing the convergence of inflation to each country's objective. Inflation in most advanced economies has fallen below their objective, mostly as a result of widespread unemployment, large output gaps, a reduction in commodities prices (in particular of oil), and, most recently in the United States, as a result of the sharp effective appreciation of the US dollar.

I believe that given the magnitude of the global financial crisis and the policy options available, UMPs were essential, and have worked well so far. Economic recovery has taken hold in the United States and the UK, and to a lesser extent in Japan, while recent figures coming out of the euro zone have been promising. Inflation expectations and core inflation have been moving toward the respective central banks' objectives.

Nonetheless, my perception is that it is too early to declare victory. To begin with, we still have to see whether the unwinding of those policies can proceed in an orderly fashion once their immediate objectives are met. Once we reach that state of affairs, the unwinding of UMPs will be unavoidable, as otherwise they would feed into inflation and induce higher than warranted interest rates and financial instability. This is why I consider that UMPs are not sustainable over the medium and long term. To assess the risks associated with the unwinding of those policies, we have to identify their unintended consequences.

The transmission of extraordinary monetary stimulus to higher economic growth was meant to work primarily by enticing more risk taking by economic agents. In the case of consumers, and in particular as a response to QE (asset-purchase programs by central banks), lower interest rates and wealth effects would stimulate their expenditure. Another important channel that would operate was that the lower interest rates, term spreads, and credit spreads that would result from QE would stimulate *real* risk taking by firms; that is, QE would induce higher corporate investment. But investment has only partially recovered from the sharp fall in the recession of 2009—the median decline from a group of advanced and EM economies has been around 2½ percentage points of GDP. Meanwhile, there have been massive investments in financial instruments of all sorts, both in local and external markets, in what has been called the search for yield, which has created considerable spillover effects of UMPs. The crux of the matter is that it seems that financial risk taking has been far more responsive to UMP than has real risk taking.

Several consequences or externalities have resulted from the above. Initially resources were directed to bonds and stock markets in advanced economies, but as the search for yield led to stretched valuations, investments in high-yield corporate bonds and EMEs' sovereign and corporate debt exploded. These responses led in turn to wider credit and term spread compressions, record high-yield debt issuance, and deteriorating underwriting standards. Most of these investments have been intermediated by nonbank financial institutions, such as asset management companies, hedge funds, and pension and insurance companies.

A novel feature of this episode of capital inflows to EMEs was that a large portion of them took place as purchases of government bonds denominated in the domestic currency by nonresident investors. This is an important feature, since it eliminates the "original sin syndrome" that haunted EMEs for several decades.[1]

Massive capital inflows into EMEs persisted for a while, fueled primarily by carry trades explained by ex ante uncovered interest rate arbitrage opportunities. The flows promoted by the excess global liquidity created a sense of exuberance, which in turn generated mispricing in some assets in many EMEs and meaningful real exchange rate appreciations, and opened the door for potential sudden capital flow reversals. These factors caused concern among many countries, in particular over the potential of capital flows to (1) induce a sharp decline in exports, given the resulting real exchange rate appreciation; (2) produce asset-price bubbles created by rapid credit expansion, which in turn could result in financial instability; and (3) eventually revert to capital outflows from EMEs, which could also be a source of financial instability. Most EMEs resorted to at least one of the following defensive policy measures: (1) the accumulation of international reserves, deviating usually from a freely floating exchange rate regime, or (2) the adoption of macroprudential policies.

The accumulation of international reserves by EMEs is a phenomenon interesting to analyze in detail. Because of the sheer size of QE in the United States, coupled with the QE implemented so far in Japan, it is not surprising that EMEs' domestic currencies underwent a sharp appreciation in response. This is the main reason why some analysts and policymakers have labeled QE "competitive easing." In a way, the aggressive accumulation of international reserves by EMEs all the way to late 2013 is at least partially the other side of the coin of "competitive easing." In fact, we might call it "competitive reserve accumulation." In most cases I would agree with this practice, given the blunt distorting effects that QE had on EMEs. The size of capital flows to this subset of countries was much larger per unit of time than the capacity of such countries to absorb them without suffering substantial distortions.

Therefore, for most EMEs it has been appropriate to "throw some gravel under the wheels" through international reserves accumulation to mitigate some of the negative externalities that could take place as a result of the sharp real exchange rate appreciation. Even the contained appreciation has had real effects, starting with a deterioration in the trade balance and going all the way to substantially handicapping some sectors in a number of countries, such as manufacturing in Brazil. There are several other recent examples of sector handicapping among EMEs.

Another important reason to accumulate reserves in the face of QE is that it might avoid financial instability in the future. As QE will be temporary, EM countries should prepare themselves for the reversals of capital, and one way to do so is by accumulating reserves and building other backstops. In addition, rapid capital inflows could be used in the recipient economy in such a way that asset-price bubbles or rich valuations could result; this is of particular concern if such flows are intermediated by the banking system of the recipient country and lead to a real estate bubble, which usually kicks off a major crisis. Avoiding this scenario through reserves accumulation has been an effective prudential instrument.

Of course, in some cases macroprudential measures applied through the banking system (e.g., loan-to-value or income-to-debt limits, the imposition of higher reserve requirements) could deliver the same results, and several EMEs have followed this path. Nevertheless, macroprudential policies are far less effective when capital flows are not channeled through the banking system, as was the case with recent cross-border flows to many EMEs, where market-based financing has been the norm. I would say that the same applies to the imposition of capital controls.

As time passed, a gradual deterioration in some EMEs' macrofundamentals, in combination with some major events in advanced economies that periodically switched the risk on to risk off, and vice versa (e.g., the problems with Greece and other countries on the periphery of the euro zone, the possibility of a fiscal cliff in the United States, the "whatever it takes" statement by Mario Draghi)[2] have made capital flows to EMEs increasingly volatile.

In April and May 2013 the first serious reality check for EMEs arrived. At that time, the global financial cycle was more clearly transmitted to

EMEs, triggered mostly by the start of the discussion of monetary policy normalization in the United States, that is, the "taper talk." This, together with the correction in commodity prices that followed the economic slowdown in China and in most advanced economies, invited a reevaluation of EMEs' prospects.

The turbulence in EM financial markets that followed was not homogeneous. The most severe turbulence occurred in countries with the weakest fundamentals, mostly judged by the size of their current account and fiscal deficits. In these cases, sharp depreciations in local currencies took place, together with disproportionate increases in interest rates and plummeting stock markets. National authorities reacted by intervening in the foreign exchange markets, facilitating the reduction of duration in investors´ portfolios, and, more important, by tightening fiscal and monetary policies. In contrast, many other EMEs managed to sail through this episode by reinforcing their policy stance and allowing the exchange and interest rates to adjust without any market interventions. We could say that many EMEs came out strengthened from this period of volatility.

Financial markets were surprisingly calm in late 2013 and the first half of 2014. The tapering of securities purchases by the Federal Reserve started in January 2014 and proceeded without unforeseen consequences. At the same time, the Federal Open Market Committee enhanced the clarity of its forward guidance, creating the expectations of policy rate adjustments until 2015. In the euro area, major concerns became evident about sluggish economic growth and massive unemployment, together with inflation rates substantially below the ECB target. This generated the expectation of significant additional monetary policy easing by the ECB. Owing to these events, together with the reactivation of the search for yield, credit spreads compressed and their dispersion fell to unusually low levels, volatility in all asset classes was suppressed, and capital flows seemed to recover.

But market conditions started to change considerably for the worse at the beginning of the second half of 2014. Again, events in the United States and the euro zone were important triggers. As the QE tapering was coming to an end in the United States, widespread speculation about potential dates and modalities of the policy rate lift-off from the zero lower bound became destabilizing, leading to higher US rates. At the same time, both the BoJ and the ECB took sequential steps toward additional monetary easing. Worth noting was that in January 2015, the ECB initiated a full-fledged QE program. The combination of the expectation of the normalization of US monetary policy and additional easing in the euro zone and Japan established conditions for euro and yen carry trades, as the United States offers higher yields and an appreciating currency, while low rates make the euro and the yen attractive funding currencies. This process feeds into itself, as the flows that it triggers have reinforced the appreciation of the US dollar. Thus it is not surprising that the US dollar effective appreciation in the nine-month span from July 2014 to April 2015 was the largest since 1973.

When the United States implemented QE, cross-border flows to many EMEs increased. But now, with the euro-zone and Japanese QE, together with the expectation of an imminent Fed tightening and stronger economic growth in the United States, even with respect to many EMEs, flows are going toward the United States, implying tighter external financial conditions for EMEs.

In addition, since mid-2014 we have also witnessed a sharp decrease in commodity prices, especially for oil, which reflects protracted low growth in the world economy, appreciation of the US dollar, and particular circumstances in specific markets. What we have seen recently in EMEs, then, are capital outflows and continued exchange rate depreciation, caused to a large extent by the strengthening of the dollar and the sharp collapse in commodity prices.

From the above, it should be clear that the start of the unwinding of the UMP in the United States, though certainly not the sole contributor, has induced a noticeable increase in volatility in financial markets, in particular those of EMEs. In a way this could be surprising, since the fact that the Fed is contemplating the full normalization of its monetary policy stance signals that the economic recovery has almost been consolidated in the context of price stability. This is good news for the United States, EMEs, and the world as a whole. But my fear is that during this transition period the overextension of financial risk taking is overwhelming the usual market responses. Let me illustrate this with a simple example. In the precrisis period, good figures for the US nonfarm payroll data generated an appreciation in EME currencies, for a strong US economy meant a positive impulse for their exports. In the postcrisis period, and more markedly in recent times, a positive surprise in US pay-roll data has generated depreciation in EME currencies, for such surprises make market participants anticipate an earlier lift-off in the US policy reference rate.

Looking ahead, and given the imminent normalization of monetary conditions in the United States, it could be expected that central banks in EMEs will increase their policy rates as the Federal Reserve adjusts the federal funds rate upward. This might happen even if the domestic economic conditions do not justify a policy rate increase. Although the baseline scenario is one of a gradual and orderly normalization of US monetary conditions, episodes of financial turbulence cannot be dis-missed. Under these circumstances, authorities might not only need to increase their policy rate but also might be forced to intervene in key financial markets, namely, the forex and money markets, performing as market-makers of last resort, in the latter case to facilitate the adjustment of duration in portfolios of domestic sovereign securities. These unortho-dox market interventions by central banks would be pertinent if, as is likely, market liquidity dries up during episodes of stress. Precisely for this reason, I have mentioned the need for EMEs to have additional back-stops, for example the IMF's Flexible Credit Line.

The fact that EMEs would have to adjust their monetary policy rate because of external conditions (i.e., Federal Reserve policy adjustments) overwhelming domestic ones (inflation and growth gaps) makes it obvi-ous that they cannot depend solely on monetary policy in the context of a freely floating exchange rate regime with full capital mobility to achieve the ultimate policy goal, which is to reach faster and sustainable growth and simultaneously consolidate financial stability. In this sense, macro-relevant structural reforms, together with strong fundamentals, become of the essence. This is the path Mexico has followed.

Let me conclude with a brief commentary on the international mon-etary system (IMS). It is fair to say that the IMS is in transition, and much remains to be done to make it more stable and to adapt it to the chal-lenges of the twenty-first century.

The global economy is becoming more multipolar and interconnected, underpinned by rapid structural growth in large EMEs. Dynamic EMEs generally exhibit lower levels of financial development and global inte-gration than advanced economies, suggesting scope for catchup. This transition raises challenges and provides opportunities, and how it will take place has important implications for financial stability and growth, and for the architecture of the IMS and its efficacy.

Despite some reforms after the global financial crisis, questions remain about the resilience of the IMS. Incremental steps have been taken to strengthen policy collaboration, monitor and manage capital flows, and broaden the financial safety net. However, more fundamental IMS reforms to address sources of instability have remained on the back burner. A key concern, one developed in this chapter, is that monetary policy decisions by advanced economies can create large spillover effects, especially for EMEs, so some form of coordination is urgently needed.

The international community has an opportunity to facilitate and shape a virtuous further integration of major EMEs into the global economy, while in the process addressing some long-standing weaknesses of the IMS. These goals can be achieved through the following measures:

First, by providing incentives and support for EMEs to join existing governance structures. Important measures include adapting those structures to the needs of EMEs and ensuring their fair representation, which would help prevent fragmentation and duplication and promote a deeper, more substantive global policy dialogue.

Second, by an orderly, well-sequenced financial deepening and opening in key EMEs, which could deliver substantial welfare gains for these countries, along with positive global spillovers and stability gains for the IMS. Deeper domestic financial markets would be expected to promote domestic demand, facilitate greater reliance on exchange rates to achieve external adjustment and thereby help reduce global imbalances, and improve EMEs' ability to cope with capital flow volatility. Increased opportunities for asset diversification, both domestically and at the global level, would provide additional welfare gains.

Third, by undertaking broad efforts to strengthen and close gaps in the global financial safety net, and avoid the need for costly and distortionary reserves accumulation. Certainly, this implies reaching the point of full implementation of the 2010 governance reforms at the IMF, which would increase its lending capacity based on quotas and enhance the voice and representation of EMEs. This would enrich the IMF's credibility, efficiency, and legitimacy, placing the institution in a stronger position to improve the functioning of the IMS.

Notes

1. The term "original sin syndrome" was coined by Barry Eichengreen and Ricardo Hausmann (1999) and refers to the propensity of Latin American countries to borrow in a foreign currency when foreign interest rates are lower than domestic ones but to disregard the potential additional cost that could be generated by local currency depreciation, which happened often in the 1980s and 1990s in the region.

2. See Mario Draghi, "Remarks at the Global Investment Conference," London, 2012.

References

Draghi, Mario. 2012. "Remarks at the Global Investment Conference." London. UK.

Eichengreen, Barry, and Ricardo Hausmann. 1999. "Exchange Rates and Financial Fragility." In *Proceedings, 1999 Economic Policy Symposium: New Challenges for Monetary Policy*. Jackson Hole, WY. Federal Reserve Bank of Kansas City.

The International Monetary and Financial
System

24

The International Monetary and Financial System: Eliminating the Blind Spot

Jaime Caruana

The design of international arrangements suitable for the global economy is a long-standing issue in economics. The global financial crisis has put this issue back on the policy agenda.

I would like to concentrate on an important blind spot in the system. The current international monetary and financial system (IMFS) consists of domestically focused policies in a world of global firms, currencies, and capital flows—but are local rules adequate for a global game? I argue that liquidity conditions often spill over across borders and can amplify domestic imbalances to the point of instability. In other words, today's IMFS not only fails to constrain the buildup of financial imbalances, but also makes it hard for national authorities to see these imbalances coming.

Certainly, some actions have been taken to address this weakness in the system: the regulatory agenda has made significant progress in strengthening the resilience of the financial system. But we also know that risks and leverage will morph and migrate, and that a regulatory response by itself will not be enough. Other policies also have an important role to play. In particular, to address this blind spot, central banks should take international spillovers and feedbacks—or spillbacks, as some call them—into account, not least out of enlightened self-interest.

Local Rules in a Global Game

Let me briefly characterize the present-day IMFS, before describing the spillover channels. In contrast to the Bretton Woods system or the gold standard, the IMFS today no longer has a single commodity or currency as nominal anchor. I am not proposing to go back to these former systems;

rather, I favor better anchoring domestic policies by taking financial stability considerations into account, internalizing the interactions among
policy regimes, and strengthening international cooperation so that we
can establish better rules of the game.

So what are the rules of the game today? If there are any rules to speak
of, they are mainly local. Most central banks target domestic inflation
and let their currencies float, or follow policies consistent with managed
or fixed exchange rates in line with domestic policy goals. Most central
banks *interpret* their mandate exclusively in domestic terms. Moreover,
the search for a framework that can satisfactorily integrate the links
between financial stability and monetary policy is still a work in progress,
with some way to go. The development and adoption of such a framework represent one of the most significant and difficult challenges for
central banks over the next few years.

Discussions of international policy seem to focus mainly on containing
balance of payments imbalances, with most attention paid to the current
account (i.e., net flows). Not enough attention is given to gross flows and
stocks—that is, stocks of debt.

This policy design does not help us to see, much less to constrain,
the buildup of financial imbalances within and across countries. This,
in my view, is a blind spot that is central to this debate. Global finance
matters—and the game is undeniably global even if the rules that central
banks play by are mostly local.

International Spillover Channels

Monetary regimes and financial conditions interact globally and reinforce
each other. The strength and relevance of the spillovers and feedbacks
tend to be underestimated. Let me briefly sketch four channels through
which this happens.[1]

The first channel has to do with the conduct of monetary policy: easy
monetary conditions in the major advanced economies spread to the rest
of the world through policy reactions in the other economies (e.g., easing to resist currency appreciation and to maintain competitiveness). This
pattern goes beyond emerging market economies (EMEs): many central
banks have been keeping policy interest rates below those implied by traditional domestic benchmarks, as proxied by Taylor rules.[2]

The second channel involves the international use of currencies. Most notably, the domains of the US dollar and the euro extend so broadly beyond their respective domestic jurisdictions that US and euro-area monetary policies immediately affect financial conditions in the rest of the world. The US dollar, followed by the euro, plays an outsized role in trade invoicing, foreign exchange turnover, official reserves, and the denomination of bonds and loans. A key observation in this context is that US dollar credit to nonbank borrowers outside the United States has reached $9.6 trillion, and this stock has expanded on US monetary easing.[3] In fact, with accommodative monetary policy intended for the United States, US dollar credit has expanded much faster abroad than at home (figure 24.1, top right panel).

Third, the integration of financial markets allows global common factors to move bond and equity prices. Uncertainty and risk aversion, as reflected in indicators such as the VIX index, affect asset markets and credit flows everywhere.[4] In the new phase of global liquidity, in which capital markets are gaining prominence and the search for yield is a driving force, risk premia and term premia in bond markets play an important role in the transmission of financial conditions across markets.[5] This role has strengthened in the wake of central bank large-scale asset purchases. The Federal Reserve's large-scale asset purchases compressed not only the US bond term premium but also long-term yields in many other bond markets. More recently, the new program of bond purchases in the euro area put downward pressure not only on European bond yields but apparently also on US bond yields, even amid expectations of US policy tightening.

A fourth channel works through the availability of external finance in general, regardless of currency: capital flows provide a source of funding that can amplify domestic credit booms and busts. The leverage and equity of global banks jointly drive gross cross-border lending, and domestic currency appreciation can accelerate those inflows as it strengthens the balance sheets of local firms that have financed local currency assets with US dollar borrowing.[6] In the run-up to the global financial crisis, for instance, cross-border bank lending contributed to raising credit-to-GDP ratios in a number of economies.[7]

Through these channels, monetary and financial regimes can interact with and reinforce each other, sometimes amplifying domestic imbal-

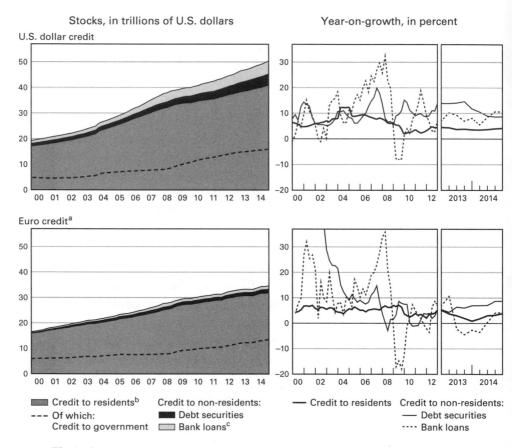

Figure 24.1
Global credit in US dollars and euros to the nonfinancial sector.
Notes: a. At constant end-Q3 2014 exchange rates. b. Credit to the nonfinancial sector in the United States/euro area from financial accounts, excluding identified credit to borrowers in nondomestic currencies (i.e., cross-border and locally extended loans and outstanding international bonds in nondomestic currencies). c. Cross-border and locally extended loans to nonbanks outside the United States/euro area. For China, locally extended loans are derived from national data on total local lending in foreign currencies on the assumption that 80 percent are denominated in US dollars. For other non-BIS reporting countries, local US dollar/euro loans to nonbanks are proxied by all BIS reporting banks' gross cross-border US dollar/euro loans to banks in the country, on the assumption that these funds are then extended to nonbanks. *Sources:* IMF, *International Financial Statistics*; Datastream; BIS international debt statistics and locational banking statistics by residence.

ances to the point of instability. Global liquidity surges and collapses as a result.

Thus, monetary accommodation at the center tended to create a global easing bias and thereby leads to spillovers and, eventually feedbacks. But these channels can also work in the opposite direction, amplifying financial tightening when policy rates in the center begin to rise, or even seem ready to rise, as suggested by the "taper tantrum" of 2013. Nevertheless, it is an open question whether the effect of the IMFS is symmetric in this regard, creating as much of a tightening bias as it does an easing bias. In both cases, it is important to try to eliminate the blind spot and keep an eye on the dynamics of global liquidity.

Policy Implications: From the House to the Neighborhood

This leads to my second point, that central banks should take the international effects of their own actions into account in setting monetary policy. This takes more than just keeping one's own house in order; it also requires contributing to keeping the neighborhood in order.

An important precondition in this regard is the need to continue the work of incorporating financial factors into macroeconomics. If policymakers can better manage the broader financial cycle, that in itself would help constrain excesses and reduce spillovers from one country to another.

But policymakers should also give more weight to international interactions, including spillovers, feedbacks, and collective action problems, with a view to keeping the neighborhood in order. How to start broadening one's view from house to neighborhood? One useful step would be to reach a common diagnosis, a consensus in our understanding of how international spillovers and spillbacks work. The widely held view that the IMFS should focus on large current account imbalances, for instance, does not fully capture the multitude of spillover channels that are relevant in this regard.[8]

An array of possibilities then presents itself in terms of the depth of international policy cooperation. They range from extended local rules to new global rules of the game.

To extend local rules, major central banks could internalize spillovers so as to contain the risk of financial imbalances building up to the point of blowing back on their domestic economies. Incorporating spillovers in monetary policy setting may improve performance over the medium term. This approach is thus fully consistent with enlightened self-interest. The need for policymakers to pay attention to global effects can be seen clearly in the major bond markets. Official reserve managers and major central banks hold large portions of outstanding government debt (figure 24.2). If investors treat bonds denominated in different currencies as close substitutes, central bank purchases that lower yields in one bond market also weigh on yields in other markets. For many years, changes in US bond yields have been thought to move yields abroad; in the last year, many observers ascribed lower global bond yields to the ECB's consideration of and implementation of large-scale bond purchases. Central banks ought to take into account these effects when setting monetary policy.

However, even if countries do optimize their own domestic policies with full information, a global optimum cannot be reached when there are externalities and strategic complementarities as in today's era of global liquidity. This means that we will also need more international cooperation. This could mean taking ad hoc joint action, or perhaps even developing new global rules of the game to help instill additional discipline in national policies.[9] Given the preeminence of the key international currencies, the major central banks have a special responsibility to conduct policy in a way that supports global financial stability—a way that keeps the neighborhood in order.

The domestic focus of central bank mandates need not preclude progress in this direction. After all, national mandates in bank regulation and supervision have also permitted extensive international cooperation and the development of global principles and standards in this area.

Conclusion

The current environment offers a good opportunity to revisit the various issues regarding the IMFS. Addressing the blind spot in the system will require us to take a global view. We need to anchor domestic policies better by taking financial factors into account. We also need to understand and to internalize the international spillovers and interactions of policies. This new approach will pose challenges. We have yet to develop an analytical framework that allows us to properly integrate financial

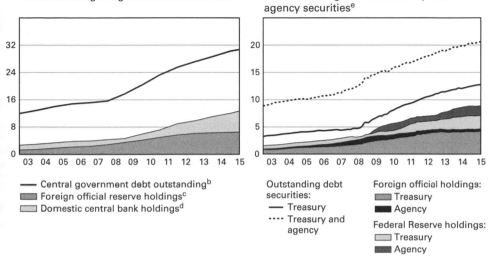

Figure 24.2
Official Holdings of US Treasury Securities (in trillions of US dollars).*
Notes: *Different valuation methods based on source availability. a. Covers the euro area, Japan, the United Kingdom and the United States; for the euro area, Japan and the United Kingdom, converted into US dollars using Q2 2015 constant exchange rates. b. For the United States, total marketable Treasury securities, excluding agency debt. c. For euro- and yen-denominated reserves, 80% is assumed to be government debt securities; for dollar-denominated reserves, as reported by the US Treasury International Capital System; for sterling-denominated reserves, holdings by foreign central banks. d. For the euro area, national central bank holdings of general government debt and ECB holdings under the Public Sector Purchase Programme and the Securities Market Programme. e. Agency debt includes mortgage pools backed by agencies and government-sponsored enterprises (GSEs) as well as issues by GSEs; total outstanding Treasury securities are total marketable Treasury securities. *Sources:* Board of Governors of the Federal Reserve System; US Department of the Treasury; Datastream; BIS calculations.

factors—including international spillovers—into monetary policy. And there is work to be done to enhance international cooperation. All these elements together would help establish better global rules of the game.

The global financial crisis has demonstrated that international cooperation in crisis management can be effective. For instance, the establishment of international central bank swap lines can be seen as an example of enlightened self-interest. However, we must also recognize that there are limits to how far and how fast the global safety nets can be extended to mitigate future strains. This puts a premium on crisis prevention. Each country will need to do its part and to contribute to making the global financial system more resilient—and I would add here that reinforcing the capacity of the IMF is one element in this regard. And taking international spillovers and financial stability issues into account in setting monetary policy is a useful step in this direction.

Notes

1. The discussion in this chapter focuses on international monetary and financial spillovers and is based on chapter V of *BIS 85th Annual Report*, Bank for International Settlements, June 2015, and Jaime Caruana, "Ebbing Global Liquidity and Monetary Policy Interactions," speech at the Central Bank of Chile, Fifth Summit Meeting of Central Banks, Santiago, November 2013. For a broader discussion of spillovers, see International Monetary Fund, "IMF Multilateral Policy Issues Report: 2014 Spillover Report," IMF Policy Paper, July 29, 2014.

2. See Boris Hofmann and Bilyana Bogdanova, "Taylor Rules and Monetary Policy: A Global 'Great Deviation'?," *BIS Quarterly Review*, September 2012, 37–49; and Boris Hofmann and Előd Takáts, "International Monetary Spillovers," *BIS Quarterly Review* (September 2015):105–118.

3. See Robert N. McCauley, Patrick McGuire, and Vladyslav Sushko, "Global Dollar Credit: Links to US Monetary Policy and Leverage," *Economic Policy* 30, no. 82 (2015): 187–229; and Benjamin Cohen and Cathérine Koch, "Highlights of Global Financing Flows," *BIS Quarterly Review* (September 2015): 17–34.

4. See Hélène Rey, "Dilemma not Trilemma: The Global Financial Cycle and Monetary Policy Independence," in *Proceedings, 2013 Economic Policy Symposium: Global Dimensions of Unconventional Monetary Policy*. Jackson Hole, WY. Federal Reserve Bank of Kansas City, August 2013.

5. See Hyun Song Shin, "The Second Phase of Global Liquidity and Its Impact on Emerging Economies," in *Proceedings of the Federal Reserve Bank of San Francisco Asia Economic Policy Conference,* November 2013, 215–224.

6. See Valentina Bruno and Hyun Song Shin, "Cross-Border Banking and Global Liquidity," *Review of Economic Studies* 82, no. 2 (2015): 535–564.

7. See Stefan Avdjiev, Robert McCauley, and Patrick McGuire, "Rapid Credit Growth and International Credit: Challenges for Asia," BIS Working Paper 377, Bank for International Settlements, April 2012; and Philip Lane and Peter McQuade, "Domestic Credit Growth and International Capital Flows," *Scandinavian Journal of Economics* 116, no. 1 (2014): 218–252.

8. See Claudio Borio, Harold James and Hyun Song Shin, "The International Monetary and Financial System: A Capital Account Historical Perspective," BIS Working Paper 457, Bank for International Settlements, September 2014; and Claudio Borio, "The International Monetary and Financial System: Its Achilles Heel and What to Do about It," BIS Working Paper 456, Bank for International Settlements, September 2014; and Claudio Borio and Piti Disyatat, "Global Imbalances and the Financial Crisis: Link or No Link?," BIS Working Paper 346, Bank for International Settlements, May 2011.

9. Related arguments are elaborated by Raghuram Rajan, "Concerns about Competitive Monetary Easing," *Reserve Bank of India Monthly Bulletin* (June 2014): 9–12.

References

Avdjiev, Stefan, Robert McCauley, and Patrick McGuire. 2012. "Rapid Credit Growth and International Credit: Challenges for Asia." BIS Working Paper 377. Bank for International Settlements, April. www.bis.org/publ/work377.htm.

Bank for International Settlements. 2015. *85th Annual Report*. Bank for International Settlements, June, www.bis.org/publ/arpdf/ar2014e.htm?m=5percent7C24.

Borio, Claudio. 2014. "The International Monetary and Financial System: Its Achilles Heel and What to Do about It." BIS Working Paper 456. Bank for International Settlements, September. www.bis.org/publ/work456.htm.

Borio, Claudio, and Piti Disyatat. 2011. "Global Imbalances and the Financial Crisis: Link or No Link?" BIS Working Paper 346. Bank for International Settlements, May. www.bis.org/publ/work346.htm.

Borio, Claudio, Harold James, and Hyun Song Shin. 2014. "The International Monetary and Financial System: A Capital Account Historical Perspective." BIS Working Paper 457. Bank for International Settlements, September. www.bis.org/publ/work457.htm.

Bruno, Valentina, and Hyun Song Shin. 2015. "Cross-Border Banking and Global Liquidity." *Review of Economic Studies* 82 (2): 535–564.

Caruana, Jaime. 2013. "Ebbing Global Liquidity and Monetary Policy Interactions." Speech at the Central Bank of Chile, Fifth Summit Meeting of Central Banks. Santiago, November. www.bis.org/speeches/sp131118a.htm.

Cohen, Benjamin, and Cathérine Koch. 2015. "Highlights of Global Financing Flows." *BIS Quarterly Review*, September, 17–34. Data available at www.bis.org/ statistics/gli.htm.

Hofmann, Boris, and Bilyana Bogdanova. 2012. "Taylor Rules and Monetary Policy: A Global 'Great Deviation'?" *BIS Quarterly Review*, September, 37–49. www.bis.org/publ/qtrpdf/r_qt1209f.htm.

Hofmann, Boris, and Előd Takáts. 2015. "International Monetary Spillovers." *BIS Quarterly Review* (September): 105–118.

International Monetary Fund. 2014. "IMF Multilateral Policy Issues Report: 2014 Spillover Report." IMF Policy Paper, July 29. https://www.imf.org/external/ np/pp/eng/2014/062514.pdf.

Lane, Philip, and Peter McQuade. 2014. "Domestic Credit Growth and International Capital Flows." *Scandinavian Journal of Economics* 116 (1): 218–252.

McCauley, Robert N., Patrick McGuire, and Vladyslav Sushko. 2015. "Global Dollar Credit: Links to US Monetary Policy and Leverage." *Economic Policy* 30 (82): 187–229.

Rajan, Raghuram. 2014. "Concerns about Competitive Monetary Easing." *Reserve Bank of India Monthly Bulletin* (June): 9–12.

Rey, Hélène. 2013. "Dilemma not Trilemma: The Global Financial Cycle and Monetary Policy Independence." Paper presented at the Federal Reserve Bank of Kansas City Economic Policy Symposium. Jackson Hole, WY,, August.

Shin, Hyung Song. 2013. "The Second Phase of Global Liquidity and Its Impact on Emerging Economies." In *Proceedings of the Federal Reserve Bank of San Francisco Asia Economic Policy Conference*, November.

25

Prospects and Challenges for Financial and Macroeconomic Policy Coordination

Zeti Akhtar Aziz

The challenges of operating in the context of the existing international monetary and financial system are clear. The world is frequently characterized by conditions of disequilibrium, financial imbalances, and at times dysfunctional markets. This chapter touches on the progress, challenges, and prospects for financial and macroeconomic policy coordination in a world that is more interconnected and interdependent than ever, with special emphasis on the perspective of the emerging market economies (EMEs).

There are several compelling reasons to advance a greater role for international cooperation and coordination: growing international interconnectivity, significant cross-border policy spillovers, and finally the immense potential benefits that can arise when countries come together for the common good. Progress has, however, been modest.

The challenges confronting international collaborative efforts arise from differences in circumstances and policy goals, and from the need to accord priority to national considerations. Additionally, the international interconnectivity and interlinkages are not well understood. The absence of clearly defined rules and explicit arrangements for such coordination further impedes international cooperation.

Finally, strong leadership is required to build an international consensus in a world environment that is highly diverse, with divergent aspirations and ideas as to how the goals of stability and sustainable economic performance might be achieved. There is therefore a need to have clarity on the objectives that are to be achieved and on the form such cooperation should take.

International Financial System Reforms

The greatest progress in international cooperation has been in the area of financial stability. The recent financial crisis in the advanced economies was marked by its international dimension, for which the policy response has been international. The crisis set in motion an international process for the fundamental reform of the financial system in terms of new international arrangements, a significant strengthening of prudential standards, a widening of the regulatory perimeter to include institutions previously not under regulatory capture, and oversight of systemically important institutions. Also significant has been the cross-border dimensions of the reforms, associated with the implementation of global recovery and resolution plans, and the stronger emphasis on macroprudential assessments to complement microprudential supervision.

Progress has also been achieved in the coordination of the overall design of the reform measures among the international standard-setting bodies. In particular, the efforts of the Financial Stability Board, the Basel Committee on Banking Supervision, and International Organization of Securities Commissions are now converging and becoming mutually reinforcing, including with respect to the framework for global and domestic systemically important banks and recovery and resolution planning.

The reforms have also created momentum for national regulatory authorities to strengthen cross-border supervisory arrangements, which have progressed significantly, including among EMEs. From the perspective of EMEs, the supervisory colleges and crisis management groups that have been established for the international financial institutions need to ensure that mechanisms for including host jurisdictions adequately take into account the importance of the banking institution in the host country, not just its importance to the home jurisdiction or to the financial group.

It is also expected that the global reform measures will reduce the incentives for national authorities to ring-fence domestic financial systems to manage the risk inherent in internationally more integrated financial systems. However, despite the focus on consistent implementation of global standards, authorities continue to be concerned about having adequate defenses against imported contagion. Such defenses have included policies regarding subsidiarization, the imposition of constraints on global funding and shared service business models, and the implementation of national resolution strategies independent of global arrangements. Such moves represent a retreat over time from globalization and result in more fragmented markets.

This situation occurs when the global standards are perceived to be incomplete and when the implementation issues are not sufficiently addressed, or when the costs and benefits are not viewed as being balanced, or when a global standard is incompatible with national priorities. As global resolution regimes develop, they will contribute to bridging the tensions between national authorities' requirement to be accountable for domestic financial stability and the need to preserve the efficiency of global business models. The level of trust and quality of cooperation between authorities across borders will, however, be highly important to avoid a retreat from the continued globalization of financial systems.

The financial stability frameworks have also become increasingly complex over a compressed period of time, with the risk that the financial institutions and supervisory authorities may not be fully prepared, particularly in terms of data, systems, and qualified resources, to effectively implement and support such frameworks. This situation has also diverted resources and management attention from the institutions to the complex implementation issues related to compliance, with less attention paid as well to the performance of their intermediation function.

A further issue has to do with proportionality. The regulation and supervision need to be commensurate with risk, so as to avoid unintended consequences, including disintermediation and financial exclusion, which may occur as a result of inappropriately stringent application of the global standards. How proportionality is to be achieved needs to be more clearly defined and supported, with practical guidance on the implementation of global standards. This approach can help preserve consistent and comparable regulatory outcomes without compromising risk sensitivity.

Finally, cumulative-impact assessments have been difficult to conduct, especially those trying to capture the interaction between new and existing standards. It is a challenge to assess the combined impact of constantly moving parts on stability, growth, and development.

Macroeconomic Policy Cooperation and Coordination

With regard to the evolving new frontiers for macroeconomic policies and the prospects for international cooperation and coordination, the issue before us is whether policymakers should have a more global perspective that takes into consideration the global implications of their policies and whether there should in fact be greater global collective action. Those skeptical of such cooperation maintain that national polices need to be based on national and domestic considerations. International cooperation and collaboration can, however, manifest in several forms that fall short of actual policy coordination. At one end of the spectrum is the exchange of information and assessments of the risks and vulnerabilities. Another form of cooperation is the adoption of an agreed-on framework of rules and standards. At the other end of the spectrum are coordinated joint policy decisions aimed at generating positive overall outcomes for macroeconomic stability and growth.

In practice, the increased intensity of such cooperation has been evident during the more recent financial crisis. The global response to such crises as late as the 1990s largely involved the multilateral agencies that dealt directly with the crisis-affected economies without facilitating much policy coordination across countries. The global financial crisis of 2007–2009, however, prompted coordinated interest rate cuts, the Fed's provision of US dollar liquidity facilities to several key central banks, and concerted fiscal expansion by several countries. While these actions did contain the depth of the crisis, they were not enough to strengthen the prospects for economic recovery. The failure to improve the prospects for economic recovery reflected not so much failure of international cooperation as the absence of a more comprehensive approach in the domestic policy action to address the consequences of the crisis.

An extensive literature has already highlighted the concern that monetary policy has been overly relied on to bring about results. Coordination of a less than optimal policy mix may then not only not yield the desired outcomes, it may also have its own unintended consequences. A second concern has to do with the underlying domestic and international environment potentially working against monetary policy. The transmission of monetary policy is affected during periods of high leverage, when balance sheets are impaired, and during periods of unstable and highly volatile financial markets. Monetary policy also cannot stimulate consumption and investment when there is no confidence over the future prospects of the economy. Thus, a macroeconomic response may avert a collapse of financial markets and the economy, but on its own it cannot deal with the challenge of raising the upside potential of the economy.

The impact of these policies has been felt beyond the borders of countries implementing them. The greatest impact has been felt by EMEs, which have been the recipient of large and volatile capital flows. No substantial progress has been made, however, in policy cooperation between the advanced economies and the EMEs. Nevertheless, the situation has led to greater efforts at cooperation and collaboration among EMEs. In Asia, this collaboration has been undertaken through a number of forums, especially the Executives' Meeting of East Asia and Pacific Central Banks (EMEAP) and ASEAN+3, in the areas of information sharing and surveillance, establishing an integrated regional crisis management framework and financial safety net arrangements (i.e., the Chiang Mai initiative of multilateralization, or CMIM, and currency swap arrangements, including in renminbi) not only to deal with the risk and vulnerabilities confronting the region but also to unlock the collective growth potential of the region.

26

Global Safe Asset Shortage: The Role of Central Banks

Ricardo J. Caballero

My assignment is to talk primarily about international liquidity provision and interlinkages of central banks' policies ... I know what I'm expected to say about these topics, and I know that most attendees and readers also know what I'm supposed to say. So we might as well skip all that and talk about something else ... although, as you will see, there are some points of contact between this something else and my mandate, but it will take a little while to get there.

I will focus on a central imbalance in global financial markets that has key implications for how we think about liquidity provision policies and central bank policies more broadly.

We currently live in a world where investment is having a hard time catching up with saving, which is leading to ever-lower real interest rates. This phenomenon started well before the subprime crisis. I often mention the Asian crisis as a defining moment, although Brad Delong has taken it further back, to the mid-1980s. In any case, this phenomenon was temporarily exacerbated by the crisis, but it seems to have a more secular nature. Larry Summers, in his irreproducible and insightful style, did a great service to this view by dubbing it the "secular stagnation hypothesis."

I believe, however, that a central aspect of this secular problem is not just an imbalance between investment and saving but a poor alignment between the financial assets that the private sector's real investment can naturally produce (or back) and the financial assets the average saver is looking for when trying to store value.

In particular, there is a shortage of *safe assets,* and when I say safe I mean mostly macroeconomic or systemic safe assets.

There are two broad implications of this shortage:

1. At the *macroeconomic level,* the shortage of safe assets puts downward pressure on safe real rates and can eventually lead to a very stubborn form of liquidity trap (a *safety trap,* if you will),[1] one that is unresponsive to forward guidance–type policies or to the emergence of financial bubbles. In a safety trap, economic agents are acutely concerned with further negative macroeconomic shocks, and it is that concern that drives their assessment of the future. In contrast, forward guidance and bubbles are promises of further riches in good future macroeconomic states and hence do not address the core problem. This form of liquidity trap is very responsive to "policy puts" as these set a floor on the states that directly concern economic agents and therefore reduce the demand for safe assets.

2. At the *microeconomic level,* this shortage generates a strong incentive for the financial system to create such safe assets, and we know that the massive effort to squeeze a safe tranche from portfolios of subprime mortgages didn't work out too well last time. It is very hard for the private sector alone, in particular for the financial sector, which is naturally levered, to create truly systemic safe assets in significant quantity.[2]

With this background in mind, let us now look for solutions to this *safe asset shortage problem,* and in particular, as they relate to the topics of international liquidity provision and policy spillover.

I want to focus on one aspect of this solution: if we can't produce these safe assets easily, at the very least we *should not be wasting them.*

When one thinks about safe assets wasting, one's thoughts immediately go to central banks, both because of the size of their portfolios and because of their buy-and-hold nature (so when they remove a safe asset from the system, they typically do it on a nearly permanent basis).

To mention one pocket: of the $18 trillion of US Treasuries more than 30 percent is stationed at central banks, two-thirds of which is at foreign central banks and one-third is at the Fed itself.

The main reasons for central bank accumulations of safe assets are international reserves accumulation and quantitative easing (QE) policies. The former is about the hoarding of foreign safe assets, and the latter is about the accumulation of domestic safe assets and occasionally riskier ones (although in the case of Japan, both policies get mixed together at times).

There are many reasons for international reserves accumulation, one of which, especially in emerging market economies (EMEs), is a precautionary motive against the sudden stop of capital flows. That is, the demand of safe assets by the central bank is for *self-insurance* purposes.

Several years ago, when Peter Diamond was president of the American Economic Association, he organized a session at the annual meeting on international financial institutions, and I was asked to talk about the future of the IMF. I felt that topic was too big for me to handle, as the IMF does many things, so I decided to interpret "IMF" as an initialism for "international market facilitator." My main point then was that self-insurance is a very inefficient form of insurance, and that the IMF has a major role to play toward completing the country-level systemic insurance market.

Of course, completing insurance markets also requires monitoring, as rogue countries can do more damage in a more complete markets environment, but that's something the IMF is accustomed to doing. I also discussed levered arrangements with the private sector, where the IMF could, in addition to playing the role of monitor, take the toxic waste layer of a special-purpose vehicle whose assets would be made of approved EMEs' debt.

At the time, I took the perspective of a country seeking insurance against sudden stops. I am now taking the perspective of a global economy facing a shortage of safe assets, but the conclusion is the same: we need to pool more global macro risks. This will cheapen the insurance cost for individual economies and reduce the massive squeeze on safe assets and its economic consequences.

Moreover, the exceptional reward received by those that can issue safe debt today makes the special-purpose vehicle structures I mentioned then even more attractive today. This is what investment banks would love to do and would be doing massively if they weren't so regulated today.

In recent years, the IMF and major central banks have made significant progress along this front through the creation of credit line and swap facilities, but there is room for a lot more. At least this is what equilibrium safe rates, which are dangerously close to sticky regions, are telling us today. In my opinion, central banks are holding too many safe assets in their reserves.

I now turn to QE, which is a very different kind of policy from international reserves accumulation. It is *not* an insurance policy. It is an ex post policy designed to compress risk spreads. In a sense, using John Geanakoplos's language, it is a policy that ought to be targeting the credit surface.

When you think about QE as a risk spread compressor, it is not clear at all that there is a role in it for the purchase of safe assets. In fact, if a shortage of safe assets is the main reason behind the liquidity trap, and the constraints on those that demand these assets to shift their portfolios into riskier assets are severe, reducing the available supply of safe assets may not only increase the risk spread but also could increase the sum of safe rates plus this spread, that is, the cost of capital for risky projects and investment.

The early QEs in the United States were very nicely targeted to risk spreads. There are aspects of the current European QE that have that feature as national central banks in periphery countries target the long and risky end of their sovereign curves.

I like much less, from the perspective of a safe assets shortage, Operation Twist–type policies (in which the central bank effectively takes out of the system the hardest safe assets for the private sector to produce, namely, long-term safe assets). For similar reasons, I don't like the purchase of Bunds among the assets targeted by European QE. Of course, there are institutional constraints necessitating this, but sometimes institutional constraints are more costly than at other times. Today they are costly, and we may well need to revisit some of them.

Hyun Song Shin has mentioned the negative real term premia in Bunds as a potential contradiction of the positive risk premium observed in high-yield spreads. I'm not so sure there is a contradiction. Long-term safe debt is very scarce and is a negative beta asset, especially during severe crises. Thus, to me, this is simply a reflection of fear and mandates, not of bullishness. As non-risk-spread-based QE promises to take Bunds away, it is only natural for the private sector to run toward them before is too late (although in these early stages of European QE, core central banks have yet to target the back end of their curves, an aspect that was missed by markets initially and probably played a role in the recent European tantrum).

There is an important footnote to all this, which is that the commitment to intervene in those long-term assets is an important factor supporting and enhancing the negative beta of long-term safe assets. But that points toward a tail policy put promise rather than to hoarding of safe assets by developed markets' central banks.

At any rate, the problems of non-risk-spread-targeted QE don't stop at their impact on the supply of safe assets, as this kind of QE also amplifies the negative spillovers that have been so frequently mentioned at the conference. When QE is not targeted to specific risk spreads, it has to be much larger to gain traction as it leaks to many assets and countries. These leakages can cause all sort of problems.

We don't have a full understanding of how non-risk-spread-targeted QE works, but it appears that an important channel is through volatility markets. It depresses *implied and realized volatilities* by anchoring an important curve for asset pricing. Once the swap curve in a major economy is pinned down, most assets look less risky, which is a paradise for all ilk of carry trades, many of which have undesirable consequences, especially for EMs trying to stabilize their capital accounts.

Note that this is a channel which is distinct from the conventional uncovered interest parity (UIP) type of effect of an interest rate cut, for it is not a movement along the UIP but operates mostly by shifting down the effective UIP for EM currencies and other risky assets.

Now, if the main purpose of QE is not risk compression but exchange rate depreciation, it may well be that intervention in safe assets is the most powerful mechanism because it operates over a smaller and more inelastic basis. Essentially, by squeezing enough of these markets so that only those unable to run away stay in it, the UIP no longer is a constraint as the safe asset market becomes segmented, and all-in returns, including an expected depreciation, can drop below international rates.

But as Agustín Carstens has said, this type of deliberate action often leads to what he wonderfully characterizes as "competitive reserves accumulation," which means that the net supply of safe assets gets hit twice, once from the QE-initiating country and another from the response of EM countries. This can't be a good outcome in the current environment of shortages. Non-risk-spread-targeted QE feels very inefficient, both from the point of view of the major safe assets imbalance we are experiencing and from the point of view of the global spillovers they cause.

In conclusion, I have argued that many of the instruments and programs created to deal with emerging market crises, such as swap lines and IMF liquidity programs, which have often been motivated from the perspective of an individual country in the past, now have another, globally systemic reason supporting them: We have a shortage of safe assets, which will keep us too close to secular stagnation unless we do something about it. One natural way to reduce this problem is by finding mechanisms for central banks to reduce their use of these scarce assets in achieving their policy goals.

Doing so requires extensive global cooperation as it involves global macro risk pooling and consideration for the policy spillovers of the different QE options available to a major economy. It may well be worth it for the world economy for developed markets to work on the institutional reforms that allow them to focus more directly on risk-spread-targeted QE rather than on the wholesale safe assets type of QE. Put differently, in the current environment (things do change, as we know), the central banks of developed markets have no business hoarding assets that have a large safe assets component beyond those required for conventional monetary policy.

Notes

1. See Ricardo J. Caballero and Emmanuel Farhi, "The Safety Trap," faculty paper, Department of Economics, MIT; Department of Economics, Harvard University; and NBER, April 6, 2015, http://economics.mit.edu/files/9543.

2. See Ricardo J. Caballero and Arvind Krishnamurthy, "Global Imbalances and Financial Fragility," *American Economic Review* 99, no. 2 (May 2009): 584-588.

27

Going Bust for Growth

Raghuram Rajan

There are few areas of robust growth around the world, with the IMF repeatedly reducing its growth forecasts in recent quarters. This period of slow growth is particularly dangerous because both industrial countries and emerging market economies (EMEs) need high growth to quell rising domestic political tensions. Policies that attempt to divert growth from others rather than create new growth are more likely under these circumstances. Even as we create conditions for sustainable growth, we need new rules of the game, enforced impartially by multilateral organizations, to ensure that countries adhere to international responsibilities.

The Conventional Diagnosis and Remedy

Why is the world finding it so hard to restore pre-global recession growth rates? The obvious answer is that the financial boom preceding the global recession left industrial countries with an overhang of debt, and debt, whether of governments, households, or banks, holds back growth.[1] While the remedy may be to write down debt so as to revive demand from the indebted, it is debatable whether additional debt-fueled demand is sustainable. In any event, large-scale debt write-offs seem politically difficult even if they are economically warranted.

How does one offset weak household and government demand if debt write-downs are off the table? Ideally, the response would be to incentivize investment and job creation through low interest rates and tax incentives. But if final demand from consumers is likely to be very weak for a considerable period of time because of debt overhang, the real return on new investment may collapse. The Wicksellian neutral real rate— loosely speaking, the interest rate required to bring the economy back to full employment with stable inflation—may even be strongly negative.[2] This typically has been taken as grounds for aggressive monetary policy. Because policy rates cannot be reduced significantly below zero (though a number of European countries are testing these limits), equilibrium long-term interest rates may stay higher than levels necessary to incentivize investment. Hence, central banks have embarked on unconventional monetary policy, which would directly lower long rates.

Another way to stimulate demand is for governments that still have the ability to borrow to increase spending. Since this will increase already high levels of government debt, proponents suggest investing in infrastructure, which may have high returns today when construction costs and interest rates are low. However, high-return infrastructure investment is harder to identify and implement in developed countries, where most obvious investments have already been made. Also, while everyone can see the need for repair and renovation of existing infrastructure, undertaking it requires far more decentralized spending and may be harder to initiate and finance from the center.

Put differently, high-return infrastructure investment is a good idea but may be hard to implement on a large scale for most advanced economy governments. To the extent that such debt-fueled spending creates a self-fulfilling virtuous cycle of confidence and activity, it can be a bridge to sustainable growth. But to the extent that it misallocates capital, it can worsen public anxieties about the future, reducing corporate investment and increasing household savings.

All this highlights another concern. Even if stimulus works in raising growth temporarily—and the above discussion suggests it may not—this growth has to be a bridge to sustained aggregate demand. But what if it isn't?

The Productivity Puzzle, Secular Stagnation, and Other Concerns

The arguments I have just enunciated for action apply to an economy where nothing fundamentally is wrong except perhaps excessive debt—what is needed is a cyclical return of growth to potential growth. Yet a number of economists, such as Tyler Cowen, Robert Gordon, and Larry Summers, have raised the possibility that potential growth in industrial countries had fallen even before the global recession of 2007–2009. Perhaps, then, the growth that we are trying to return to is unachievable without serious distortions.

The term "secular stagnation" used by Larry Summers to describe the current persistent economic malaise has caught on.[3] But different economists focus on different aspects and causes of the stagnation.[4] Summers emphasizes the inadequacy of aggregate demand, and the fact that the zero lower bound, as well as the potential for financial instability, prevents monetary policy from being more active. Among the reasons for weak aggregate demand are aging populations that want to consume less and the increasing income share of the very rich, whose marginal propensity to consume is small.

Tyler Cowen and Robert Gordon, on the other hand, emphasize a weak supply potential.[5] They argue that the post–World War II years were an aberration because growth was helped in industrial countries by reconstruction, the spread of technologies such as electricity, telephones, and automobiles, rising educational attainment, higher labor participation rates as women entered the workforce, a restoration of global trade, and increasing investments of capital. However, postwar total factor productivity growth—the part of growth stemming from new ideas and methods of production—was lower than its 1920–1950 high. More recently, not only has productivity growth fallen further (with a temporary positive uptick toward the end of the 1990s because of the IT revolution), but growth has been held back by the headwinds of plateauing education levels and labor participation rates, as well as a shrinking labor force. It is obvious from these lists of factors that it is hard to disentangle the effects of weak aggregate demand from slow growth in potential supply.

Structural reforms, typically ones that increase competition, foster innovation, and drive institutional change, are the way to raise potential growth. But these hurt protected constituencies that have become accustomed to the rents they get from the status quo. Moreover, the gains to constituencies that are benefited are typically later and uncertain. No wonder Jean-Claude Juncker, then Luxembourg's prime minister, said at the height of the euro crisis, "We all know what to do, we just don't know how to get reelected after we've done it!"

The Growth Imperative

If indeed fundamentals are such that that the industrial world has, and will, grow slowly for a while before new technologies and new markets come to the rescue, would it be politically easy to settle for slower growth? After all, per capita income is high in industrial countries, and a few years of slow growth would not be devastating at the aggregate level. Why is there so much of a political need for growth?

One reason is the need to fulfill government commitments. As the sociologist Wolfgang Streeck writes, in the strong growth years of the 1960s, when visions of a "Great Society" seemed attainable, industrial economies made enormous promises of social security to the wider public.[6] The promises have been augmented since then in some countries by politically convenient (because hidden from budgets) but fiscally unsound increases in pension and old-age health care commitments to public-sector workers. Without the immediate promise of growth, all these commitments could soon be seen as unsustainable.

Another reason is that growth is necessary for intergenerational equity, especially because these are the generations that will be working to pay off commitments to older generations. Insofar as these are also the cohorts that can take to the streets, growth is essential for social harmony.

Not only are the benefits of growth unequally distributed across generations, they are also very unequally distributed within generations. Because of changes in technology and the expansion of global competition, routine repetitive jobs, whether done by the skilled or the unskilled, have diminished greatly in industrial countries. With every percentage point of growth creating fewer "good" jobs for the unskilled or moderately skilled, more growth is needed to keep them happily employed. Equally, the rapid deterioration in skills for the unemployed is an additional reason to push for growth.

The Deflation Fear

Finally, a big factor persuading authorities in industrial countries to push for higher growth is the fear of deflation. The canonical example here is Japan, where many are persuaded that the key mistake it made was to slip into deflation, which has persisted and held back growth.

A closer look at the Japanese experience suggests that it is by no means clear that its growth has been slower than warranted, let alone that deflation caused slow growth. It is true that after its devastating crisis in the early 1990s, Japan may have prolonged the slowdown by not taking early action to clean up its banking system or restructure overindebted corporations. But once it took decisive action in the late 1990s and early 2000s, Japanese growth per capita or per worker looks comparable with that of other industrial countries (table 27.1).[7]

What about the deleterious effects of deflation? One worrisome effect of deflation is that if wages are downwardly sticky, real wages rise and cause unemployment. Yet Japanese unemployment has averaged 4.5 percent between 2000 and 2014, compared to 6.4 percent in the United States and 9.4 percent in the euro area during the same period.[8] In part, the Japanese have obtained wage flexibility by moving away from the old lifetime unemployment contracts for new hires to short-term contracts. While not without social costs, such flexibility allows an economy to cope with sustained deflation.

Another concern has been that moderately low inflation spirals down into seriously large deflation, where the zero lower bound on nominal interest rates keeps real interest rates unconscionably high. Once again, it is not clear this happened in Japan (figure 27.1).

Even if deflation is moderate, it may cause customers to increase savings in anticipation of a lower price in the future, especially if the zero lower bound raises real interest rates above their desired value. Figure 27.2 plots household savings as a share of GDP in Japan against the deflation rate. Again, it is hard to see a sustained pattern of higher savings with higher deflation.

Table 27.1
Growth in Real GDP per Capita, Advanced Economies, 1996–2014

	Japan	United States	Euro Area
1996–2000	0.63	3.10	2.41
2001–2005	1.05	1.56	0.99
2006–2010	0.35	−0.12	0.41
2011–2014	0.91	1.38	0.13

Source: World Economic Outlook Database, IMF, April 2015.

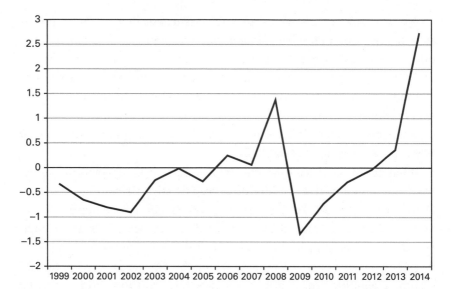

Figure 27.1
Japan: CPI Inflation Rate (period average, in percent). *Source*: *World Economic Outlook Database,* IMF, April 2015.

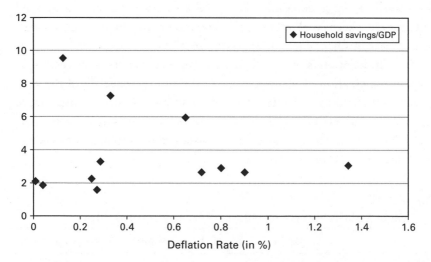

Figure 27.2
Household Savings and Deflation Rate: Japan.
Note: This chart plots the deflation rates and savings ratios for Japan for all years with negative inflation rates since 1980–1995, 1999, 2000–2005, and 2009–2014.
Source: World Economic Outlook Database, IMF, April 2015.

Finally, it is true that deflation increases the real burden of existing debt, thus exacerbating debt overhang. But if debt is excessive, a targeted restructuring is better than inflating it away across the board.

Regardless of all these arguments, the specter of deflation haunts central bankers. When coupled with the other concerns raised above, it is no wonder that the authorities in developed countries do not want to settle for low growth, even if that is indeed their economy's potential.

So the central dilemma in industrial economies has been how to reconcile the political imperative for strong growth with the reality that cyclical stimulus measures have proved ineffective in restoring high growth, debt write-offs are politically unacceptable, and structural reforms have the wrong timing, politically speaking, of pain versus gain. There is, however, one other channel for growth—exports.

Emerging Markets' Response

If industrial countries are stuck in low growth, can emerging markets (I use the term broadly to also include developing or frontier markets) take up the global slack in demand? After all, EMEs have a clear need for infrastructure investment, as well as growing populations that can be a source of final demand. EMEs have no less of an imperative for growth than industrial countries. While many do not have past entitlement promises to deliver on, some have aging populations that have to be provided for, and many have young, poor populations with sky-high expectations of growth. Ideally, EMEs would invest for the future, funded by the rich world, thus bolstering aggregate world demand.

The 1990s were indeed a period when EMEs borrowed from the rest of the world in an attempt to finance infrastructure and development. It did not end well. The lesson from the 1990s crises was that EMEs' reliance on foreign capital for growth was dangerous.

Following the 1990s crises, as the dotted line in figure 27.3 indicates, a number of EMEs went further to run current account surpluses after cutting investment sharply, and started accumulating foreign exchange reserves to preserve exchange competitiveness. Rather than generating excess demand for the world's goods, they became suppliers, searching for demand elsewhere.

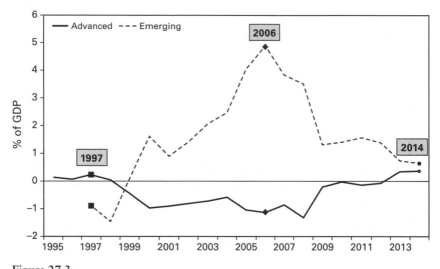

Figure 27.3
Current Account Balance (as percent of GDP).
Note: Emerging economies include "emerging and developing" countries. *Source: World Economic Outlook Database,* IMF, April 2015.

In 2005, Ben Bernanke, then a governor of the Federal Reserve, coined the term "global savings glut" to describe the current account surpluses, especially of EMEs, that were finding their way into the United States.[9] Bernanke pointed to a number of adverse consequences to the United States from these flows, including the misallocation of resources to non-traded goods such as housing and away from tradable manufacturing. He suggested that it would be good if the US current account deficit shrank, but that primarily required EMEs to reduce their exchange rate intervention rather than actions on the part of the United States.

Prior to the global financial crisis, then, EMEs and industrial countries were locked in a dangerous relationship of capital flows and demand that reversed the equally dangerous pattern before the EM crises in the late 1990s. Sustained exchange rate intervention by EM central banks, as well as an excessive tolerance for leverage in industrial countries, contributed to the eventual global disaster. But in the wake of the most recent financial crisis, the pattern is reversing once again.

Industrial countries have curtailed their investment without increasing their consumption (as a fraction of GDP), thus reducing their demand for foreign goods and their reliance on foreign finance. The counterpart of

(a)

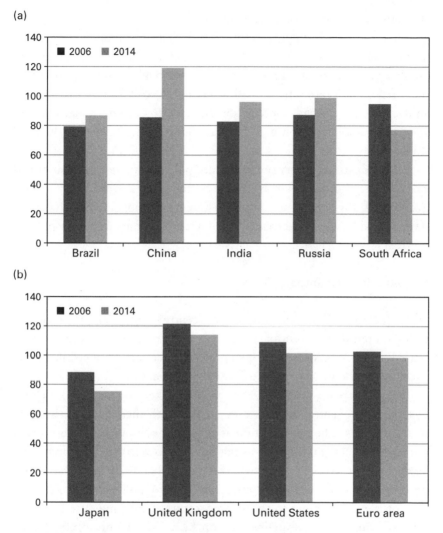

(b)

Figure 27.4
Real Effective Exchange Rate Movements, 2006–2014.
Notes: a. Selected emerging economies (REER index, 2010 = 100). b. Advanced economies (REER index, 2010 = 100). *Source: World Economic Outlook Database,* IMF, April 2015.

this shift of advanced economies from current account deficit (demand creating) to surplus (supply creating) has been a substantial fall in current account surpluses in EMEs. This relative increase in demand for foreign goods from EM countries has come about through a ramp-up in investment from 2008 rather than a fall in savings. Facilitating or causing this shift has been a broad appreciation of real effective exchange rates in EMEs and a depreciation in industrial country rates between 2006 and 2014.

Have industrial country central banks' policies, similar to the sustained exchange rate intervention by EMs' central banks in the early 2000s, accelerated this current account adjustment? Possibly, and likely candidates would be what are broadly called unconventional monetary policies (UMPs).

Unconventional Monetary Policy

UMPs include both policies whereby the central bank attempts to commit to hold interest rates at near zero for long and policies that affect central bank balance sheets, such as buying assets in certain markets, including exchange markets, in order to affect market prices.[10]

There clearly is a role for UMPs: when markets are broken or grossly dysfunctional, central bankers may step in with their balance sheets to mend markets. The key question is what happens when these policies are prolonged long beyond repairing markets to actually distorting them. Take, for instance, the zero-lower-bound problem. Because short-term policy rates cannot be pushed much below zero, and because long rates tack on a risk premium to short rates, central banks may use UMPs to directly affect long rates. Direct action by a risk-tolerant central bank, such as purchasing long bonds, effectively shrinks the risk premium available on remaining long assets.

This has two effects. First, those who can rebalance between short and long assets now prefer holding short-term assets because, risk adjusted, these are a better deal. Thus, as the central bank increases bond purchases under quantitative easing, the willingness of commercial banks to hold unremunerated reserves increases. Second, those institutions that cannot shift to short-term assets, such as pension funds, bond mutual funds, and insurance companies, will either continue holding their assets and suffer a relative undercompensation for risk or turn to riskier assets. This *search for yield* will occur if the relative undercompensation for risk in more exotic assets is lower, or simply because institutions have to meet a fixed nominal rate of return.

None of this need be a problem if everyone knows when to stop. Unfortunately, there are few constraints on central banks undertaking these policies. If the policy does not seem to be increasing growth, one can simply do more. All the while, the distortion in asset prices and the misallocation of funds can increase, which can be very costly when the central bank decides to exit.

Equally important, though, is that domestic fund managers can search for yield abroad, depreciating the sending country's currency, perhaps significantly more so than ordinary monetary policy. This may indeed cause the increase in domestic competitiveness that could energize the sending country's exports. But such increases in competitiveness and "demand shifting" can be very detrimental for global stability, especially if unaccompanied by domestic demand creation.

Spillovers to Emerging Markets and Musical Crises

If UMP enhances financial risk taking in the originating country without enhancing domestic investment or consumption, the exchange rate impact of UMP may simply shift demand away from countries not engaging in UMP, without creating much compensating domestic demand for their goods. If so, UMP would resemble very much the exchange rate intervention policies of the EMEs before the global financial crisis of 2007–2009.

Indeed, the post–global crisis capital flows into EMEs have been huge, despite the best efforts of EMEs to push them back by accumulating reserves.[11] These flows have increased local leverage, not just through the direct effect of cross-border banking flows but also through an indirect effect, as the appreciating exchange rate and rising asset prices make it seem that EM borrowers have more equity than they really have. Bernanke's concerns in 2005 about malinvestment in the United States resulting from capital inflows have surfaced in EMEs post-crisis as a result of capital inflows from industrial countries.

Have crises in EMEs in the 1990s been transformed into crises in industrial countries in the 2000s, and once again into vulnerabilities in

EM countries in the 2010s, as countries react to the problem of inadequate global demand by exporting their problems to other countries? The "taper tantrum" in July 2013 certainly seemed to suggest that EM countries that ran large current account deficits were vulnerable once again.[12] Is the world engaged in a macabre game of musical [chairs] crises as each country attempts to boost growth? If possibly yes, how do we break this cycle?

Good Policies ... and Good Behavior

In an ideal world, the political imperative for growth would not outstrip the economy's potential. But as we do not live in such a world, and because social security commitments, overindebtedness, and poverty are not going to disappear, it is probably wiser to look for ways to enhance sustainable growth.

Clearly, the long-run response to weak global growth should be policies that promote innovation, as well as structural reforms that enhance efficiency. Policies that improve the domestic distribution of capabilities and opportunities without significantly dampening incentives for innovation and efficiency are also needed.

In the short run, though, the need for sensible investment is paramount. In industrial countries, green energy initiatives such as carbon taxes or emission limits, while giving industry clear signals on where to invest, also have the ability to move the needle on aggregate investment and help long-run goals on environment protection.

Most EM countries have large infrastructure investment needs. We still need to understand how to improve project selection and finance, for too much public-sector involvement results in sloth and rent seeking and too much private-sector involvement leads to risk intolerance and profiteering. Going forward, well-designed public-private partnerships, drawing on successful experiences elsewhere, should complement private initiatives.

Clearly, sensible investment has a much better chance of paying dividends when macroeconomic policies are sound. And such policies are easier when the adverse spillovers from cross-border capital flows are limited. This may require new rules of the game for policymaking.

New Rules of the Game?

How do we focus on domestic demand creation and avoid this game of musical crises, with countries trying to depreciate their exchange rate through sustained direct exchange rate intervention or through UMPs (where demand-creating transmission channels are blocked)? It might be useful to examine and challenge the rationales used to justify such actions.

Rationale 1: Would the world not be better off if we grew strongly?

Undoubtedly, if there were no negative spillovers from a country's actions, the world would indeed be better off if the country grew. But the whole point about policies that primarily affect domestic growth by depreciating the domestic exchange rate is that they work by pulling growth from others.

Rationale 2: We are in a deep recession. We need to use any means available to jump-start growth. The payoff for other countries from our growth will be considerable.

This may be a legitimate rationale if the policy is a "one-off" and if, once the country gets out of its growth funk, it is willing to let its currency appreciate. But if the strengthening currency leads to a continuation of the UMPs as the country's authorities become unwilling to give back the growth they obtained by undervaluing their currency, this rationale is suspect. Moreover, policies that encourage sustained unidirectional capital outflows to other countries can be very debilitating for the recipient's financial stability, over and above any effects on their competitiveness. Thus, any "one-off" has to be limited in duration.

Rationale 3: Our domestic mandate requires us to do what it takes to fulfill our inflation objective, and UMP is indeed necessary when we hit the zero lower bound.

This rationale has two weaknesses. First, it places a domestic mandate above an international responsibility. If this were seen to be legitimate, then no country would ever respect international responsibilities when it was inconvenient to do so. Second, it implicitly assumes that the only way to achieve the inflation mandate is through UMP (even assuming UMPs are successful in elevating inflation on a sustained basis, for which there is little evidence).

Rationale 4: We take into account the feedback effects on our economy from the rest of the world while setting policy. Therefore, we are not oblivious to the consequences of UMPs on other countries.
Ideally, responsible global citizenship would require a country to act as it would act in a world without boundaries. In such a world, a policymaker should judge whether the overall positive domestic and international benefits of a policy, discounted over time, outweigh its costs. Some policies may have largely domestic benefits and foreign costs, but they may be reasonable in a world without boundaries because more people are benefited than are hurt.

By this definition, rationale 4 does not necessarily amount to responsible global citizenship because a country takes into account only the global "spillbacks" for itself from any policies it undertakes, instead of the spillovers also. So, for example, country A may destroy industry I in country B through its policies, but it will take into account only the spillback from industry I purchasing less of country A's exports.

Rationale 5: Monetary policy with a domestic focus is already very complicated and hard to communicate. It would be impossibly complex if we were additionally burdened with having to think about the effects of (unconventional) monetary policies on other countries.
This widely heard rationale is really an abandonment of responsibility. It amounts to asserting that the monetary authority has only a domestic mandate, which is rationale 3 above. In an interconnected globalized world, "complexity" cannot be a defense.

Rationale 6: We will do what we must; you can adjust.
Adjustments are never easy, and sometimes they are very costly—one reason why Ben Bernanke placed the burden of change in his "savings glut" speech outside the United States. EM countries may not have the institutions that can weather the exchange rate volatility and credit growth associated with large capital flows—for instance, sharp exchange rate depreciations can translate quickly into inflation if the EM country's

central bank does not have credibility, while exchange rate depreciations may be more easily endured by an industrial country.

The bottom line is that multilateral institutions such as the IMF should reexamine the "rules of the game" for responsible policy and develop a consensus around new ones. No matter what a central bank's domestic mandate may be, international responsibilities should not be ignored. The IMF should analyze each new UMP (including sustained unidirectional exchange rate intervention) and, based on its likely effects and the agreed-upon rules of the game, declare it in- or out-of-bounds. By halting policies that primarily work through the exchange rate, it will also contribute to solving a classic prisoner's dilemma problem associated with policies that depreciate the exchange rate—once some countries undertake these poli-cies, staying out is difficult (the country that eschews these policies sees its currency appreciate and demand fall). Exit is also difficult (the exiting country faces sharp appreciation). Therefore, in the absence of collective action, these policies will be undertaken even when they are suboptimal, and will be carried on too long.

Of course, we clearly need further dialogue and public debate on the issues that have been raised, while recognizing that progress will require strong political leadership.

Conclusion

The current nonsystem in international monetary policy is, in my view, a source of substantial risk, both to sustainable growth as well as to the financial sector. It is not an industrial country problem or an EM country problem; it is a problem of collective action. We are being pushed toward competitive monetary easing and musical crises.

I use Depression-era terminology because I fear that in a world with weak aggregate demand, we may be engaged in a risky competition for a greater share of it. We are thereby also creating financial sector risks for when unconventional policies end.

We need multilateral institutions with widespread legitimacy to moni-tor new rules of the game. And each one of us has to work hard in our own countries to develop a consensus for free trade, open markets, and responsible global citizenry. If we can achieve all this even as recent eco-nomic events make us more parochial and inward-looking, we will truly have set the stage for the strong sustainable growth we all desperately need.

Notes

The chapter draws on Governor Raghuram Rajan's panel presentation during the "Rethinking Macro Policy III" conference, as well as remarks before the Economic Club of New York on May 19, 2015. Rajan thanks Dr. Prachi Mishra of the Federal Reserve Bank for very useful comments and research support.

1. See the interesting evidence in Atif Mian and Amir Sufi, *House of Debt* (Princeton, NJ: Princeton University Press, 2014), and the cross-country evidence in Carmen Reinhart and Kenneth Rogoff, *This Time Is Different: Eight Centuries of Financial Folly* (Princeton, NJ: Princeton University Press, 2008). For an illuminating overall view of the global financial crisis and the policy remedies, see Martin Wolf, *The Shifts and the Shocks: What We've Learned and Have Still to Learn from the Financial Crisis* (New York: Penguin, 2015).

2. Though see a thoughtful piece by Claudio Borio and Piti Disyatat, "Low Interest Rates and Secular Stagnation: Is Debt a Missing Link?" (blog post *VoxEU*, Centre for Economic Policy Research, June 25, 2014, http://www.voxeu.org/article/low-interest-rates-secular-stagnation-and-debt), suggesting that the real neutral interest rate may be influenced by low policy rates.

3. Larry Summers, "U.S. Economic Prospects: Secular Stagnation, Hysteresis and Zero Lower Bound," speech before the National Association for Business Economics, Economic Policy Conference, February 24, 2014, http://larrysummers.com/wp-content/uploads/2014/06/NABE-speech-Lawrence-H.-Summers1.pdf.

4. See, for example, Wolfgang Streeck, "The Crises of Democratic Capitalism," *New Left Review* 71 (September/October 2011), or Raghuram Rajan, "The True Lessons of the Recession: The West Can't Borrow and Spend Its Way to Recovery," *Foreign Affairs* 91, no. 3 (May/June 2012).

5. Tyler Cowen, *The Great Stagnation How America Ate All The Low-Hanging Fruit of Modern History, Got Sick, and Will (Eventually) Feel Better* (New York: Dutton, 2011); Robert J. Gordon, "Is US Economic Growth Over? Faltering Innovation Confronts Six Headwinds," NBER Working Paper 18315 (Cambridge, MA: National Bureau of Economic Research, August 2012).

6. See Streeck, "The Crises of Democratic Capitalism."

7. I first learned of these facts from Jean-Claude Trichet. For a more comprehensive look at deflation, see Claudio Borio, Magdalena Erdem, Andrew Filardo, and Boris Hofmann, "The Costs of Deflations: A Historical Perspective," *BIS Quarterly Review*, March 2015.

8. Data from *World Economic Outlook Database*, IMF, Washington, DC, April 2015.

9. Ben S. Bernanke, "The Global Saving Glut and the U.S. Current Account Deficit," remarks by Governor Ben S. Bernanke before the Virginia Association

of Economists, the Sandridge Lecture, Richmond, VA, March 10, 2005, http://www.federalreserve.gov/boarddocs/speeches/2005/200503102.

10. For an excellent overview, see Claudio Borio and Piti Disyatat, "Unconventional Monetary Policies: An Appraisal," *Manchester School* 78, no. S1 (2010): 53–89. September 2010.

11. Indeed, similar to the behavior of commercial banks, the willingness of EM central banks to hold short-term paper in response to capital inflows enhances the ability of the industrial country central bank to engage in further UMPs. In a sense, EM central banks provide liquidity for foreign investors by holding precautionary reserves.

12. For those who advocate allowing exchange rate adjustment as central to macromanagement, it should be sobering that countries that allowed the real exchange rate to appreciate the most during the prior period of quantitative easing suffered the greatest adverse impact to financial conditions (see Barry Eichengreen and Poonam Gupta, "Tapering Talk: The Impact of Expectations of Reduced Federal Reserve Security Purchases on Emerging Markets," faculty paper, Department of Economics, University of California, Berkeley, 2013; and Prachi Mishra, Kenji Moriyama, Papa N'Diaye, and Lam Nguyen, "The Impact of Fed Tapering Announcements on Emerging Markets," IMF Working Paper [Washington, DC: IMF, 2014]).

Conclusion

28

Rethinking Macro Policy: Progress or Confusion?

Olivier Blanchard

On April 15 and 16, 2015, the IMF hosted the third conference on "Rethinking Macroeconomic Policy." I had initially chosen as the title and subtitle "Rethinking Macroeconomic Policy III. Down in the Trenches." I thought of the first conference in 2011 as having identified the main failings of previous policies, the second conference in 2013 as having identified general directions, and this conference as a progress report.

My subtitle was rejected by one of the co-organizers, Larry Summers. He argued that I was far too optimistic, that we were nowhere close to knowing where were going. Arguing with Larry is tough, so I chose an agnostic title and shifted to "Rethinking Macro Policy III: Progress or Confusion?"

Where do I think we are today? I think both Larry and I are right. I do not say this for diplomatic reasons. We are indeed proceeding in the trenches. But where the trenches will eventually lead remains unclear. This is the theme I shall develop in these concluding remarks, focusing on macroprudential tools, monetary policy, and fiscal policy.

Macroprudential Policies

Let me start with macroprudential tools. If anything, the crisis has convinced most of us that they have to be part of the basic macro toolkit. And much progress has been made, both in terms of research and in terms of policy. Measures of systemic risk are being developed, with an eye on implied instruments. A recent survey by the US Office of Financial Research identified thirty-one methods to identify particular dimensions of systemic risk, and there are no doubt many more. Most countries have put in place macroprudential authorities, sometimes at the central bank, such as in the UK, sometimes outside with central bank participation, such as in the United States. More and more countries are experimenting with loan-to-value ratios and other tools to affect housing demand and prices.

But where are these trenches going? We do not know the shape of the future financial system, for example the degree to which it will be institution- or bank-based or market-based. Of course, the same uncertainty applies to, say, the high-tech sector, and we do not worry; we just observe, and we will see where it goes. But finance is different. Policymakers cannot be simple observers, as what the financial system will be depends very much on regulation. And we do not have a good sense of what regulation should be.

Consider the distinction between financial regulation and macroprudential policies, which, for these purposes, I define, borrowing from Paul Tucker's presentation, as "dynamically adjusted financial regulation."

Take, for example, capital ratios. In principle, variable capital ratios (macroprudential) sound better than fixed ones (financial regulation). But is the trade-off really that clear? The difficulty of identifying when and how to move the ratios, and the political economy complications associated with such changes, make the answer far from obvious.

The preliminary conclusions from a study by an IMF team that looked at banking crises since 1970 in advanced economies are that a capital ratio of 15 to 22 percent (a bit higher than what is coming out of Basel III) would have been sufficient to fully absorb losses in 90 percent of them. Maybe a constant 15 percent is better than a ratio that varies between, say, 10 percent and 30 percent.

Very much the same set of issues arises with respect to cross-border flows. Much work is going on revisiting the effects of the various types of capital flows, and the efficacy of various forms of capital controls and foreign exchange intervention. As we heard from the speakers in the session on capital flows, there is fairly wide agreement that capital flows can be disruptive, and that it may make sense to use foreign exchange intervention and capital controls. But again, the ultimate question, namely, the degree of openness of the capital account, remains unanswered. Should some flows be permanently banned, if that were indeed possible? We do not know.

Monetary Policy

Let me turn to monetary policy. Central banks have experimented with and researchers have explored monetary policy, often in that order. We have learned a lot, namely, that the zero lower bound can be reached and is hard to get away from, that financial assets are truly imperfect substitutes, that quantitative easing can affect the term premium, and that bank runs happen to nonbanks as well. In the trenches, a lot has been done and is being done. But again, it is not clear where the trenches will lead.

Take two related issues—the size and the composition of central bank balance sheets. (I will leave out one of my favorite issues, such as how to avoid the zero lower bound in the future, and the optimal rate of inflation. Not much progress has been made here, but I don't think the issue has gone away. I will also leave aside the central issue of coordination of monetary and macroprudential tools.)

I will focus on the Fed, but the arguments apply to the other central banks just as well. At this time, the balance sheet of the Fed is about $4.5 trillion, roughly five times larger than it was before the crisis in 2007. T-bills, which accounted for about 25 percent of the total, are gone from the balance sheet. Nearly all Treasury securities that the Fed holds have a maturity of more than one year, and more than half have a maturity of more than five years. Relative to where we are, what should the balance sheet of the future look like?

For the moment, the issue is largely moot. The required direction of movement is clear, and it will take a long time for the balance sheet to adjust to whatever it should be. But should it go back to its precrisis size, or perhaps even smaller, given the steadily decreasing demand for currency for transaction purposes? Or should it remain larger, with interest paid on the excess reserves that banks would have to hold? I see no argument for a large central bank balance sheet, but the discussion has not yet taken place.

Should the Fed return to intervening only at the short end of the yield curve, or are there good reasons for continuing to intervene along the curve? Put another way, what are the advantages of affecting both the short rate and the term premium on longer-maturity bonds? How solid is the argument that, to the extent that the Fed holds T-bills, it is depriving the private sector of precious collateral? I do not know the answer to those questions, yet they are central to where we want to go in the end.

Fiscal Policy

Let me move to a brief discussion of the third pillar, fiscal policy. We have learned many things. Fiscal stimulus can help. Public debt can increase very quickly when the economy tanks, but even more so when contingent—explicit or implicit—liabilities become actual liabilities. The effects of fiscal consolidation have led to a flurry of research on multipliers, on whether and when the direct effects of fiscal consolidation can be partly offset by confidence effects, through decreasing worries about debt sustainability. (There has been surprisingly little work or action where I was hoping to see it, namely, on a better design of automatic stabilizers. It is explored in this spring's *Fiscal Monitor* [IMF 2015, but so far there have been no actual policy changes.)

Admittedly, navigation by sight may be fine for the time being. The issue of what debt ratio to aim for in the long run is not of the essence when there is a large consensus that it is too large today and the adjustment will be slow in any case—although even here, Brad DeLong has provocatively argued that current debt ratios are perhaps too low. (I shall not embark on the debate over secular stagnation and whether we can act under the assumption that r will be less than g for the indefinite future.)

But how to assess what the right goal is for each country? This remains to be done. It has become clear that there is no magic debt-to-GDP number. Depending on the distribution of future growth rates and interest rates, on the extent of implicit and explicit contingent liabilities, one country's high debt may well be sustainable, while another's low debt may not. Conceptually and analytically, the right tool is a stochastic debt sustainability analysis (something we already use at the IMF when designing programs). The task of translating this into simple, understandable goals remains to be done.

In short, though the trenches are being dug, we still do not have a good sense of where they will ultimately lead. We clearly need to have another conference in two years.

Reference

IMF. 2015. "Now Is the Time: Fiscal Policies for Sustainable Growth." *Fiscal Monitor*. Washington, DC, IMF, April. http://www.imf.org/external/pubs/ft/fm/2015/01/pdf/fm1501.pdf.

List of Contributors

Viral V. Acharya is the C. V. Starr Professor of Economics in the Department of Finance at New York University Stern School of Business.

Anat R. Admati is the George G. C. Parker Professor of Finance and Economics at the Graduate School of Business at Stanford University. She is a Fellow of the Econometric Society, the recipient of multiple fellowships, and a past board member of the American Finance Association. She has served on a number of editorial boards and is currently a member of the FDIC Systemic Resolution Advisory Committee and the CFTC Market Risk Advisory Committee.

Zeti Akhtar Aziz is the Governor of the Bank Negara Malaysia.

Ben Bernanke served as Chairman of the Federal Reserve's Board of Governors, after serving as Board member from 2002 to 2005. Bernanke also served as Chairman of the President's Council of Economic Advisers from June 2005 to January 2006. He has also held a number of academic positions, including as Professor in Princeton's Economic Department from 1985 to 2002. He is currently a Distinguished Fellow in Residence at the Brookings Institution.

Olivier Blanchard is the first C. Fred Bergsten Senior Fellow at the Peterson Institute for International Economics. He is also the Robert M. Solow Professor Emeritus at MIT, and served as Economic Counsellor and Director of the Research Department of the IMF from 2008 to 2014.

Marco Buti is the Director General for Economic and Financial Affairs of the European Commission.

Ricardo J. Caballero is the Ford International Professor of Economics and Director of the World Economic Laboratory at the Massachusetts

Institute of Technology, an NBER Research Associate, and an advisor of QFR Capital Management LP.

Agustín Carstens serves as Governor of the Banco de Mexico. Currently he is Chairman of the International Monetary and Financial Committee at the IMF and of the Global Economic Meeting and the Economic Consultative Council at the BIS, where he is also a board member. Among other distinguished positions, he has also served as Deputy Managing Director at the IMF and Minister of Finance of Mexico.

Jaime Caruana is the General Manager of the Bank for International Settlements since 2009. Previously, he was Director of the Monetary and Capital Markets Department of the International Monetary Fund. From 2000 to 2006, Mr Caruana was the Governor of the Bank of Spain and served on the Governing Council of the European Central Bank in that capacity. He was also the Chairman of the Basel Committee on Banking Supervision from 2003 to 2006. Prior to joining the Bank of Spain, Mr Caruana worked in the private financial sector for nearly ten years.

J. Bradford DeLong is Professor of Economics at the University of California, Berkeley and was Deputy Assistant Secretary for Economic Policy of the US Treasury during the Clinton administration.

Martin Feldstein is the George F. Baker Professor of Economics at Harvard University and President Emeritus of the National Bureau of Economic Research, Cambridge, Massachusetts.

Vitor Gaspar is Director of the Fiscal Affairs Department of the IMF. Prior to joining the IMF, he held a variety of senior policy positions at the Banco de Portugal, the ECB and European Commission, and served as Minister of State and Finance of Portugal during 2011 to 2013.

John Geanakoplos is the James Tobin Professor of Economics at Yale University. He is a founding Partner of Ellington Capital Management, and an External Professor of the Santa Fe Institute. He was Director of the Cowles Foundation from 1996 to 2005 and Chairman of the Science Steering Committee of the Santa Fe Institute from 2009 to 2015.

Philipp Hildebrand is Vice Chairman of BlackRock. Until January 2012, he served as Chairman of the Governing Board of the Swiss National Bank and Vice-Chairman of the Financial Stability Board.

Gill Marcus served as Governor of the South African Reserve Bank from 2009 to 2014.

Maurice Obstfeld is the Economic Counsellor and Director of the Research Department of the IMF. He is on leave from the University of California, Berkeley, where he is the Class of 1958 Professor of Economics.

Luiz Awazu Pereira da Silva is former Deputy-Governor at the Central Bank of Brazil, from 2010 till 2015, in charge of Economic Policy and at present Deputy General Manager at the Bank for International Settlements.

Rafael Portillo is a Senior Economist in the Research Department of the IMF and at the Joint Vienna Institute.

Raghuram Rajan is the twenty-third Governor of the Reserve Bank of India. Prior to that, he was Chief Economic Advisor, Government of India, the Eric J. Gleacher Distinguished Service Professor of Finance at University of Chicago's Booth School of Business, and Chief Economist at the IMF (2003–2006).

Kenneth Rogoff is Thomas D. Cabot Professor at Harvard University. From 2001 to 2003, Rogoff served as Chief Economist at the IMF. He is also an international grandmaster of chess.

Robert E. Rubin served as the seventieth US Secretary of the Treasury, from 1995 until 1999, and was the first Director of the National Economic Council from 1993 to 1994. He was Co-Chairman at Goldman Sachs and senior adviser to Citigroup. He is currently the Co-Chairman of the Council on Foreign Relations. In June 2014, he completed a twelve-year term as a member of the Harvard Corporation.

Hyun Song Shin is the Economic Adviser and Head of Research at the Bank for International Settlements. Before joining the BIS, he was the Hughes-Rogers Professor of Economics at Princeton University.

Lawrence H. Summers is the Charles W. Eliot University Professor and President Emeritus of Harvard University. During the past two decades, he has served in a series of senior policy positions, including as the seventy-first US Secretary of the Treasury for President Clinton, Director of the National Economic Council for President Obama, and Vice President of Development Economics and Chief Economist of the World Bank.

Lars E. O. Svensson is Visiting Professor at the Stockholm School of Economics and Affiliated Professor at the IIES, Stockholm University. He has previously served as Deputy Governor of Sveriges Riksbank (2007–2013), Professor of Economics at Princeton University (2001–2009), and Professor at the IIES, Stockholm University (1984–2003).

John B. Taylor is the Mary and Robert Raymond Professor of Economics at Stanford University and the George P. Shultz Senior Fellow in Economics at Stanford's Hoover Institution. He is also the Director of Stanford's Introductory Economics Center. He has held several policy positions, including as US Under Secretary of the Treasury for International Affairs from 2001 to 2005.

Paul Tucker is Chair of the Systemic Risk Council and a fellow at the Harvard Kennedy School. He was Deputy Governor at the Bank of England from 2009 to October 2013, having joined the bank in 1980. When this chapter was written, he was also a fellow at the Harvard Business School.

José Viñals is currently the Financial Counsellor and Director of the Monetary and Capital Markets Department of the IMF. He is a member of the Financial Stability Board, representing the IMF. Prior to the IMF, he served as the Vice-Governor of the Central Bank of Spain, after holding successive positions there.

Paul A. Volcker worked in the US federal government for almost thirty years, his service culminating in two terms as Chairman of the Board of Governors of the Federal Reserve System from 1979 to 1987. He has held several other positions, including as Chairman of the President's Economic Recovery Advisory Board from November 2008 to 2011. Mr. Volcker launched the Volcker Alliance in 2013.

Index